The War in the Peninsula, 1808-1814

THE DUKE OF WELLINGTON

The War in the Peninsula, 1808-1814

The Battles with Napoleonic France in Portugal, Spain, The Pyrenees & Southern France

Alexander Innes Shand

The War in the Peninsula, 1808-1814
The Battles with Napoleonic France in Portugal,
Spain, The Pyrenees & Southern France
by Alexander Innes Shand

First published under the title
The War in the Peninsula, 1808-1814

Leonaur is an imprint of Oakpast Ltd
Copyright in this form © 2011 Oakpast Ltd

ISBN: 978-0-85706-605-3 (hardcover)
ISBN: 978-0-85706-606-0 (softcover)

http://www.leonaur.com

Publisher's Notes

The opinions of the authors represent a view of events in which he was a participant related from his own perspective, as such the text is relevant as an historical document.

The views expressed in this book are not necessarily those of the publisher.

Contents

Introduction	9
Invasion of Portugal and Revolt of Madrid	15
The Rising in Spain: The Capitulation of Baylen	26
Roliça, Vimeiro and the Convention of Cintra	32
Moore's Advance—His Retreat and the Battle of Corunna	42
The Siege of Zaragoza and Affairs in Portugal	53
The Surprise of Oporto and Soult's Retreat	60
Invasion of Spain, Victory of Talavera and Spanish Defeats	70
Fall of the Frontier Fortresses and Battle of Busaco	81
Torres Vedras, Barossa, Fuentes d'Oñoro and Albuera	92
The Storming of Ciudad Rodrigo and Badajoz	109
Operations in Aragon And Catalonia	118
Operations Before the Campaign of Salamanca	124
Campaign of Salamanca	133
Salamanca and Burgos	147
The Allies Fall Back on the Portuguese Frontier	160
In Winter Quarters	167
Joseph Abandons Madrid, and Suchet is Checked in Valencia	174

The Rout of Vittoria	180
Operations in the East and Siege of San Sebastian	191
Battles of the Pyrenees	199
Fall of San Sebastian	209
Passages of the Bidassoa and Nivelle	217
Battles of the Nivelle and Surrender of Eastern Fortresses	228
Battle of Orthes and Submission of Bordeaux	237
The Battle of Toulouse, and Close of the War	245

Necessarily this condensed narrative is based on Napier, the historian of the War, and on the Wellington Despatches. Southey and other English writers have been consulted, and references will be found in the text to the Memoirs of French soldiers who served in the campaigns, and to the observations of the Emperor himself at St Helena. Perhaps I may add that I had the advantage of talking over some of those 'Operations of War' with the late Sir Edward Hamley, though, as I must trust to memory for the recollection of the conversations, he is not to be held responsible for opinions expressed.

Introduction

The dramas of great wars must always have an irresistible fascination. Students who follow them intelligently are absorbed even more in the results of well-devised strategy or prompt decisions than in the swift vicissitudes of thrilling episodes or eventful situations. Moreover, combinations and events are always at the mercy of Chance, and, as Napier says, in war Fortune will assert her supremacy. It is true that in the wars of the past the catastrophe is foreknown, which eliminates the elements of suspense and expectation. But, on the other hand, the subject has been flooded with light from a host of historians, military and civil; history has been as thoroughly revised as can be reasonably expected, and we have the feeling that we are dealing with actual facts and not with probabilities or hazardous presumptions.

There is a remarkable variety of interests attaching to the Peninsular War, and it must always have a special attraction for Englishmen. It was the turning point of the fortunes of Napoleon, and the conqueror of Europe took the first step towards political suicide when he rashly decided to pass the Pyrenees. Britain was supreme on the seas; Buonaparte had made himself master of the Continent. After the peace of Tilsit, it is impossible to surmise how the map of Europe might have been recast had he been satisfied to rest on the maxim, *quieta non movere*. But his ambition was boundless as his self-confidence was not unreasonably overweening. He could feel himself neither satisfied nor safe so long as England was prosperous and consequently formidable. While circumstances gave her the monopoly of commerce, she could subsidise his unwilling tributaries, and encourage them to fresh efforts for independence.

The fighting which began at Vimeiro and ended at Waterloo was really a prolonged battle for markets. The insurrections in Spain and

Portugal were merely episodes which influenced the direction and course of operations. The decree of Berlin, followed by the decree of Milan in December 1807, had declared England in a state of blockade. The immediate response was the Orders in Council. France and the countries dependent on her were to be blockaded in turn. All vessels trading between hostile or neutral ports, or under such a certificate as was required by the decree of Berlin, were declared liable to seizure; and neutral ships, bound to or from any hostile port, were required to touch and pay duties at some port in Great Britain. Then the combatants found themselves face to face. Buonaparte could close the northern harbours, though smugglers and receivers drove a thriving trade, but the prohibited goods were poured into the Peninsula through the free port of Gibraltar, and notably through Portugal; in fact, Portugal, as historians of the time have defined it, was but an outlying province of our own.

Portuguese independence must be suppressed if the continental system was to be effectively carried out. Hence the secret treaty of Fontainebleau, which tempted its author to the invasion of Spain. We are far from asserting that our country, and even our Cabinets, were not actuated by nobler and more generous motives. They sympathised warmly with the revolt of the Peninsular nations against unprovoked invasion and intolerable oppression. They were indignant at the arbitrary pressure put on their ally, the Regent of Portugal, and shocked by the treachery which, having secured the Spanish fortresses under the guise of friendship, had ensnared the whole of the royal family at Bayonne. But free commerce was the very life-blood of the British Isles, and when they embarked the first detachment of troops for the Peninsula, they committed themselves to a death-struggle from which the will and the victories of Wellington made it difficult and well-nigh impossible to draw back.

Buonaparte's motives for the conquest of Portugal were clear, and had he been content to stop there his schemes might have been successful. But his aggression on Spain was so ill-timed and ill-advised that it is difficult to reconcile it with the far-sighted sagacity of his genius. His warmest admirers have sought in vain to explain his reasons or defend his policy. He appears to have been drawn on, step by step, to take resolutions from which he could not recede without compromising his prestige and his reputation for infallibility. Warning after warning came to him in vain, sign after sign was disregarded. Ségur marvels at the blindness which failed to foresee that the rising of the 2nd of May in Madrid was the spark which could only be extinguished beneath the ruins of his crumbling empire. Escoiquiz, the able though servile envoy of Ferdinand and the Council of Castille, summoned courage at the last to speak out like a sage and a patriot. With rare prescience he described all the difficulties and troubles which would beset the invaders; he predicted the consequences of the inevitable interposition of the English, although he could not foretell that they would be commanded by Wellington. But when he spoke it was towards the eleventh hour, and the autocrat refused to listen. Already Joseph had peremptory orders to exchange the crown of Naples for that of Spain, though Joseph knew he was being sacrificed to his brother's ambition, and would have refused had he possessed the nerve and wealth of his brother, the Prince of Canino.

Had his statecraft not failed him for once, Napoleon might have governed Spain, for a time at least, through the Bourbons, leaving Charles or Ferdinand a shadowy supremacy. When they called him in to arbitrate in the scandals of the palace, they had abdicated all free will and placed themselves absolutely at his disposition. The Prince of Peace, the all-powerful favourite, trembling for the consequences of his contumacy before the Battle of Jena, was his obsequious tool, ready to sell his master and the liberties of the nation. Doubtless the prudent course was Napoleon's first idea. But with more familiar knowledge his contempt had increased for the senile king and the hereditary prince. He saw that the courtiers and aristocracy were corrupt to the core; that the ministers and place-hunters were venal as Godoy, and would have been as base had they enjoyed Godoy's opportunities. It seemed well to get rid altogether of a dynasty, who might easily be intimidated but were never to be trusted. And it would be as gratifying to his ambition as to his pride to succeed where Louis the Grand had failed, to efface the Pyrenees and to annex another kingdom for the aggrandisement of the Buonapartes.

He reckoned without the Spanish nation, and, strange to say, he seems to have taken slight account of the remarkable defensible capabilities of the country. He told the Abbé de Pradt that he would never undertake the venture, were it likely to cost him 80,000 men; but that even if all Spain were to rise, the insurrection could be suppressed at a sacrifice of 12,000 soldiers. The Spaniards of the lower orders were ignorant and indolent, but they were warlike, careless of life, passionate for their independence, and vindictive as Orientals. Sober and frugal, they could sustain long fasts and endure extreme privations. In their climate, through great part of the year, the shelter of a roof was matter of indifference. Living far away from the corruption of the Court, their loyalty was a deep traditional sentiment, unshaken by centuries of gross misgovernment. In short, the Spanish people were still of the same stuff which had recruited the armies of Cortez and Alva: and if anything was likely to fire their pride, it was insolent aggression by their formidable neighbours.

That Spain was an agglomeration of semi-independent kingdoms was a source at once of weakness and of strength. The jealousies were detrimental to any broad scheme of regular warfare; but, on the other hand, in a guerrilla insurrection, the Peninsula was like a steamship built in compartments. One province might be swamped by the rush of invasion, but the next, behind its mountain barriers, was comparatively indifferent. The patriotism was provincial, not national. As for those barriers, the successive ridges of parallel sierras, traversed by few and difficult roads; the rivers, rarely bridged and seldom fordable in flood; the gorges through which those roads are carried, were so many fastnesses or almost impregnable lines of defence, assuming that they were held by resolute men. Nor were the cities, as a rule, less defensible, thought except on the northern frontiers, or on the borders of Portugal, few were regularly fortified.

The stubborn, resistance of Zaragoza through the siege showed what effective use might be made of the flat-roofed palaces and massive convents, mutually supporting each other, and only to be taken by sap or storm. The *plazas* were so many rallying centres, where troops could bivouac or deploy, and which, by simply barricading the issues, could be turned into entrenched camps. In Portugal, a small and narrow country, the isolated risings could be speedily crushed by rapid concentration. In Spain, which could only be comparatively weakly occupied, there were vast distances to be traversed from the several headquarters, over barren mountains and inhospitable plains. The Juntas had leisure to drill their levies, or they could rally the fugitives after defeat in *dehesas* and *depoblados*, heaths and wastes, which were practically inaccessible.

The first invasion, undertaken to escort Joseph to his capital, was planned on the assumption of the acquiescence of the nation, or at least in the belief that the French need deal with nothing more serious than local *émeutes*, which could be easily put down. Napoleon relied with reason on the superiority of disciplined troops, under veteran leaders, over raw levies wretchedly commanded. Nevertheless he knew that his own forces were chiefly composed of conscripts who fell easy victims to disease, or of foreigners pressed into the ranks and always ready to desert. His grand plans were worthy of his genius; but he had reckoned without the Spanish temperament, and had forgotten to count with the chapter of accidents. His generals would seldom act in concert, and his first and best combinations were baffled by the unexpected disaster of Baylen. The usurper fled from his capital to the Ebro; the army of invasion was standing on the defence; the Emperor's schemes were to be entirely remodelled, and the occupation was to be recommenced more methodically and on an infinitely more formidable scale.

That brings us to the point where the English ministers decided to assume the offensive on land. It was no light undertaking, nor is it wonderful that the Cabinet had hesitated. The difficulties were great and the circumstances discouraging. The Emperor had put forth stupendous efforts. The numerical superiority of the French was overwhelming, for Portuguese and Spaniards were an undrilled rabble. Theirs was no longer an army of conscripts. Eighty thousand veterans, habituated to victory, had been drawn from Germany, celebrating the victories to come in a triumphal progress through France. In 1808 the conscription of 1810 had been already anticipated, so behind these were practically inexhaustible reserves. The advance was securely based on the northern fortresses, where the magazines were being filled to repletion. Eight *corps d'armée*, each complete in its several parts, were under the command of eight distinguished generals; above all, the Emperor was at headquarters in person, to overrule their rivalries and repair their mistakes.

The French generals had been schooled in war; their soldiers were flushed with conquest. The English Army was under a cloud since the treaty of Utrecht; ill-planned expeditions, often under incompetent chiefs, had damaged its reputation; the nation, ever susceptible to moods and fancies, had almost been brought to doubt its fighting qualities. There were no leaders who loomed large in the public eye like the French marshals, and the hero of Assaye, of subordinate rank, was slightingly spoken of as the Sepoy General. There was no master mind at the War Office or the Horse Guards—no organised plan. The contingents were at first sent out in driblets. As for the cavalry, it was a mere handful, whereas the French were especially strong in that arm.

It might have been assumed that our forces would have one great advantage, as they were operating in friendly countries. That was far from being the case. Napoleon, although never neglecting his magazines, made the war, as far as possible, support itself, and his generals were unsparing in levying contributions. The British had to carry their supplies or buy them. Often their allies not only refused to sell provisions or hire animals for transport, but expected to be fed from the British cruisers. The French were assured of effective mutual support, when jealousy did not interfere. The British generals must reckon with confederates who seldom scrupled to play them false, and with shadowy *corps d'armée* absurdly magnified, or sometimes existing only in report. Far from getting reliable information, as might have been expected, they moved in an atmosphere of suspicion and mendacity, and the Government envoys and official despatches were the least trustworthy of all. Their communications rested on seas and sails, and on a rocky coast-line which, through the prevalent winds from the south-west, was always perilous and .often impracticable. The more we weigh the conditions of that most unequal match, the more we marvel at the genius which achieved such unparalleled results. But the Austrian war withdrew Napoleon from Spain, and Providence gave us a Wellington to direct the allied operations.

CHAPTER 1

Invasion of Portugal and Revolt of Madrid

NOVEMBER 1806—MAY 1808

We retrace our steps to give a summary of the events that led immediately to the great war. Effect had to be given in the Peninsula to the oppressive Berlin decree, and it was followed up by the treaty of Fontainebleau. The Spanish Court, submissive to servility, had invited the interposition of Napoleon in domestic affairs. There was a shameful unveiling of the scandalous secrets of the palace. The Prince of the Asturias had been charged with conspiring against the lives of his royal parents. His mother regarded him with undisguised malignity, and Godoy, the Prime Minister and all-powerful favourite, was his bitter enemy. Professing to believe his life in danger, as indeed it probably was, he appealed to Napoleon for protection. On his side, Godoy, Prince of the Peace, was eager now to make any terms with the French Emperor. By summoning the Spaniards to arms on the Prussian declaration of war, he had provoked an enemy apt to be implacable, and feared he had sinned beyond forgiveness. To be restored to favour, to secure his personal safety and have his ill-gotten fortune guaranteed, he was willing to consent to any sacrifice.

Napoleon welcomed the opportunity of interposing as mediator, for it precisely forwarded his views. With that high-handed and flagitious treaty he began his course of spoliation and treachery. That it deprived the House of Braganza of its ancestral dominions might be fair enough, for undoubtedly had the Regent of Portugal been free from French menaces and pressure he would have cast in his lot unreservedly with the English. But the Queen of Etruria, daughter of the

Spanish King, was arbitrarily expelled from the Tuscan territory with her infant son, being promised compensation in Northern Portugal. As to the semi-tropical province of Algarve in the south, that was to be erected into a principality for Godoy. As Napoleon robbed the Tuscan Queen, so from the first he meant to befool his obsequious Spanish tool. It is as clear that Godoy was effectually deceived as that the autocrat had no intention of fulfilling his promises. With the promptitude to which he had hitherto owed his successes, the Emperor lost no time in carrying out his decision. Nine days before the treaty was signed the French had passed the frontier on their march to Lisbon. The command was confided to Junot—to console him for the loss of his position on the Imperial staff—a general as audacious as he was ambitious; easily elated by the victories he was swift to follow up, and capable of admirable strategical combinations.

But, as subsequent events were to show, he was depressed and paralysed by adverse circumstances. His march, after receiving his orders to leave Salamanca, was a brilliant military achievement. In a month to a day after leaving Bayonne his advance guard had entered Portugal. Over miserable roads, in late autumn and early winter, he pressed forward without giving his forces breathing time. If there was a certain number of seasoned soldiers, for the most part they were conscripts. Proclamations with fair promises were scattered broadcast, but the assurances were belied by pillage and rapine. The guns were brought forward, but the commissariat train fell behind, and the army supported itself precariously by living on the inhabitants. The natives who offered desultory resistance were easily disposed of, but fatigue and hunger had done their work, and the general struggled into the capital at the head of 2000 footsore and famished veterans, with their cartouche boxes in many cases as empty as their bellies. It was a rash venture, but he had a great prize in view.

It was known that the royal family contemplated flight to their colony of Brazil: the object of the forced marches was to secure their persons, or at all events the treasure with which their vessels were to be freighted. In that latter purpose Junot partially succeeded, but he had the mortification of barely being in time to see the leading ships of the squadron standing across the bar of the Tagus. There was an English squadron off the mouth of the river, the city was filled with an excited population lamenting the departure of the Royal House, and there was a considerable number of regular troops under arms. The people of Lisbon have been blamed for not rising on the French and annihilating the stragglers, as they might easily have done. But the accusation is unfair. Behind that feeble and exhausted advance guard was the whole strength of Napoleon's veteran hosts, with the terrible prestige of the conqueror who had never yet succumbed to defeat. So the Three *Uhlans* captured Rheims, because they represented the armies of United Germany.

Junot took advantage of the panic and surprise to occupy the posts of strength and make menacing dispositions. As his regiments straggled in his position was assured. Possibly, had he possessed the humanity and self-restraint of his subordinate, Travot—almost a singular exception to the truculence of his *confreres!*—Junot might have reduced the Portuguese to acquiescence and obedience. The French were present in irresistible force; the Portuguese had no faith in effective succour from England, and the Spaniards were under the French colours as allies. Mild and generous government would have paid in every sense. Napoleon had chosen well when he sent that dashing leader to annex, but the choice proved singularly unfortunate when Junot came to administer. He carried the system of governing by terror—of making serfs instead of subjects of subjugated nations—to excess. He was the plunderer *par excellence* among predatory generals, compelled by their imperious master to live up to their opportunities, and almost constrained to enrich themselves by pillage.

Junot was resentfully denounced by the exile of St Helena, in the memoirs dictated to Las Casas, as 'a monster of rapacity.' The proof is that when he embarked after the Convention of Cintra, he asked for five ships to carry his personal baggage, and had actually emptied the stables of the Prince Regent of Portugal. His subordinates, detached in command of districts, emulously followed his example. The soldiers, in their degree, imitated their superiors. What with public contributions, private exactions, outrages on property, insults to women, and, above all, by the sacrileges which scandalised the pious and alienated the priests, the Portuguese passed from despondency into desperation, and were driven by despair into open insurrection.

Isolated outbreaks might have been easily suppressed, and the reign of terror effectually established, had not the conflagration suddenly broken out in Spain. In Spain the policy of Napoleon in a very few months had turned a nation of cordial allies into deadly enemies. The warlike Spaniards had followed with admiration the achievements of the great captain. Among the more intelligent his name had become a household word, like that of the Cid. They sympathised in his hatred of the English. The occupation of Gibraltar was a perpetual outrage on the national pride, and more recent offence had been given by the questionable capture of their frigates. When Junot was sent on his mission of annexation, considerable Spanish forces were engaged as his auxiliaries, and were well content to march under the tricolour. But in the early days of 1808 the nation began to take alarm. Under pretext of supporting the army of Portugal a stream of regiments continued to turn the western Pyrenees, and troops were even poured into Catalonia, remote as that province was from the scene of operations. A scheme, perfect from the military point of view, had been devised as a preliminary, by which the fortresses, which were the keys of Northern Spain, were to be transferred to French hands by infamous treachery. The commandants were generally patriotic, and their suspicions had been excited.

But the orders of the Prime Minister were peremptory. The French were to be received everywhere as friends, and everything was to be done to gratify their wishes. At Pamplona, the strong capital of mountainous Navarre, the French by a trick were actually smuggled into the fortress in numbers sufficient to overpower the garrison. At Barcelona, Alvarez, who commanded in the almost impregnable fort of Monjuich, built originally to dominate the city, was a man of courage and determination, and would have taken measures to baffle the plot he had penetrated. But he knew that he would assuredly be disavowed by Godoy, and that successful resistance would have involved his disgrace, and probably be punished by death, unless he were prepared to break out in rebellion. Before the end of January the seizure of that northern chain of strong places had given the invaders a secure base of operations, and the Pyrenees were lost as a line of defence. In February Napoleon could venture to throw off the mask with a demand for Spanish territory in exchange for compensation in Portugal. The violent *émeute* of Aranjuez precipitated events. By his greed, his infamous morals and the influence he had vilely abused, Godoy had long been justly odious. To a great extent he had been hoodwinked by Napoleon's professions, but now he was generally accused of venal treason and the popular indignation was not to be controlled.

The Court had prepared to leave Aranjuez for Seville; it was believed that they meant to follow the example of the Braganza family, and, without the excuse of submitting to irresistible force, desert their subjects in this crisis of their fate. For Seville was on the road to Cadiz, whence they could embark for Vera Cruz. The mob burst into the precincts of the palace, cut the traces of the mule teams, and refused to let the sovereigns go. Nevertheless the veneration for the throne was profound; it still respected degraded royalty, but the pent-up indignation vented itself on the Minister. Dragged from his hiding-place by the people, he was rescued by the royal guards. He found temporary safety in ignominious hiding; he was afterwards escorted out of the country under protection of the French, whose policy was never to abandon an instrument. But irretrievably discredited, he had become useless for their purposes. Having no longer a supple agent at his service, who controlled the Court and governed the State, it was then that Napoleon took the fatal resolution of securing all the Bourbon family by threats or guile.

Nothing was to be apprehended, in the meantime, from the impotent Charles who had abdicated in favour of his son. It was true that Ferdinand had been the first to appeal to Napoleon; but now he represented the principle of royalty, already he was doubtless receiving assurances of loyal devotion, for the execrated favourite had been his bitter enemy, and his temper might have changed with the altered circumstances. He had been proclaimed king. He was at Madrid, where the Council of Castille was sitting as the Central Junta, and it was impossible to tell what mischief might be brewing. Prompt action was necessary, and Murat was ordered to occupy the capital in force. The riots of Aranjuez accelerated his movements. He made his public entry on the 23rd March, accompanied by Savary, Duke of Rovigo, perhaps the ablest and least scrupulous of the Emperor's counsellors. Beauharnais was already in residence as imperial envoy.

Ten thousand soldiers were introduced into the city; the rest of the army was encamped outside. Clouds of cavalry swept the surrounding country, cutting off all communications with the provinces, and a detachment was sent forward to Aranjuez. As Junot had been an unfortunate choice to effect the subjugation of Portugal, so Murat was the worst possible selection to carry out the crafty instructions of his master. Napoleon had no wish to precipitate matters. Already he had evidently come to realise that he was treading the crust of a volcano. In a remarkable despatch, he orders his impetuous brother-in-law to treat the Spaniards with consideration and leniency, 'so that they may not suspect the course I intend to pursue.' All manner of civility was to be shown to the old King, the Queen and Godoy; above all, Napoleon was not to be committed to granting Ferdinand an interview *within Spain*. He added this prophetic warning, 'If war once break out all is lost' But Murat was not the man to temporise. He believed in military force, and he was irritated by the sullen bearing of the citizens and their ill-devised attempts at futile resistance. Possessing the real power, absolutely controlling the situation, he put himself ostentatiously forward, in place of using Spanish statesmen as a screen. He was indiscreet enough to have himself elected a member of the Central Junta, thereby accepting gratuitous responsibility for the unpopular measures he meant to inspire. But perhaps still more significant of the diplomacy of the tactless and headstrong *sabreur* was his urging the surrender of the sword of Francis I., treasured as a national heirloom in memory of the victory of Pavia, for it was an idle provocation to Spanish vanity.

At that time Murat had no fears for the future. His despatches are full of jubilant self-confidence; but the unfortunate Ferdinand was in extreme perturbation. He had made his entry into the capital, and his reception by the people had been all he could desire. He came prepared to play the humiliating *rôle* of toadying the civil and military French chiefs, but his flatteries were wasted. The French Ambassador paid him no royal honours. Murat, when questioned, declared he could take no steps in the matter till he received further instructions. Nevertheless, both Beauharnais and Savary were lavish of civilities in private. They posed as the friendly advisers of the young King, and their kindly advice was invariably the same—that he should seek an immediate interview with the Emperor. Then all would be well, and the Emperor would come to Burgos to meet him. Distracted between hopes and fears, Ferdinand was terrorised into his fatal decision, and on the 11th April he set out for Burgos.

At his own earnest request, Savary was the companion of his journey. The part assigned to the Duke, and he played it excellently, was to lull the victim into false security. Reaching Burgos, Ferdinand's fears got the upper hand, on learning that the Emperor was still at Bayonne. When he was reluctantly induced to proceed to Vittoria, it was too late to turn back. His Spanish counsellors, whose eyes were opened at last, tried hard to persuade him. As previously at Aranjuez, the populace rose and cut the traces of the carriage. But Ségur, who was there and pitied him, and who unhesitatingly condemns the conduct of his master, explains how, in obedience to orders, the French had closed in behind him, preventing a retreat. Yet it is possible that even then he might have been suffered to pass back, in fear of the grave responsibility of a public scandal. But Savary, always at his elbow, felt it was no time for scruples. He solemnly pledged his personal honour to a

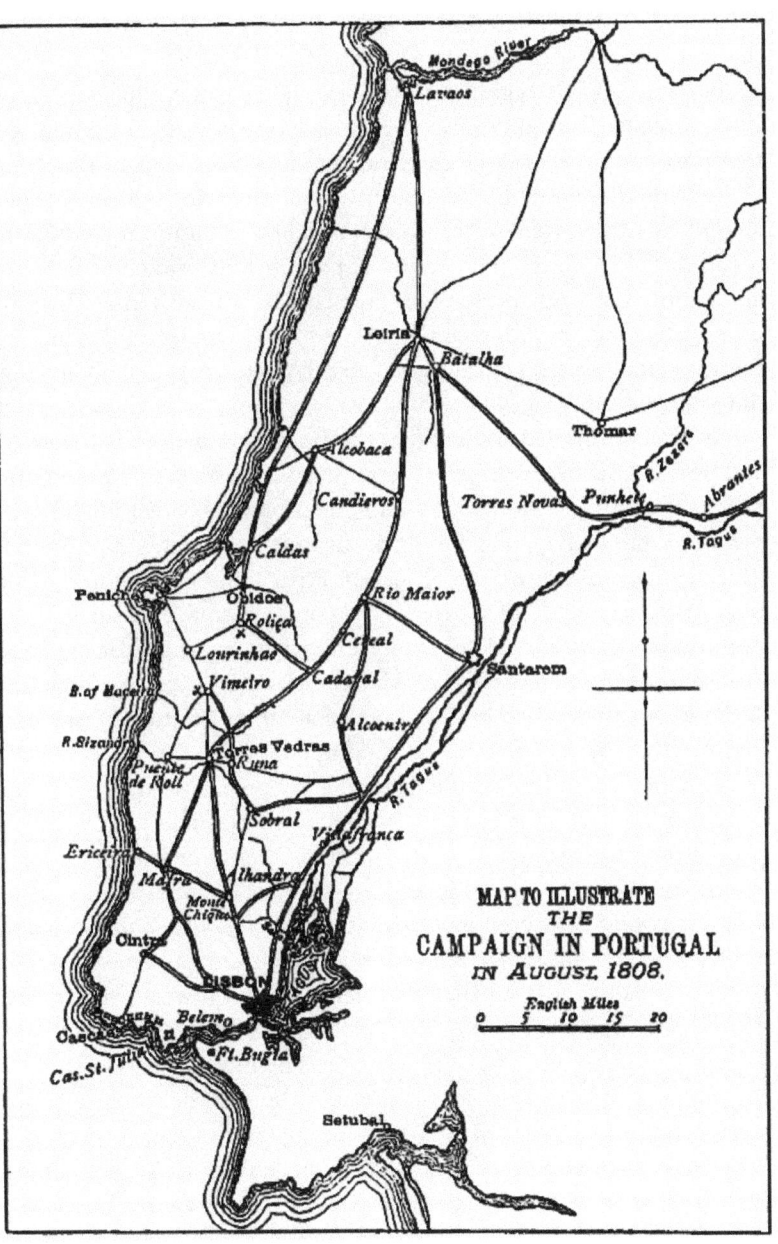

safe-conduct. Whatever the result of an interview, which could not fail to be satisfactory, whether as King or Prince he should be received as an honoured guest—be free, at his pleasure, to return as he had come. Ferdinand's eyes were finally opened to the fact of his captivity by the slights which he met with after crossing the Bidassoa.

Betrayed and outraged, the prisoner proved less complaisant than the tyrant had hoped. Consequently orders were sent to Murat to transport the old King, the Queen and Godoy forthwith to Bayonne. The scenes that ensued in the stormy family meetings, where Napoleon sat as arbiter, were so scandalous as to appear almost incredible. It is said that the Queen, in a tempest of passion, told Ferdinand, in presence of her husband and the Emperor, that he was no son of Charles. The upshot was that Charles surrendered his crown into the hands of the Emperor, which was followed next day by the formal abdication of Ferdinand.

As it had been determined that the Bourbons were to be deposed and interned in France, it became imperative to secure all the members of the family. The *Infante* Carlos, next brother to Ferdinand, had preceded him to Bayonne. Fresh instructions had been sent to Murat, ordering him to forward the Queen of Etruria and her children, with Don Francisco, a boy of fourteen, the youngest son of Charles. They were under Murat's hand, for they were occupying the palace at Madrid. On the memorable 2nd of May, the travelling carriages drew up at the palace doors. The French have been falsely accused of provoking the troubles, as a pretext for making a bloody example, probably because they had made no adequate military preparations. The charge is false on the face of it, for they had left their hospitals unguarded. A great crowd had gathered on the spacious *plateau* before the palace. When they saw the weeping Queen and her children come forth, with the young Prince who was the sole remaining hope of the kingdom, then grief turned to frenzied indignation.

The knives which all the Madrileños of the lower orders carry flashed out; the escort was overpowered in a simultaneous rush, and again the traces of the carriages were cut. The mob surged down into the city; the insurrection spread through the crowded quarters; the foreign garrison was taken unawares; stragglers and detached parties were massacred, and the sick in the hospitals were ruthlessly butchered. The fiery Spaniards had been wrought up to frenzy, but never was revolt more insane. The French closed in on the city with guns and cavalry, and though the resistance was desperate, it was soon over.

The slaughter was great, though it has been probably exaggerated, and next day there were summary executions of prisoners who were court-martialled and condemned on slight evidence. Napoleon's presage was to be fulfilled, for war had broken out. One of the immediate consequences was that Charles's brother, Don Antonio, who had hitherto presided over the Council of Castille, resolved to depart for Bayonne to share the fortunes of his family. Remonstrances were unavailing. Doubtless he felt that as prince and patriot his position had become intolerable, since a river of blood had flowed between his countrymen and the foreign invaders.

Chapter 2

The Rising in Spain: The Capitulation of Baylen
May—July, 1808

The trouble in Madrid precipitated the impending insurrection. The Spaniards had been already irritated by the betrayal of the royal family and the treacherous occupation of the fortresses. Friendship had changed to mistrust, and mistrust had given place to patriotic indignation. The Spanish blood was heated to fever point, and the fire broke out in a general conflagration. At first it was essentially a popular movement. The nobles and those who had anything to lose were naturally disinclined to risk everything in a cause which they considered doubtful, if not desperate. The most experienced among their inexperienced generals realised the military strength of the French and were anxious to repress popular demonstrations. Some, like Cuesta, though sincerely patriotic, exerted themselves to avert a movement which seemed destined to be stifled in blood. Others who, like Solano, were suspected of truckling to the invaders, of being faint-hearted or lukewarm, fell victims to the popular fury. The flames of patriotism were fanned by truculent demagogues, and a reign of terror was established, to which the national leaders had to bow.

Yet many prominent men were tempted to canvas for office by the prospects of pay, patronage and popularity; the more cautious or far-sighted, who would gladly have held back, were constrained to come forward under penalty of proscription. On the whole, the *Juntas*, which were formed everywhere, were composed of local notorieties. But the civilians with any knowledge of affairs were mere clerks or bureaucrats, and few of the soldiers had seen war. Nor either then or afterwards could there be unity of action. Spain is still an agglomeration of independent kingdoms. The Asturian has nothing in common with the Andalusian, and even near neighbours like the Aragonese and Catalans, separated only by the wall of the *Sierras*, cherish the memories of ancient feuds. To such an extent was local jealousy carried, that the *Juntas* of districts in the same province were often at dagger's drawn. No province would share foreign supplies or remittances with the next; one army could never be relied upon to support another, and so a common scheme of operations was impracticable, even had there been a strategist capable of conceiving and directing it.

On the other hand, although the French were comparatively few in the first invasion, and for the most part raw levies, they were directed by the genius that, with what seemed superhuman prescience, foresaw and provided for every contingency. Had Savary carried out Napoleon's ideas, and struck effectually before the revolt had gathered head, the result might have been very different. The plan was simple. Bayonne and Perpignan were the bases of operation in France. The passes through the Pyrenees into Navarre and Aragon were relatively unimportant The line through Vittoria and Burgos, where there were to be great magazines and strong reserves, must be kept open at any cost, as on the eastern side Barcelona was of supreme importance. The Catalonian capital was the centre of a rugged country, teeming with a warlike peasantry, and could communicate by sea with the English in Sicily and the Balearic Isles. But Madrid was to be the centre and pivot of operations.

Thence corps were to be detached, in various directions, which should menace important cities in the south and sever the communications between the provinces. They should have been disposed so as to render mutual support and to crush any hostile efforts within their spheres by sudden converging movements. But Savary let his forces get out of hand and showed himself incapable of appreciating or adhering to the plan so ably traced out. Not one of the generals but was guilty of blundering, except Bessières, who took matters into his own hands and acted in the north-west with skill and energy. At the first outbreak he effectually scattered the forces opposed to him, but he had afterwards to face a more formidable combination. Cuesta, routed by him before, had assembled a second army, and was joined at Benevente by Blake with the levies raised in Gallicia. Of the two, Blake was the better general. But Cuesta's obstinacy was as great as his undeniable courage; his seniority gave him a certain authority, and he was at the head of by far the larger contingent.

Though weak in the cavalry arm, in which the French were always strong, he determined on advancing towards the plains of Castille and again offering battle. Bessières, on his part, combined prudence with daring. He gradually strengthened his force by withdrawing garrisons, though even then it barely numbered 15,000, and he waited to bring up some heavy guns. The Spaniards, who offered battle in a strong position, with 25,000 regulars and a mob of about 17,000 ill-armed peasants, were scattered with great slaughter. The killed and wounded amounted to 6000, and there were many prisoners. The Spaniards are said to have fought well, yet the French reports returned only 50 killed. The loss of material of war was serious, for Cuesta had carried fatuity so far as to form his magazines in the plains instead of in the mountains. It is significant of the state of discipline among the patriots that Blake's strategy is supposed to have been influenced by the fact that his soldiers had just murdered their former leader, Filangieri. The importance of the seasonable victory could scarcely be overrated. It removed all danger from the French communications, leaving the road to Madrid open to Joseph, and it crushed the patriots of the north-western provinces who had taken the lead in the war of liberation.

Zaragoza was only second in strategic importance to Barcelona. There, three out of the four routes from France to Madrid converged; separated from a suburb by the Ebro, which was navigable for gun-boats, it was a centre for operations on either bank. It had been entered but immediately evacuated, as there was no citadel to overawe the city; nor did the invaders desire needlessly to excite alarm by leaving an adequate garrison. They would have acted differently had they foreseen the future. Now General Lefebre-Desnouettes was detached from Pamplona to take possession. With 4000 men he forced the passage of the Ebro, as cruelly as impolitically shot the leaders he had made prisoners, dispersed 10,000 of the Spaniards who barred his way, and delivered an assault on a city with 50,000 inhabitants. It is asserted that had he followed up his first advantage he might have taken the place when the defenders were panic-stricken. Palafox, who has been exalted into the hero of the siege, had left by one gate—to seek for succour, as he said—as the French were forcing another. But it must be allowed that, according to the rules of war, and looking at things by the light of subsequent events, Lefebre-Desnouettes would have been severely blamed for a disaster. Retiring after his first partial success, he fell back upon the siege in form, which was not raised till after the French reverses and retreat.

In Catalonia, General Duhesme was in possession of Barcelona. He also held Figueras. But he had committed the palpable and strange mistake of neglecting to secure the intervening fortresses of Gerona and Hostalrich, which effectually closed the high road from Perpignan. His tardy attempts to retrieve the error were unfortunate. The first assault on Gerona failed, chiefly owing to the shortness of the scaling ladders. The result of the second siege was still more mortifying. The French, advancing from Figueras on the one side, and from Barcelona on the other, found themselves severed from their respective bases by irregulars swarming down from the mountain spurs and forming behind the rugged banks of the Llobregat, and by the fire of the British warships blockading Barcelona. The dashing though rash action of the Count Caldagues at the head of a relieving force had better fortune than it deserved, and Duhesme was driven to a hasty retreat, in which he abandoned his artillery and munitions. In Valencia, the veteran Marshal Moncey had no better luck, though he was guilty of nothing worse than an error in judgement. Considering his numerical weakness, it was no discredit to be repulsed from a city containing 80,000 people; nor was it a necessary part of the plan that he should occupy it. But he seems to have believed that it had been sold to him by traitors within the walls, and that no serious opposition would be offered. Moreover, the Valencians were the reverse of the Catalans, for the Spanish proverb says the men are women and the women nothing. Moncey withdrew in perfect order, and his corps again occupied the position assigned to it.

But the coming calamity, which was to counterbalance Bessières' victory of Rio Seco, was Dupont's humiliating surrender at Baylen. When that general was ordered to occupy Andalusia, no serious opposition was anticipated. He passed the Sierra Morena, to find all the conditions changed. A patriotic junta at Seville had proclaimed war against France. He could no longer count on the Spanish and Swiss veterans assembled in the camp at San Roque as allies; on the contrary, Castaños who commanded, was in friendly communication with the English in Gibraltar. All Andalusia was up in arms, and, finally, the supports he expected from Portugal were returning to Lisbon. Probably Junot was by no means eager to assist him. Nevertheless he crossed the Guadalquivir, routed as usual the undisciplined Spaniards who opposed him when he recrossed the river at Alcolea, defeated them again at Cordova, stormed the city and sacked it. The fugitives spread consternation in Seville. Castaños who had come up from San Roque and been appointed captain-general, was already embarking his artillery and stores with the intention of descending the river to Cadiz, and had Dupont followed up his success, Seville must have surrendered. He can hardly be blamed for not doing so, as he was in ignorance of the state of affairs. But he hesitatingly chose the middle course, which, notwithstanding the proverb, is often the most dangerous; a good general of division, he was an execrable commander. He wrote urgently to Savary for reinforcements, and irresolutely loitered away ten precious days in Cordova.

Then he decided to withdraw to Andujar, relieving by his retreat the apprehensions of the Spaniards. Having once fallen back, it is incomprehensible that he did not retire to Baylen, where he would have had his back to the ridges of the *Sierra*, and kept open the pass of Despeñas Perros, through which he would receive the succours and supplies from La Mancha. In place of that he remained for a month at Andujar, leaving the enemy ample room to manoeuvre between his headquarters and his supports under General Vedel. That was precisely what the Spaniards did, when he had given them leisure to recover themselves and organise. Meantime his young soldiers, inactive and disheartened, were rapidly filling the hospitals. The enemy was closing around him, and then at the eleventh hour he resolved on further retreat. The march was disorderly, and the men were demoralised. He was taken between two fires, and at last he was forced into action. Seldom has a battle been fought under more singular conditions. He was attacked in the front by Castaños, in the rear by Reding, and Reding was interposed between him and Vedel, who had been marching aimlessly backwards and forwards. The comedy of strategical blunders ended in favour of the Spaniards.

A comedy of blunders it was, for Dupont carefully made his dispositions to be beaten in detail; the Spanish generals were too chivalrous to take advantage of his error, and Castaños, whose wish had been to fall back upon Cadiz, was spurred on to the battle and the victory by the civilian junta of Seville, profoundly ignorant of war. When his ammunition was exhausted and his troops were without food, Dupont was reluctantly persuaded to a capitulation. When the pen was in his hand, he had nearly thrown it down at the sound of the guns of Vedel, who was in full tide of success. Indeed, there is little doubt that had Vedel pursued his advantage he might have cut a way for his chief through the obstructing forces. But the capitulation was so complete that it embraced not only the victorious division of Vedel, but the scattered supports in La Carolina and the villages of La Mancha. It has been said that Vedel should have repudiated it and saved his division, and indeed he hesitated; but that would have been a rash course to adopt, for the Spaniards had threatened to massacre their prisoners in the event of the surrender not being according to stipulations, and in their temper there can be little question they would have kept their word. On their side they had conceded terms to the vanquished which the generals must have known they were powerless to keep, and they not only laid themselves open to the reproach of treachery, but the soldiers covered themselves with disgrace by their atrocious brutality to the prisoners.

It was the only victory won even nominally by the Spaniards in the war, and it was won chiefly by the Swiss mercenaries and the Walloons. By the irony of fate the battle was fought the very day on which Joseph entered Madrid in triumph, and on which Napoleon left Bayonne for Paris, expressing his conviction that the rebellion was stamped out. The news of Baylen, magnified by the national boasting and *magnilóquence*, put heart into the insurgents all over the country, yet it may be questioned whether it was of advantage to the cause in the end. For by inflating Spanish vanity and overweening self-confidence, it led to the most culpable neglect and temporarily crushing disasters. Meanwhile, when the intelligence reached King Joseph several days after it was common talk among the patriots, it decided him hastily to abandon the capital which he had entered in triumph ten days before.

CHAPTER 3

Roliça, Vimeiro and the Convention of Cintra
JULY, AUGUST, 1808

In the summer of 1808 the relations of Spain and Britain were peculiar. War had never been proclaimed, yet a state of hostilities existed. In the spring the Asturian deputies had been cordially welcomed; assistance was promptly and liberally offered. Yet General Spenser was at sea with 5000 men intended for the capture of Ceuta on the Morocco coast. As has been said, Sir Hew Dalrymple, the Governor of Gibraltar, was on the most friendly terms with Castaños, actually supplying him with 2000 barrels of powder. Castaños had invited Spenser to disembark his forces at Cadiz, but the *Junta* under Morla were opposed to the measure, and ministers at home, from political considerations, hesitated to sanction our active interference in Andalusia. In the meantime, they contented themselves with sending agents to the Spanish *juntas*—the precursors of our present-day Intelligence Department—and they responded freely to even unreasonable appeals for money, arms and clothing. The national feeling was running high then, and there was no surer road to popularity than supporting the Spanish revolt against Napoleon.

The inevitable farther step was to render armed assistance. The revolt had altered circumstances to our advantage. The defection of the Spaniards under Junot's command had gravely compromised his position. Those in the north of Portugal had retired across the frontier, after disarming their French comrades; those in the south had been disarmed themselves, and the Frenchmen were mounting guard over them. The north, with Oporto for its centre and the bellicose bishop for its chief, was in open insurrection; and the Portuguese, like the Asturians, were asking for aid. The opportunity seemed favourable, and it was decided to despatch an expedition. The chief of the English Cabinet was a mere figure-head, but Canning was Foreign Minister and Castlereagh Secretary-at-War. The former had a generous sympathy with Portuguese and Spaniards, and Castlereagh, although essentially an aristocrat, detesting and dreading measures originating with the democracy, was inveterately opposed to Napoleon's ambition. Unfortunately those brilliant statesmen may be said to have been personal enemies, which must go far to account for conflicting plans, diverging counsels, the multiplication of envoys constantly at cross purposes, and the supersession of commanders in the hour of crisis. The English forces available for service were estimated at 80,000.

It seemed obvious that anything effectual could only be achieved by concentration, yet they were gratuitously squandered all over Europe. We had troops in Sicily; we sent Sir John Moore to place himself at the disposition of the insane King of Sweden. Spenser, with another contingent, went cruising in the Mediterranean, and finally mismanagement was to culminate in the disastrous Walcheren expedition, when the soldiers died like flies in the pestilential swamps of Zealand. After many delays, and with no little difficulty, 9000 men were embarked at Cork for the grand Peninsular venture, which, with a force so manifestly inadequate, seemed a doubtful leap in the dark. For even then, including those under Junot, there were 100,000 French in the Peninsula, and behind them were all the legions of the Grand Army, from which they were to be reinforced in the following year by 300,000 seasoned soldiers.

Nor could anyone have realised then that the Titanic struggle between Britain's sea power and Napoleon's veterans was to be decided by the choice of the commander of that insignificant advance guard. Notwithstanding the distinction the General of *Sepoys* had won at Seringapatam and Assaye, he owed his appointment chiefly to family influence, for his brother. Lord Wellesley, believed in him, and had much weight with the Cabinet. And a weaker man might well have resigned, after the fashion in which he was treated by ministers, and the indifference with which they received his appeals.

Sir Arthur left the fleet and sailed with Mr Stewart, the British envoy, in a swift frigate to Corunna. The Gallician *Junta* gave him no encouragement to land his troops there. They were urgent, as usual, for money and supplies, but declared that the patriots only needed

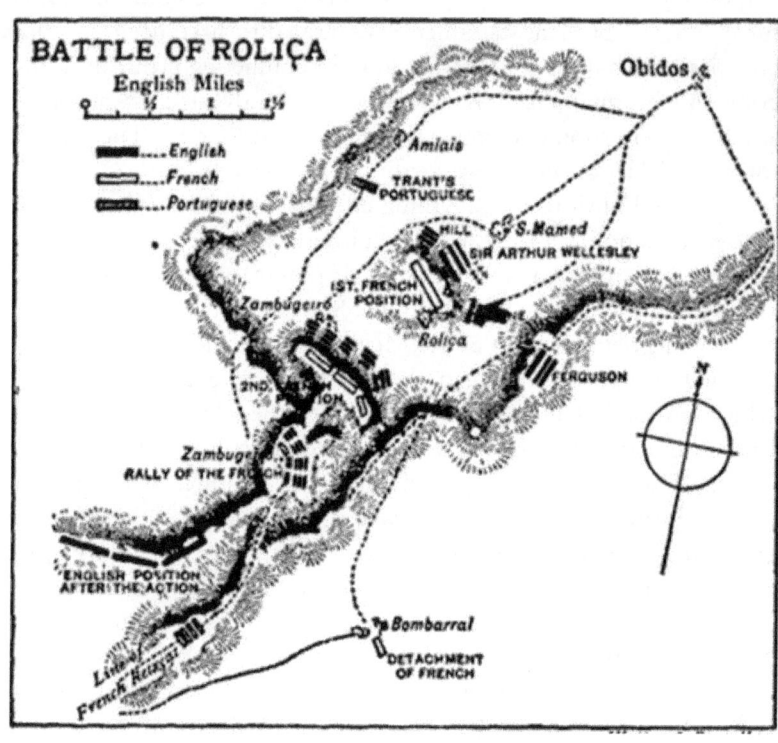

equipments. They gave glowing reports of the strength and spirit of the Oporto insurgents, and, desirous to get rid of him, advised him to co-operate with them. At that time our generals were still in the dark as to the reliance to be placed on Peninsular assurances. The Bishop of Oporto had confirmed the Gallician reports by asking equipments for 40,000 infantry and 5000 cavalry, pledging his word that the English auxiliaries should be fed and supplied with ox-teams for the artillery and commissariat. Yet the mendacious prelate had barely 5000 tatterdemalions under his orders; and when the English general claimed fulfilment of his pledges, neither food nor the draught animals were forthcoming.

Ministers in England had formed no definite plan. Sir Arthur had, in fact, the responsibility of a roving commission, yet his discretion was limited, for the admiral had authority to control the land service. He might go to Cadiz if he pleased, but that idea was promptly dismissed, for political and other reasons. Ministers had suggested a landing at Lisbon. But it was clearly impracticable to force the Tagus, with a hostile Russian squadron lying in the river, and then to disembark under the fire of the batteries. Peniche was the only safe harbour to the north of Lisbon in that rock-bound and weather-beaten coast, but the anchorage was commanded by a fort, and the fort was strongly garrisoned. The next best alternative was landing in the estuary of the Mondego River, and, fortunately, the fort at the mouth had fallen shortly before to the dashing enterprise of some Portuguese students, and was now held by our marines. The landing commenced on the 1st August, but it was not completed till the 5th. A sudden gale would have brought the expedition to shipwreck, but the weather was favourable, and by a happy chance General Spenser arrived at that critical moment.

Thus the force at Sir Arthur's disposal was raised to 12,000 men, for a part of General Spenser's detachment was destined for Gibraltar. Even so, the enterprise seemed daring to desperation: he had thrown himself into a country unknown to him and devastated by the invaders; communication with the fleet was dependent on the weather, and possibly even Sir Arthur might have hesitated had he realised how delusive were the assurances of his Portuguese allies. He must feel his way with extreme circumspection, for he was lamentably deficient in cavalry, and the few horses on board had suffered greatly from seasickness.

Junot, on his side, was seriously embarrassed. His troops were dispersed or shut up in garrisons. Having passed from extreme self-confidence to depression, he exaggerated the strength of the patriots, but he knew that Lisbon was ready to rise; that insurgents from Algarve were mustering on the south of the Tagus, waiting to answer a summons from the citizens. Moreover, he had heard of the disasters in Andalusia. His dispositions have been blamed by capable critics; it has been said that, scattering his forces, he had left them exposed to be beaten in detail, but it is hard to see how he could have acted differently. He promptly recalled Loison from Almeida, and Loison pressed forward with such forced marches that he was compelled to halt for two days in Leiria to get his men in fighting condition. The advance of the English had to be observed and obstructed, and Laborde, who handled an inadequate force with equal skill and courage, was detached for that purpose. Having taken every precaution for the security of Lisbon, Junot followed himself with two or three thousand men—all that could be spared to form the reserves.

Even had Napoleon been in command, he must have assumed that the English would, in common prudence, act *en masse* and cling to the seaboard. Understanding the situation and the value of time, Sir Arthur pressed onwards rapidly, and Laborde was compelled to dispute the passage with his very inferior numbers. Had he marched eastward to join hands with Loison, or fallen back upon Junot and the reserves, the direct road to Lisbon would have been left unguarded. The first encounter of the hostile nations was at Roliça, where he made the most of an exceptionally strong position, withdrawing in excellent order after a protracted and bloody combat. Having disputed each inch of ground, and leaving three of his guns behind him, he made a night march to gain Montechique on the south-east, and thus the road leading to Torres Vedras was left open to the victors.

The road to Torres Vedras was open, and Sir Arthur prepared to follow up his success. He had resolved to press the beaten army and prevent its rallying. Roliça had been decided in the afternoon of the 17th August. News had come that Loison was within five miles of his left flank, but he believed that, having rallied the troops of Laborde, the united forces would fall back upon Montechique and Junot. On the 18th he meant to march to Torres Vedras, the centre of the foremost of the mountain barriers crossing the peninsula formed by the sea and the Tagus, and situated on the road leading straight to Lisbon. Circumstances induced him to change his intention before nightfall. He learned that a fleet with reinforcements had arrived, and he resolved to see to their landing at the adjacent Bay of Maceira. The landing was safely effected, and on the 18th the English advanced to Lourinham by the more circuitous coast road, for Junot, who realised the importance of the commanding position which was the key to operations, had had time to win the race. Crossing the line of Laborde's retreat, having picked up Loison's corps on the way, he occupied Torres Vedras late on the same day. But Sir Arthur had a second plan in reserve, characterised by his habitual celerity of movement.

It was to turn the position of Torres Vedras, so formidable that it could hardly be assailed from the front: to throw forward a strong advance guard to Mafra, and, occupying the intervening heights with his main body, to menace the French flank and the line of march to Montechique. Unfortunately at that critical moment came a frigate with Sir Henry Burrard. The victor of Roliça went on board to communicate with his new superior, who was necessarily ignorant of everything. Before leaving the Mondego, Wellington had written to Sir Henry, recommending that Sir John Moore, who was expected with the army he had saved from Sweden, should land there, and that he should operate independently on the northern bank of the Upper Tagus. Thence he could cut the communications between Lisbon and Almeida, and threaten the line of Junot's march, should that general retreat to Spain by way of Elvas. Burrard disapproved. Moore was off the coast, and should be directed to disembark at Maceira. Meanwhile the army must remain on the defensive in the positions it occupied, with Vimeiro for the pivot.

But it was Junot's intent to force the fighting, and he was determined to bring on the inevitable battle. Decisive it must be in any case. If the British were beaten, they must re-embark under the onslaughts of a triumphant enemy, with no such anchorage as Corunna, and no armed works to cover their escape. On the contrary, if the day went against Junot, there was nothing for him but capitulation or evacuation of the country. The British occupied positions on heights that were more or less commanding, and the precipitous mountain covering the left flank was further protected by a deep ravine, invisible to the enemy, which played an important part in the subsequent engagement. Junot had made a night march, intending to attack at daybreak, and the strength of his position at Torres Vedras is shown by the fact that the narrow defile by which any attack must have been delivered in his centre had delayed his advance for several hours. The combatants were not unequally matched in point of numbers, though the

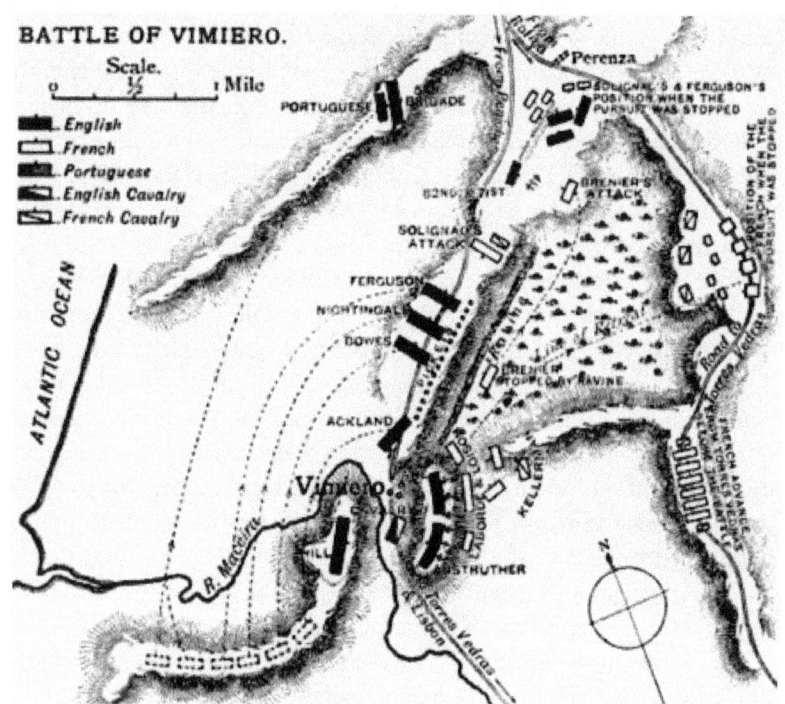

English had somewhat the superiority. But, on the other hand, whereas all the French were brought into action, but a part of the British were actively engaged. Junot showed great personal courage, but his dispositions were faulty. He formed up in two columns of attack, in place of concentrating his attack upon our left Sir Arthur had been halted in a situation where he had never intended to offer battle. For several hours the road of retreat to Lourinham was inevitably left unguarded. Had Junot occupied it with the bulk of the French, the English must have been forced back upon the sea. As it was, his right column of attack, coming on the ravine that formed the ditch of the precipitous mountain, gave the English time to strengthen the defence, and it was ultimately repulsed with heavy loss, leaving several guns behind. But the serious fighting was in the centre, and very desperate it was. The French scaled the heights, sweeping the English skirmishers before them, to face a crushing artillery fire, followed up by headlong bayonet charges. Driven down far faster than they had climbed, they rallied and returned gallantly to the attack. The copses, vineyards and ravines were filled with the dead and wounded. Guns were taken, retaken, and taken again.

Finally Sir Arthur learned, to his relief, from the questioning of a general taken prisoner, that the enemy had brought his last man into action. Junot, on his side, realised that his attempt had failed; but though his troops were beaten, they were, scarcely disorganised, or, at least, they rallied at once under the protection of the guns and cavalry. Moreover, the able and prudent dispositions of Kellerman, who commanded the reserves, induced Sir Arthur, dashing as he was, to decline to listen to heated advisers, who urged him to strike again and without an hour's delay.

Yet it was his full intention to follow up his victory. It was barely noon, and the day was before him. But three of his eight brigades had borne the brunt of the battle; the others had either suffered slightly or not been engaged at all. His original superiority in numbers had been considerably increased, and his scheme was to turn Junot upon either flank, forcing him back from Torres Vedras on the Tagus, and cutting him off from Lisbon. That it would have driven the French general to a more hurried and disastrous retreat than that of Sir John Moore can scarcely be doubted, the rather that he seems to have done nothing to guard his left and observe the coast road, which, turning the lofty Torres Vedras range, would have led the English to those natural lines of defence in his rear which stretched from Mafra to Montechique.

But responsibility had devolved upon Burrard, and having generously left Wellesley all the credit of winning Vimeiro, now he rightly assumed the direction.

It is needless to enter into the considerations which induced him to disapprove the proposed strategy; suffice it to say that they are admitted to have been weighty and were approved by the experienced officers of his staff. Yet he would have adopted Sir Arthur's proposals, though with hesitation, and when it was comparatively too late; but by this time a third commander-in-chief had appeared on the scene. Sir Hew Dalrymple was an able general, if he had not the genius of Wellesley; he had done much to foment the insurrection in Andalusia and to equip Castaños for the victory of Baylen. But being profoundly ignorant of the position in Portugal, he had to wait to be instructed by his predecessors in command. Meantime Kellerman appeared at the outposts, under a flag of truce, with propositions from Junot. The result was the Convention—miscalled—of Cintra, for it was really arranged and signed at Torres Vedras. Briefly, the French army capitulated. It was to evacuate Portugal with the honours of war. It was to be transported to France in English shipping, with no restrictions as to serving again. The article by which the French were permitted to carry away their personal effects gave rise to serious trouble and many misunderstandings.

Unquestionably it was grossly abused, and the pillagers secured the bulk of their plunder. But, in the circumstances, exhaustive search was impracticable; the tension in Lisbon was becoming unendurable; and it was of paramount importance to get rid of the still formidable invaders on any reasonable terms. The convention was virulently abused both in Portugal and England. The Portuguese authorities, who had done nothing for their auxiliaries except draw upon their stores and decline to act with them, indignantly protested that they had not been consulted. The populace of the capital complained, with better reason, that their oppressors had been let off too easily with their booty. And in England the malice of party, acting upon popular misapprehensions and irrational annoyance, secured the appointment of a parliamentary committee to investigate all the circumstances. Dalrymple, Burrard and Wellesley were summoned home to give evidence, or, in other words, to defend themselves; the army was deprived of its chiefs; Portugal, when seething with disturbances from one end to the other, lost the benefit of their local knowledge and experience. Yet the misfortune might have been greater had not the arrival of Moore placed a capable general in supreme command.

As for the maligned convention, it was as cordially approved by Sir Arthur Wellesley as by Sir Hew Dalrymple. Both from a military and political point of view, the gains were immense. Portugal was relieved from the firm hold of a formidable army, still strongly secured in a military sense. Not only the capital with its forts, but the frontier fortresses of Elvas and Almeida, facing Badajoz and Ciudad Rodrigo, were given over without bloodshed, and instead of Junot withdrawing to reinforce his compatriots in Spain, and transfer his energies to the ill-defended Andalusian, he was sent out of the way of doing immediate mischief Several thousand Spanish prisoners, confined in hulks on the Tagus, were set at liberty, and given a free passage to Spain, and, moreover, there was a surrender of the Russian squadron in the river, to be held in deposit till the conclusion of a peace. The moral effect both in Spain and Portugal was incalculable. Following Baylen, it gave another blow to the prestige of Napoleon and his hitherto invincible armies, and the effect throughout the Peninsula was the greater, that the Portuguese were pleased to claim no little of the credit.

CHAPTER 4

Moore's Advance—His Retreat and the Battle of Corunna
SEPTEMBER 1808—JANUARY 1809

After the Battle of Baylen, and the abandonment of the capital by the usurper, the Spaniards had a great opportunity, for there were no French to the south of the Ebro. It is needless to say that they did not avail themselves of it. There was energy or rather excitement enough, but the innumerable local *juntas* were acting independently of each other, and often at open enmity. It would be tedious to trace the history of these miserable squabbles, nor is it necessary. The upshot was that it became evident, even to the jealous Council of Seville, which would gladly have usurped supreme authority, that something in the nature of a parliament must be assembled, which might exercise some authority over the nation. Yet it was chiefly owing to the persistent representations of the British agents that a central *Junta* was assembled at Madrid, composed of thirty-five members from the provinces. A very mixed assemblage it was, comprising patriots of spotless reputation, such as Florida-Blanca, the superannuated president, and some men of notoriously infamous character, like the envoys sent up by Seville.

The practical wisdom of the proceedings is illustrated by the proposal that they should raise half-a-million of infantry forthwith, besides 50,000 cavalry. Had the men been forthcoming, and probably there were never more than a fourth of that number in the field, they had neither arms nor ammunition, nor clothing, and for filling the military chest they must trust to English liberality, Spaniard-like, while broaching these magnificent schemes, they did not make the most modest attempts at organisation. Throughout the course of the protracted war there never was any regular commissariat, which explains why the armies of undisciplined men, though individually brave and animated by fervid detestation of the French, often were scattered from sheer starvation. The levies were unclad in the bitter winter cold, and had to go unshod in the snows unless they found themselves in sandals. A Carnot with a free hand would have been invaluable at Madrid, but there was neither organiser, general nor statesman. Sir John Moore and the British envoys lost no opportunity of urging the necessity of appointing a general-in-chief. The *Junta* admitted the propriety of the measure, but could never come to a decision.

Blake, like Cuesta, was discredited by defeat, yet the choice lay between Cuesta and Castaños. Cuesta, though the old man's indomitable courage won the affection of his soldiers, was arbitrary, impracticable, and what may be called cross-grained. He brooked no crossing of his will, and to offer a suggestion went far towards having it rejected. At that time he had outraged the dignity of the *Junta* by the illegal arrest of one of its most honoured members, and he was not only under a cloud, but had been ordered into a kind of honourable captivity. Castaños might possibly have obtained the post, and he had the advantage, although some considered it an objection, of being personally acceptable to the British. But he was unambitious and indolent, although it was taking a step in the right direction when he was gazetted Captain-General of Madrid.

Meantime the *Junta* indulged in endless talk, issued inflated proclamations, and gave orders which were generally ignored. Each local leader did what seemed right in his own eyes, when he did not take instructions from his soldiers under pain of summary execution. And Napoleon, drawing veterans and even some of the Old Guard from Germany, was preparing to send 200,000 soldiers over the Pyrenees to reinforce the French already in Spain. The conscription of two years in advance, as we said, had been anticipated—evidence sufficient of his fixity of purpose—and Champigny, who conducted foreign affairs, had avowed in State papers that State policy was synonymous with justice, and that the end justified the means.

But at that juncture, by an excellently-planned *coup*, Spain recovered some efficient defenders. According to Napoleon's system, when professing himself her ally he had drained her of the flower of the army to fight his battles elsewhere. One body was in Tuscany under O'Farrel, and there were 14,000 good soldiers in Denmark commanded by the Marquis of Romana. Thanks to British initiative and by the interposition of venturesome agents, the bulk of Romana's corps was embarked on British ships and transported from the Danish islands to the harbours of Gallicia. They were destined to co-operate with a Gallician force which was to make an effective diversion and to give the Spaniards fresh breathing time if they cared to avail themselves of it. The English Government had finally decided to follow up Vimeiro and the convention by an advance into Spain. Nor did the enterprise appear anything but hopeful. It is evident that they persistently under-rated the strength Napoleon could bring to bear, and, misled by the optimism of their subordinate agents, they still put faith in Spanish statistics and promises.

On the 6th October a momentous despatch was received at Lisbon. It appointed Moore to the command of a nominal force of 30,000 infantry and 5000 cavalry. Ten thousand were to be sent from England, under Sir David Baird; the rest, it was assumed, might be drawn from the depleted army in Portugal. In what manner Moore was to enter Spain was left to his own judgement. He might take the army by sea to the northern ports, or march through the interior. The former plan would effect an immediate junction with Baird's contingent, nevertheless he elected for the latter, chiefly because Sir Hew Dalrymple had already made some arrangements for a march on Almeida. Moore's hopes were never high, as were those of the Ministry; as a soldier, he had a more lively appreciation of the French power, nor did he put implicit faith in the reports of the patriots. Still these reports were so circumstantial as to the support he would receive that he could not refuse them a certain credence.

At all events, his instructions were peremptory—the difficulty was to decide on the method of the advance. Wellesley had been guided by excellent maps when marching in the Torres Vedras peninsula, but north-east of the Tagus the country was virtually a *terra incognita*. All reports agreed that the roads over the mountains to Almeida and Ciudad Rodrigo were impracticable for artillery. As it proved, these reports were fallacious, but they induced Moore reluctantly to violate a fundamental rule of war, and, separating from his heavier guns and cavalry, send them by a southerly route, under Sir John Hope to Talavera. Thence, crossing the Guadarama, they were to meet him at Salamanca. He found the roads practicable for guns, but the difficulties otherwise had not been exaggerated. Though the army marched in three columns, it was hard to find means of bare subsistence; the baggage had been cut down to a point engendering the discontent which afterwards culminated in mutinous indiscipline, yet it was impossible to procure sufficient transport animals. As Moore wrote bitterly, 'The army runs the risk of finding itself in front of the enemy with no more ammunition than the men carry in their pouches.'

Everything had to be paid for in a friendly country, but the military chest was so low that it was with the utmost difficulty that £8000 could be spared to Baird, who had landed penniless. By the way, he was detained on the transports for a full fortnight till the formalities insisted upon by our allies could be fulfilled. Yet when the British generals were in such dire financial straits, two millions of dollars were being landed at Corunna, consigned to the Gallician Junta. They were brought by Mr Frere, who had arrived with the fleet which disembarked Romana and his men. Mr Frere came to supersede Mr Stewart as plenipotentiary. He was a brilliant man of letters, the early friend of Canning, the admired familiar of Scott and Southey, yet the selection was unfortunate. Emotional, romantic and unpractical, he lost credit as a diplomatist; his despatches on Peninsular affairs fostered the illusions of his superiors at home, and impracticable suggestions in intemperate language aggravated the embarrassments of Moore when he had to come to prompt and critical decisions.

But the advance of the army was happily timed, for it arrested the French in full swing of victory, and deranged the far-sighted calculations of the Emperor. Had he only had the Spaniards to deal with, the country would have been rapidly overrun, although the irrepressible guerrilla warfare would have gone on smouldering everywhere. All along the line, from Biscay to the Catalonian coast, discipline and skilful combinations—notwithstanding some slight and trivial successes of the patriots—had triumphed over ignorant rashness and unregulated valour. Joseph's defence had been almost as feeble and ill-advised as the Spanish attack, but all changed when Napoleon in person came on the scene. His generals forgot their jealousies under the master's immediate eye. Eight corps were actively employed in concert. The Battles of Espinosa and Gamonal, in which Blake again illustrated his incapacity, subjugated the north of Spain, and assured the French communications with Bayonne, while Burgos, in place of Vittoria, became the centre of offensive operations.

Thence the powerful cavalry could sweep the plains of Castille, driving back the broken bands of the patriots upon the mountains. Then Marshal Lannes inflicted a crushing defeat on the army of the

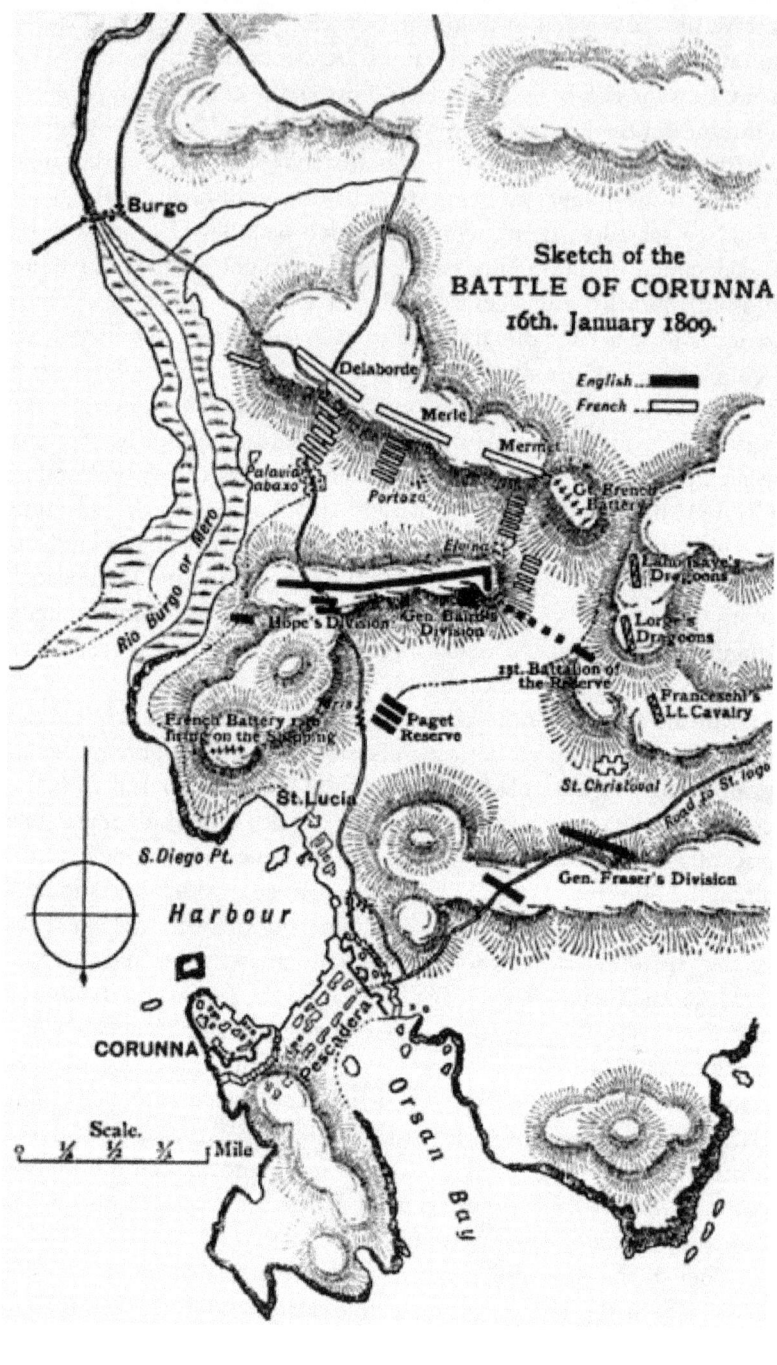

Spanish centre at Tudela on the Ebro. He surprised it when the leaders were clamouring in discordant councils, much like the Covenanters at Bothwell Bridge. Castaños had been checked and overruled by the incompetent and vain-glorious Palafox. The rout was complete, yet the disaster would have been greater had not Ney been in one of the occasional fits of lethargy which sometimes palsied the indomitable energy that covered the retreat from Moscow. Castaños saved a portion of his troops, and a still more important result was that 15,000 of the fugitives under Palafox found their way to Zaragoza.

Assuming that the news of his success would induce the English to retreat, Napoleon detached Lannes to follow up Palafox and summon Zaragoza, while he himself hurried forward to occupy the capital. The pivot of operations was to be advanced from Burgos to Madrid, for political as much as for military reasons. The short road lay over the Somosierra Pass, a formidable position at all seasons, virtually impregnable in the winter if resolutely defended. And the Spaniards for once had made due preparation. The gorge and its surroundings were held by General St Juan with 12,000 men, a battery of sixteen pieces swept the precipitous ascent, and the more open ground, above and behind, was raked by the cross fire from redoubts and entrenchments. According to all principles of war, to assail the pass was to invite disaster. The French column of attack was flanked and preceded by skirmishers on either side; it was received with a warm, running fire of musketry, and the battery of guns was there in readiness to pour showers of grape on the head of the column.

Napoleon rode up to survey the situation. At that moment his sight was obscured by a dense fog, thickened by the powder smoke hanging over the guns. He had one of those rare and original inspirations, which only come to leaders like himself and Wellington. He ordered his Polish lancers to take the battery. The gallant Poles charged up the pass, and the leading squadron went down almost to a man. They broke, fell back, rallied and charged again under cover of the fog and smoke. The gunners were slaughtered, the guns were seized, and in another moment the Spaniards were in headlong flight, throwing away their arms and abandoning their baggage. The French cavalry followed fast in pursuit: the bulk of the runaways fled to Talavera, and there they celebrated their safety by murdering their general. In six weeks Napoleon had scattered the Spanish armies. The stroke of brilliant audacity opened the way to Madrid, and in a few days the French cavalry were before the capital. There was a fierce attack on the suburbs, and Napoleon menaced the city with a bombardment.

But he had no mind to destroy his brother's capital, if indeed he did not for a time entertain the idea of superseding Joseph and administering Spain as a dependency of France. He still hoped that by an affectation of mildness he might induce the panic-stricken people to accept his supremacy. Threats were judiciously blended with promises, and the negotiations were not suffered to drag. Madrid was surrendered by the double-minded Morla and his vacillating colleagues. Doubtless Morla had already resolved to play the traitor; but indeed the miscellaneous inhabitants of La Corte were not of the stuff to make determined resistance. The regular troops and the patriotic irregulars had time to withdraw, and on the 4th December the Emperor made his entry, to find himself in undisputed possession. Whether the Spaniards gave him further trouble or no, he had assembled an imposing force to overawe the country. His *corps d'armée*, operating in concert, had each its allotted work. But his plans were upset by Moore and Zaragoza. He learned to his disappointment that Moore, in place of falling back on the report of his victories, was advancing on Salamanca and threatening his communications. Therefore, instead of prosecuting his designs on the south, he directed every available man against the British, and hurried westward himself to direct the movements in person.

That Moore did not lack audacity, as his disparagers averred, is evident. Had the Spaniards arrested the progress of Napoleon, had they even avoided crushing defeat, he was prepared to detach himself from his base at Lisbon and throw himself into the heart of Spain. As it was, the advance from Salamanca towards Sahagun was daring enough, for it must draw upon him all the available French forces. But his courage was largely tempered by prudence, and when his allies failed him in every respect, though his purpose was partially achieved, retreat could only be a question of time, routes and celerity. His despondency as to great results was too well grounded. Napoleon, with far superior strength, followed him up as far as Astorga. There the Emperor handed over the pursuit to Soult, chiefly because he was preoccupied by the intelligence from Austria, partly, perhaps, because he was disinclined to be present at a possible reverse in the passes of Gallicia.

Moore's retreat was conducted under no ordinary difficulties. Some of the superior officers were disaffected and almost mutinous; the rank and file were discontented when ordered to turn their backs on the enemy. There were no sufficient magazines to fall back upon. Unlike the Frenchman, who is a disciplined marauder, the English, when reduced to forage for themselves, broke loose from discipline and refused to obey. The peasants drove their cattle to the hills, and the pinch of hunger became daily more severe. The wine vaults in the towns were an irresistible temptation. Villa Franca was found to be full of the rabble that was the bulk of Romana's broken army, though Moore had begged the Spaniard to avoid his line of march. Yet still, when danger pressed, the troops showed a bold front. The pursuers had a serious check at Benevente; and at Lugo, having rallied the army on the heights, for two days Moore vainly offered battle. When the precipitate retreat was resumed, it degenerated into something like flight from sheer scarcity of food.

When they entered the higher mountains, in the depth of a bitter winter, the men were thoroughly demoralised. The absurd provisions of the service had cumbered them with women and children. The transport animals gave out, and could not be replaced. Guns and ammunition waggons were abandoned; barrels of dollars were broached and the contents started down the precipices, tempting the soldiers to fill their pockets and sacrifice their lives. All the time Soult warily followed, pressing hard on the retreat, but avoiding fighting. Moore had nothing to gain by insisting on a battle, since victory could have gained him nothing but a brief delay. Between Lugo and Betanzos disorder had come to a head, and the losses were great.

After leaving the former town in a blinding tempest of rain and sleet, the landmarks were obscured, the guides lost their way, and two of the three divisions strayed from the main road. Many of the numerous stragglers never rejoined the ranks, and when the main body found shelter in Betanzos, it arrived in utter confusion. There Moore halted for a day, and when the march was resumed it was soldierlike and orderly. There were 14,000 infantry with the colours when the head of the column looked down upon Corunna. The general anxiously gazed out to sea, but no fleet was to be seen in the roadstead or the offing. Adverse winds had delayed the ships which were to come round from Vigo. That Soult would seize his last chance of striking was certain, and all preparations were made for repelling the attack. Had the British force been sufficient, it might have occupied positions almost impregnable in the semi-circular heights enclosing the rocky arena in which the battle was to be fought.

As it was, that advantage had to be abandoned to the French, and on these heights they formed the batteries which raked the plain with the lower eminences on which our battalions were posted. In men,

SIR JOHN MOORE

guns and cavalry, and notably in the two latter arms, the French marshal had an overwhelming superiority. Before the battle was engaged he had brought 20,000 combatants into line, and to face the fire of his heavy guns we had only a few light field-pieces. For when the fleet had at last come into the bay, the bulk of our artillery was embarked with the best of the few serviceable horses. On the other hand, thanks to Spanish negligence, our men had an unexpected stroke of good fortune. The muskets, battered and rusted on the march, were replaced with new pieces found in the arsenal, and there was an ample supply of the ammunition which happily was failing with the enemy. At two in the afternoon of the 16th, Soult ordered a simultaneous advance. Moore's dispositions were imperatively dictated by the nature of the ground.

The infantry was solidly aligned in a front stretching from Elvina on the right to the bank of the Mezo River. But Baird at Elvina was raked by the great battery on the ridge to his right front, and further to his right the French cavalry was outflanking him. However, the horsemen, who could scarcely act on such ground, were also held in check by Eraser's division and Paget's reserve. Between Baird and the Mezo was Hope's division. The fighting was fiercest at Elvina, and there our losses were most severe. But at nightfall the doubtful contest there had been decided in our favour, though the gallant leader of the division had been seriously wounded. The attacks of the other French columns had equally failed. Foy on their right made but feeble resistance when Hope assumed the offensive, and on their left our skirmishers, followed closely by supports, were actually threatening to take in reverse the formidable battery on the hill.

The victory nobly retrieved the reputation of the army, somewhat imperilled by the disorders of the hurried retreat. But it was dearly bought by the death of Moore, struck from his horse by a cannon shot when watching the fight at Elvina. He was buried by torchlight in a bastion of the citadel, and the volley over the grave was fired by the guns of the enemy. The command devolved on Sir John Hope, who, resisting the temptation to complete Soult's discomfiture, wisely turned his attention at once to the embarkation. Ere daybreak two of the divisions were on board, while the third, which held the citadel and carried the operations on, quietly embarked in course of the afternoon.

Up to a certain point it seems that Moore's generalship was irreproachable. He could hardly have formed magazines on his line of retreat, from the difficulty of filling them. Yet, had his temperament been sanguine, the upshot might have been very different. In place of writing to Cradock for empty transports, he would rather have pressed for reinforcements. The victors of Corunna would have won a more decisive battle, and hurled Soult back into the Gallician defiles. With supplies pouring into Corunna and Ferrol from the sea, we should have held another position like Torres Vedras, and escaped a temporary eclipse of prestige and false imputations of timid faithlessness. But no soldier could have desired a nobler death than that of Moore, and his chivalrous opponent did him ample justice. Almost simultaneously with the battle of Corunna, nominal hostilities ceased between Britain and Spain, and a formal treaty of alliance was concluded with the Supreme *Junta*.

CHAPTER 5

The Siege of Zaragoza and Affairs in Portugal
DECEMBER 1808—MAY 1809

The heroic and obstinate defence of Zaragoza was the second obstacle which upset the French plans. Fifteen thousand fugitives from Tudela had sought refuge there, and had the victory been promptly followed up, possibly the place would have fallen. As it was, the reduction of that bulwark of the east was an object of supreme importance. Moncey began the siege operations, to be replaced by Mortier, who resigned the command to Junot finally superseded in turn by Lannes. On the 20th December the French began to close in. It was no light task they had undertaken. Thirty-five thousand men, exposed to incessant alarms from irregulars swarming in the mountains, were to contain a garrison half as numerous again and to storm a city exceptionally defensible. The defence of Zaragoza continually reminds us of the siege of Jerusalem by Vespasian. There were the fanatics excited by the monks, corresponding to the Zealots. There were the armed peasants from the hills, answering to the Idumeans of John of Gischala. There were the regular soldiers under Palafox and St Marc, and there were the citizens who fought manfully for their homes, but who were, nevertheless terrorised by their more desperate comrades.

There were the same feats of reckless courage, similar ferocity, and the same indescribable horrors. Patriotism inspired the defence, but it was patriotism under a reign of terror. St Marc was an excellent general, and St Genis an engineer of rarely adaptive genius. But it was monks of the lowest orders—men of the people—who coerced the constituted authorities, and directed the resistance. The French were in front and there were gibbets behind, daily garnished with fresh batches of suspects. For the faintest breath of suspicion was a death sentence, and the timid found it safer to fight than to flinch.

The city was girdled on one side by the Ebro, and guarded on the other by ancient walls. But its real strength was in the massive solidity of its buildings, and in the stupendous convents and public edifices, which seemed to have been constructed with a view to this crisis. It would speedily have succumbed to the tremendous bombardment had it not been virtually fire-proof, and almost bomb-proof. Massive blocks of buildings were divided by broad thoroughfares, and each of these was raked by batteries. All the outer doors and lower windows of the houses were built up, the walls were loopholed and the roofs barricaded. So the siege resolved itself into a struggle of the engineers, and the Spaniards had found a Cohorn to confront the French Vauban. The talents of Lacoste had been appreciated by Napoleon, but perhaps St Genis, a Zaragozan by birth, showed the higher qualities of inventive genius. For he adapted his plans to his means, and regulated his operations by circumstances. It was a dramatic climax to the protracted struggle in which they played the leading parts, that those great engineers fell almost simultaneously.

Palafox has had the chief honours of the defence; yet there are few characters in history as to whom we are more puzzled. Both French and English authorities are in absolute antagonism. Some present him as the chivalrous hero, others as a mere puppet and a cowardly sensualist. He is praised by the Frenchman Lejeune, and bitterly censured by Napier. Of course the truth lies between these extremes. Like all the chief Spanish commanders he was no general; and his feebler will bent to the ferocious energy of Tio Gorge, and the fanatics who were the elect of the dregs of the populace. St Marc was the soul of the strategy and St Genis inspired the engineering. Yet had Palafox not been a patriot and a man of courage, he must have lost his place and probably his life.

The weather fought at first against the Zaragozans. They had reckoned upon the winter frost and cold to carry death into the French lines. As it happened, the winter was one of the mildest on record, and the muggy fogs rising each morning from the river valley masked the operations of the sappers. So the siege they had hoped would have been raised went on, but the prolonged resistance had a double effect. On the one hand, like the victory of Baylen, it flattered the national vanity as it kept up the national spirit, and encouraged in England a delusive faith in Spanish determination. But calmer reflection led to depressing conclusions. Zaragoza and Gerona, which behaved almost more heroically, proved to be altogether exceptional instances. No serious efforts were made to succour either city, though each night the French were kept on the alert when they saw from their leaguer the signal bonfires blazing along the uplands.

The trenches had been pushed forward; the attacking columns had been alternately successful and repulsed; all the outlying positions had been carried with the great convent of St Joseph, which projected from the walls like a Titanic bastion. On the 10th of January the bombardment began, to go on uninterruptedly to the end. On the 23rd Lannes took over the command, communicating his own fiery energy to the operations. After a contest for every foot of ground, the assailants mastered the ramparts, making them their first line of defence, yet even then their troubles were only beginning. Each house, with the ingress blocked, the stairs destroyed, and its own store of hand grenades and ammunition, had become a separate fortress. They were the flanking works of the convents and public buildings, which were so many formidable citadels. Each broad thoroughfare, being searched by the fire of raking batteries, could only be crossed under cover of travises or by subterraneous galleries.

Above ground work was impossible in the day, when each roof and steeple was occupied by the deadly marksmen who had come down from the *Sierras*. Mine met mine, and appalling explosions were of hourly occurrence. When the stormers rushed forward to occupy a shattered house, they were shot down to a man. Then Lacoste betook himself to adjusting his charges of powder so that only one side of the house should fall. With powder the besiegers were amply supplied; it was with explosions of some 3000 lbs. that they breached their way into the massive convents. A glance at one of these affairs may suffice to give an idea of the rest. It is borrowed from the graphic narrative of the artistic Lejeune. The scene was the convent of St Francis. The explosion destroyed half the building, choking with *débris* the subterraneous chambers in which many families had taken refuge.

The French rushed in through blinding clouds of dust, and in the old Gothic church and through the side chapels a desperate hand-to-hand combat ensued, when soldiers and peasants were mingled with monks and women. The grenadiers followed the defenders up the stairs to renew the fighting on the roofs, where quarter was neither given nor asked, and the grotesque gargoyles were belching out the blood that flowed from the gutters in the lead.

The French pillaged anything that fire or powder had spared, not so much for the sake of plunder as for protection from bullets and the weather. The folios from the monkish libraries were easily built up as breastworks; the varnished canvases from altars and chapels made excellent protection against the rain, and the parchment leaves torn from precious manuscripts were spread between the sleepers and the damp ground. Repeatedly the despondent soldiers were on the point of mutiny, and had any of their generals but Lannes or Soult been in command, it is doubtful whether the siege would not have been raised. But Lannes sustained the spirit of his men by keeping them actively employed, and by representing the desperate case of the besieged. Nor would it have been easy to exaggerate that. Only the stronger of the famished garrison were fit for duty; famine had brought epidemics in its train; malignant typhus was raging, and the mortality was greatest among the women and children, who had been confined for weeks in pestilential cellarage.

The corpses filled the cellars and choked the streets; fortunately the colder weather preserved them, so that they could be made useful for barricades, when the defenders were too feeble to tear up the heavy paving stones. Surrender had become a matter of necessity, and it had become possible through the death of the democratic chiefs. Yet there were still stubborn enthusiasts who refused to yield, and the negotiations had to be conducted with craft and secrecy. Fair terms were granted, considering the desperate circumstances. And even the French, who were naturally resentful of that ruthless strife, were moved by pity when they saw some 12,000 sickly and starving tatterdemalions, survivors of a force of four times that number, limp painfully out of the city to lay down their arms.

The embarkation of Moore's army had complicated the situation in Portugal, the base of the British operations in the Peninsula, and the surrender of Zaragoza discouraged Spain, as it set free 25,000 French soldiers. Sir John Cradock was in command at Lisbon. His position had always been difficult; the forces at his disposal were numerically weak; he was subordinated to the authority of the civilian envoys; for months he had no communication with the War Office; his instructions were not only indefinite but conflicting, and he was drifting in circumstances which could not have been foreseen. The justice he deserved has scarcely been done him. Wellington was a soldier of genius, Moore was a soldier of talent, Cradock was a soldier of capacity and resource. Had affairs then been directed by a timid man or a blunderer, undoubtedly Portugal must have been evacuated.

Cradock had barely 10,000 men with which to garrison the frontier fortresses and to secure Lisbon, which was the point of supreme importance. Even when he received reinforcements he could never put half that number in the field, and the long frontier he was supposed to defend was easily assailable by an enterprising enemy. He had efficient irregular leaders in Wilson and Trant, but their undrilled Portuguese levies were in no way reliable. There was sedition, with something like anarchy, in Oporto, nor was the condition of Lisbon much more reassuring. The central Government there was at open enmity with the turbulent Bishop of Oporto and his delegates. Cradock's instructions were, in case of necessity, not only to embark his troops but to carry off the Portuguese fleet and the contents of the arsenals.

While events were in suspense he made extraordinary efforts, not only to send succours to Moore, but regiments to strengthen the garrison of Cadiz, thus establishing, according to the desires of the Cabinet, a second base of operations in the south of Spain, from which the British might direct the defence of Andalusia. The succour never reached Moore, since he had severed his communications with Portugal; the vanity and jealous imbecility of the Spanish *Junta* baulked the other scheme, and the negotiations of Frere and the energetic Sir George Smith were fruitless. Moreover, the French interest was always strong in the south, and there were traitors in the Spanish Council. The troops sent out on these missions returned or were recalled when Cradock needed every man at his disposal. For as reverse followed reverse, invasion became certain in the north of Portugal, and imminent in the west. It was known that Soult meant to pass the Minho. Victor, with the first corps, was in Estremadura, threatening Badajoz, which was even less prepared to stand a siege than the Portuguese frontier fortress of Elvas. The division of Lapisse was to operate between, menacing Ciudad Rodrigo and Almeida.

The utmost Cradock could do was to concentrate troops and efforts for the defence of the capital, with the always probable alternative of evacuation. The preparations in case of the worst were perhaps unnecessarily ostentatious. The Portuguese, not unnaturally, were alarmed and excited at the prospect of being abandoned. The Englishmen were insulted, and an outbreak was not improbable. Cradock took his precautions carefully. The forts of Lisbon were strongly garrisoned, and, adopting the schemes of Junot's staff officers in somewhat similar circumstances, he secured the commanding heights of Saccavem without the city. In fact, in some degree, he anticipated Wellington's idea by entrenching himself in a Torres Vedras on a smaller scale.

But just when it seemed certain that evacuation must become an accomplished fact, the tension was suddenly relieved. The English Government, which had seriously contemplated abandoning Portugal before the impending French advance, changed its policy, and simultaneously the Portuguese authorities became more hopeful and conciliatory. Despatches reached Cradock announcing that he was to be speedily reinforced. Generals Sherbrooke and Mackenzie brought their divisions to Lisbon, raising the effectives to 14,000 men. The Portuguese had offered the command of all their troops to an English officer. After Wellesley had declined the appointment, General Beresford was selected. He landed at Lisbon, was gazetted a Portuguese marshal, and lost no time in taking all necessary measures for training and disciplining excellent raw material.

His task was the easier that he had only to have recourse to the admirable military polity which had fallen into disuse. Briefly, the whole fighting strength of the country was to be brought under arms as regulars, militia or reserves. The reforms were carried out with promptitude and some severity, and the ultimate results were eminently satisfactory. Indeed, any trouble mainly arose from the system of placing Englishmen in command, which from cautious beginnings was gradually extended. Yet the wisdom of that measure was conspicuously and immediately shown in the firm resistance to the French advance in the districts south of the Douro.

Cradock had no lack of advisers as to the strategy to be adopted. Oporto, the second city in the kingdom, was immediately threatened by Soult. The danger from Victor was somewhat less pressing, yet he might any day advance from Estremadura on Lisbon. The *Junta* and the Bishop of Oporto were naturally clamorous for help. The central authorities were solely concerned for Lisbon. Mr Frere actually proposed that Cradock should take the initiative, and move forward to the assistance of the Spaniards. To the suggestions of Marshal Beresford he was bound to give more serious consideration. Beresford was all for a daring game. He averred that there was time enough to beat Soult and save Oporto, and yet return southward to intercept Victor. It cannot be doubted that Cradock was only simply prudent in declining to imperil Lisbon on the chance of saving Oporto. He could not trust Cuesta, who was supposed to be holding Victor in check.

Events speedily justified his sagacity, Soult passed the Minho, and took Oporto by storm; Victor routed Cuesta at Medellin; Sebastiani scattered the army of La Mancha at Ciudad Real, and had these generals, who had been joined by Lapisse, combined to press their successes, even brilliant victory in the north might have been succeeded by fatal disaster.

CHAPTER 6

The Surprise of Oporto and Soult's Retreat
March—May 1809

The Duke of Wellington made two remarks to Lord Stanhope which throw an interesting light on Soult's invasion of Portugal. He said that Soult, next to Masséna, was the most formidable antagonist to whom he had been opposed in the Peninsula, and that Napoleon, when far removed from the scene of war, would nevertheless insist on directing even the movements of a battalion. Perhaps the Duke of Dalmatia had never shown greater military capacity, whether in advance or retreat. Although naturally not anticipating the incredible, he suffered himself to be surprised by the passage of the Douro. The Emperor, in anticipation of the embarkation of the British, before leaving Valladolid sent Soult a valedictory despatch. In that he assumed the loyal co-operation of Victor and Lapisse, to whom he sent simultaneous instructions. Soult's orders were peremptory. He was to invade immediately, and he was timed almost to a day in the stages from the frontier, by way of Oporto, to Lisbon.

No account was taken of possible difficulties—of the season, of the condition of the country, of the contingencies of serious resistance. The despatch reached the Marshal when he was in no condition for prompt obedience. It is true that both Corunna and Ferrol were in his hands; the one had yielded upon honourable terms, and the other had been betrayed. He had enrolled part of the regular Spanish garrisons in his own army, and the stores of the arsenals, supplied by England, were at his disposal. But his soldiers had suffered on the march, and been demoralised by defeat. They were sickly, half-famished, shoeless and footsore. The gun-carriages had been shaken to pieces in the Gallician defiles, and powder was still scarce, even when the Spanish magazines had been emptied. Immediate obedience being out of the question, he moved southward to St Jago di Compostella, where he halted to recruit and reorganise. The nominal strength of his corps was nearly 50,000 men, but what with detachments and other deductions he could barely muster half that number.

It was the 1st of February before he was in a position to set out, and he decided for the shortest road to Oporto. He hoped, by descending the northern bank of the Minho, to pass it near the mouth, where the fortified Spanish town of Tuy was faced by a Portuguese fortress. Both, of course, were dilapidated, and the French easily made themselves masters of Tuy. But as the month was February the Minho was in raging flood, and Soult was foiled by the gallant defence the Portuguese militia opposed to his passage. The check, with the consequent delay, proved to be of supreme importance. Before he established a base at Oporto, Cradock's attenuated battalions had been reinforced, and the spirit of the patriots had risen accordingly.

Meantime, Soult was in a dilemma. In any case he had to retrace his steps and cross the Minho somewhere in its upper course. The natural difficulties were formidable: the tributaries of the river, running south-west, flowed between parallel ranges of *sierras*; the roads were impracticable for guns, and scarcity of provisions enforced celerity of movement, for the Gallicians, pillaged by both French and English, had driven their remaining cattle to the mountains. When hours were precious, with characteristic promptitude he came to an original and audacious resolution. He determined to advance, severing himself absolutely from his base till he could re-establish communications after the capture of Oporto. He left Tuy behind, in charge of General Martinière, with a slender garrison of 500 sound men and 1000 invalids.

There he left the greater part of his guns and ammunition, pressing forward with his forces in perilously light marching order. He could not count on an unopposed march, although he calculated on the instability of the patriots in holding even the strongest positions. Nor was his confidence misplaced. Romana, who had rallied another army, was acting in conjunction with the Portuguese under Silveira. Neither general, though they had all the advantages of ground, made any creditable stand; both were routed with great slaughter, and the French passed the river. Their march along the southern bank might have been contested at every step, but they were suffered to thread a succession of defiles with impunity. The Portuguese, who occupied Braga in some strength under Freire, gave orders to their general instead of accepting them, refused to retire when prudence advised retreat, and ended by murdering their unfortunate commander. In fact, three Portuguese generals within as many weeks fell victims to the ferocity and suspicions of their troops.

On the 27th February Soult was before Oporto, where great preparations had been made to receive him, though the approaches had been left practically undefended. The bishop, who was even less of a strategist than a churchman, leaving the passes open, had gathered upwards of 40,000 combatants for the defence. Many of them were regular troops, and the peasants of those districts who had responded to his appeals were as good fighting material as the Aragonese, who had so gallantly defended Zaragoza. His dispositions were faulty, not to say absurd. He had fortified and entrenched a long line of sandhills, bending in an arc around the north of the city. Several hundred pieces of cannon had been mounted, and the men who held the trenches were resolute and even desperate. They foresaw all the horrors of this second invasion. The lines were weakened by being unduly prolonged; nevertheless, the position was formidable.

Had the bishop acted up to his brave words, and fanned the enthusiastic patriotism of his flock, notwithstanding mistakes, the result might have been more fortunate. But in the hour of peril he withdrew to those convent-crowned heights on the southern bank, which Wellington used to very different purpose. Leaving the command to his subordinates, from thence he looked on passively at the calamities he had done his utmost to invite. Soult's dispositions, on the contrary, were masterly as they were dashing. Had he been defeated, or even held in check indefinitely by forces doubling his own, who could have fallen back, as at Zaragoza, upon a line of streets, he might have sacrificed his army. The very evening of his arrival, although his men were fagged, he made a feint against either flank of the works on the sandhills, at the same time holding back his centre, with strong reserves behind. The double feint answered its purpose. In the night the Portuguese were busy shifting reinforcements to the threatened points.

Moreover, as at Zaragoza, the elements fought against them. A tremendous thunderstorm burst in the darkness. The defenders mistook the artillery of the skies for that of the French, and opened an answering fire from all their batteries, backing it up with incessant discharges of musketry. Kept idly on the alert, they wasted ammunition and, what was no less important, squandered nerve and strength. The French were up and stirring with the dawn. The feints were renewed on either flank; they were insisted upon but not pressed, till the concentrated and serious assault had cut the Portuguese communications in the centre. Then the French generals of division, closing in on either side, drove the defenders back into the city, except those who took flight towards the sea. Oporto was connected with its suburb on the southern bank by a single bridge of boats. Soult's strategy had been directed to seizing this passage, and so cutting off the retreat.

The victorious French columns entered pell-mell with the fugitives; the panic-stricken citizens made a rush *en masse* for the bridge; the mob of men, women and children were choking the narrow passage, when a panic-stricken squadron of Portuguese horse came charging headlong down the main street, trampling under hoof all who were in the way. The chains of the boat-bridge snapped under the excessive strain, and the nearest pontoon was sunk. In the mad rush to escape hundreds were hurled into the water, and the Douro was choked with corpses. It is said that the French, struck with horror at the sight, exerted themselves nobly to save the drowning; but it is certain that the city was given up to all the horrors of a sack, although the excesses of the soldiers could scarcely have been worse than those of the British at Badajoz and San Sebastian. Houses were gutted and fired; women were violated; and neither age nor sex was spared in the indiscriminate massacre.

Whether from policy or humanity, in the march on Oporto, Soult had treated the peasantry with exceptional leniency. Now, as soon as possible, he got his men under command, but he was no more master of the immediate situation than Wellington after the storming of the Spanish fortresses. There is something like grim satire in the proclamations by which he invited the citizens who had succeeded in saving themselves to return and trust to the mercies of soldiers who, reeking with their kinsfolk's blood, had been guilty of unmentionable atrocities.

Nor can anything be more suggestive of the terrors of such a war than the fact that not only many of the citizens did come back to their desolated homes, but that Soult made himself relatively popular. It seems not improbable that he was aiming at the succession to the Braganzas, and ere long there were not a few influential Portuguese who were far from unwilling to forward his candidature. They had lost confidence in English support; they were weary of anarchy, bloodshed and invasion, and would have welcomed a firm hand at the helm. Nor were his aspirations irrational, but the crown of Portugal could only be the reward of the occupation of the capital and the expulsion of the English. Lisbon was 200 miles from the Douro, but Cradock was enfeebled to the last degree, and the only troops to obstruct the advance were some corps of ill-disciplined Portuguese and partisans. But the jealousies or incompetency of the Marshal's colleagues again, as on many other occasions, upset the plans that had been devised by the genius of the Emperor.

Victor, as has been said, had been instructed to co-operate with Soult. After the victories in Estremadura and La Mancha he remained inexplicably inactive. But Lapisse with his division had been directed to maintain the communications between the armies, and that was all-important. He advanced to threaten Ciudad Rodrigo. He found in his front Sir Robert Wilson, with a battalion of the Lusitanian Legion and a few irregular levies. That able and daring partisan, with no reliable force, played a masterly and most judicious game of bluff. Lapisse, forgetting or ignoring his instructions, after a variety of futile demonstrations, turned southward to join Victor with his 10,000 men. Even that unexpected accession of strength failed to stir Victor to action, but it left Soult in isolation and destitute of intelligence. He dared not risk the movement upon Lisbon which had been contemplated. He sent a detachment to relieve Tuy and recover his artillery. Meanwhile, Franceschi was detached to push into the country to the southward, and that general would have been more successful had he not been opposed by Trant, for the Portuguese at first were panic-stricken.

But Soult's most important operations were to the eastward, to keep open a line of retreat. Caulaincourt was sent thither with the cavalry, and Loison, of Lisbon notoriety, was in command of the infantry column. Laborde, who had distinguished himself at Roliça, followed afterwards in support. The central point on that side was the bridge over the Tamega at Amarante—the Tamega flows into the Tagus from the north. If the bridge were secured and held, retreat would be comparatively easy. The bridge was the scene of one of the most romantic episodes of the war. The Portuguese fully realised the essential importance of the position. Their batteries concentrated a converging fire on the passage; moreover, the western arch had been mined, and a wire was attached in readiness to explode the mine. To venture on the bridge seemed certain death. Colonel Brochard of the engineers devised a scheme which was only made possible by the over-confidence of the defenders. Powder casks draped in grey cloth were rolled forward by sappers shod with felt and in similarly coloured clothing. The train was laid, the powder was fired, the wire was snapped and the mine was flooded. Loison was left master of the disputed pass, and the Marshal reckoned with misplaced assurance on an unobstructed march in case of necessity.

Meantime, his politic leniency had been bearing fruit. Petitions, which appear to have been spontaneous, had been addressed to him, inviting him to take over the government, and hinting that he might aspire to the vacant throne. He had actually raised several native battalions. What his real intentions were must always be doubtful. He declared that he merely met these advances in the desire to establish the peaceful supremacy of the French. The Emperor accepted his subsequent explanations with the ambiguous answer that he could only remember the day of Austerlitz. But when all seemed tolerably fair sailing, the situation changed. A formidable conspiracy broke out at his headquarters, and Sir Arthur Wellesley landed at Lisbon. The return of the new actor to the scene of his former triumphs assured Soult that he must face a daring and resourceful antagonist; moreover, it indicated that England was in earnest and intended to meet invasion by attack.

If Soult was alarmed and on the alert, Cradock had some reason to complain. He had done excellent work with inadequate means in the face of no ordinary difficulties, and he was summarily and unceremoniously superseded. But the wisdom of the new selection was justified at once, for the enthusiasm in Portugal was extraordinary. And Sir Arthur started with advantages which Cradock never enjoyed. He brought reinforcements, and in particular, four regiments of cavalry. The exertions of Beresford, Wilson and Trant had already drilled the Portuguese army into some efficiency. Yet Wellesley was confronted by the dilemma which had embarrassed his predecessor. It was desirable to deal promptly with Soult, who occupied the second city in the kingdom and had overrun the richest province. Yet no immediate danger was apprehended from that Marshal, for the march from Oporto to Lisbon was obstructed by flooded rivers and formidable defiles. Besides, Wellesley, as afterwards in the Talavera campaign, underestimated his enemy's strength.

To Victor, on the contrary, the road to Lisbon lay comparatively open; the only difficulty was the Tagus, and the Tagus could be forded or ferried. Cuesta might have given Victor occupation in Spain, but

Cuesta notoriously detested the English, and was not to be trusted. Victor had 30,000 effectives; Soult was supposed to have 20,000—he really had considerably more; and the numbers of the united British and Germans were barely 22,000. Still the British general, with Lisbon and the sea for a base, had the commanding advantage of a central position. Something must be risked, and he decided that there was time to deal with Soult without serious danger from Victor. The expulsion of Soult would not only recover northern Portugal, but probably, and as it proved, liberate Gallicia. He believed that Silveira still held the bridge of Amarante, which was the keystone of his original idea. Beresford was directed to cross the Tamega there, and thence move on Oporto along the northern bank of the Tagus.

Meanwhile Wellesley carried on the operations already begun by Cradock. Detaching a body of Portuguese to Alcantara, with orders to defend the passage of the Tagus, and blow up the bridge in case of Victor's advance, by the 5th of March he had concentrated his army at Coimbra. It numbered 25,000, but of these more than a third were Portuguese. While at Coimbra, the news that Silveira, repulsed by Loison, had lost Amarante compelled him to modify his plans. His idea had been, by uniting Beresford's corps to the Spanish and Portuguese, to interpose a formidable army between Soult and Tras os Montes, forcing him either to fight when assailed both in front and rear, or to fall back upon the Minho and Tuy.

Now, on the 16th May, Beresford was still despatched to distract the French Marshal's attention and act upon the upper Douro, by way of Viseu and Lamego. But the direct attack was to be made on Oporto by his own army from Coimbra. With the bulk of his forces he followed the direct road. The left wing, under General Hill, was to take the coast road, and turn the right flank of the French, which rested on the Lake of Ovar. From information received, he had reason to believe the lake had been left unguarded, although it extended for twenty miles behind the enemy's lines. The manoeuvres of both wings were entirely successful. Loison, in place of holding to the passage, had weakly fallen back before Beresford, and both flanks of the French were turned. Meantime the main army had attacked Franceschi, and it was only by an accident, of which he made masterly use, that the French general withdrew in safety to Oporto.

He brought his troops into the city, destroying the bridge of boats, for the British were pressing hard on him. The Marshal, overwhelmed with anxiety, had already resolved on retreat. The conspiracy, to which allusion has been made, had been discovered. It aimed at nothing less than the subversion of Napoleon's autocracy, and proposed to replace Soult, who was staunch to the Emperor, by Gouvion St Cyr. D'Argenton, who was at the head of it, had been in repeated communication with the British headquarters. In fact his last visit had been to Coimbra a few days before, when he had invited British co-operation and offered an armistice. Unfortunately for him, when arrested, English passports were found upon him. His guilt was clear; indeed, he confessed it. Although he firmly refused to betray his accomplices, he told all he knew of the English strength and plans. Happily, and thanks to Sir Arthur's shrewd precautions, that was very little.

Nevertheless, Soult learned that he had the whole of the English army in front of him; and he learned it at the critical moment when his confidence in all his subordinates was shaken. The citizens were excited by the approach of their friends. The insurgents of the country were closing in on him from behind. Ten thousand of his veterans were under him in Oporto, but his lines of defence were drawn out from Amarante nearly to the river mouth. Knowing already that his flanks were turned or seriously threatened, retreat became more urgent than before, but he had to recall his outposts from the lower Douro. Not a moment was lost in directing his guns and military train upon Amarante; but sending orders to Loison—of whose mistakes and misadventures he was still in ignorance—to draw in his detachments, he determined to remain in Oporto over the 12th, in order to give that general time to carry out his instructions.

He might well believe his position assured. Before him was the broad and bridgeless river in flood, and every boat upon it had been carefully secured. But the fortunes of war depend on trivial chances. A barber brought about the capture of Oporto, as a pedlar afterwards saved Soult from capitulation. The barber, eluding the vigilance of the sentinels, had crossed to the southern bank in his skiff. Wellesley, coming to the front, was surveying the situation from the heights of Sarco whither the bishop had withdrawn when his city was being sacked. Being at a sharp bend of the river, these heights were not visible from the town. The English general saw no soldiers on the opposite side, but in the distance, through clouds of dust, columns in retreat were to be distinguished. No time was to be lost, if the passage were possible. And beneath him, on the other bank, was an unfinished building, which seemed to have been planned for a *tête de pont*, if the Tagus could be bridged. It would shelter a considerable force, and to the west there was a *pleine terre*, which could be swept by musketry and artillery fire.

The question was how to throw the head of a column across? There was the skiff, and Colonel Waters volunteered to accompany its owner. Colonel Waters, among many dashing actions, was famous afterwards for a daring escape, when, being refused his *parole*, he was lashed to a gun-carriage. The Duke knew him so well, on that occasion, that he ordered his baggage to be brought along, saying that Waters will be sure soon to rejoin us. A third adventurer was the Prior of Amarante, and the three returned with some capacious boats in tow. ' Let the men embark,' said the general, brusquely, when someone suggested difficulties. The guns, as they were dragged up to the heights, successively opened fire, covering the crossing as well as the improvised outworks, but a considerable time had elapsed before the French took the alarm. Then they swarmed from the town, preceded by clouds of skirmishers, but the British forlorn hope had been rapidly reinforced, and the guns mounted on the commanding eminence dominated the fire of the hostile cannon.

In the confusion, the citizens, left to themselves, brought their boats over to the suburb where the pontoon bridge had been destroyed. So there were simultaneous attacks on the centre and away to the left, while General Murray had passed the river some miles higher up and was descending the northern bank. Soult had been fairly taken by surprise; believing that the urgent danger must be on the lower Douro, he had established his quarters in a house away to the west end of the city. When he awoke to the reality, the surprise was complete. All that was left was to direct and facilitate the retreat, and had it not been for the inaction of Murray, who contented himself with looking on as column after column of the enemy swept past, discomfiture must have ended in crushing disaster. The dusk found the British in possession of the French quarters, with the incredibly slight loss of 20 killed and 100 wounded.

Sir Arthur was compelled to delay for a day, while he refreshed his troops, exhausted by hard marching and fighting, and waited for his baggage and ammunition train. Soult withdrew in perfect order, rallying to him the force he had detached to the west. Beresford had seized on Amarante almost simultaneously with the surprise of Oporto, and both Soult and Wellesley believed that the retreat of the French was open. Sir Arthur, when he was able to move, had lost touch of the French, but he presumed that they were falling back upon Amarante.

Had he realised the circumstances, the wisdom of pressing them hard would probably have overridden all other considerations. For Soult found himself in an almost desperate situation. He had relied upon Loison's tenacity, and Loison had failed him. He was between the Tagus and Sierras, believed to be impassable. His choice seemed to lie between surrender or attempting to force the Tamega against Beresford, with Wellesley coming up on his rear. At that moment the unpatriotic Spanish pedlar interposed. He offered to guide the Marshal by a track leading over the Sierra de Catalina to Guimaraens. Soult lost not a moment in taking his decision. Deaf to the murmurs of the disaffected and the desponding, he destroyed his guns with the greater part of his ammunition, and, following the pedlar, plunged into the mountains.

At Guimaraens he had the good luck to meet with Loison; the cavalry he had detached to Braga had joined him during the previous night, and consequently he had rallied his whole army in the lightest marching order. Making sure that the British would take the main road to Braga, he resolved to avoid that town. Again he threw himself into the mountains to the right, leading his troops along breakneck goat paths, but gaining nearly a day by the unexpected movement. Till he found himself safe in Orense on the 19th, there was incessant fighting in front and rear; Portuguese and Spaniards were driven from a succession of bridges and precipitous defiles, where skilful and determined resistance would have given time for Sir Arthur to bring him to battle under desperate conditions. In person he took the direction of his rearguard, and Loison, who had distinguished himself by his atrocities, led the advance; he was assured that Loison, of all men, dare not surrender. But if Soult's own advance on Oporto had been characterised by exceptional humanity, in his retreat he rivalled the cruelties of Loison. The pursuers could track him by the smoke of burning villages, and the peasantry were mercilessly butchered.

The inhuman outrages were as savagely avenged. Exhausted by constant alarms, fatigues and hunger, the soldiers fell out of the ranks by hundreds, although they must have known that their fate was to be mutilated and murdered. He brought 19,000 men back to Orense, having lost his guns, his stores and his baggage. He left 6000 men behind, half having been captured in hospital, and the other half slaughtered on the march. Yet that he saved so much was infinitely to his credit as a general, for on the Souza River he was in far more desperate case than Dupont at Baylen or Junot after Vimeiro.

CHAPTER 7

Invasion of Spain, Victory of Talavera and Spanish Defeats
MAY—DECEMBER, 1809

The operations that preceded the final evacuation of Gallicia by the French must be briefly dismissed, and with some disregard for chronology. On the 20th May Soult had brought his troops to Orense, but on the following day they were again in motion. The Gallicians, moved to energy at last by the destruction of their villages and the capture of their cattle, had been giving Ney and the 6th Corps infinite trouble. Romana, although no great general, was an honest patriot, and a man of decision and action. Gallicia is the wildest province of Spain, and the most dangerous campaigning ground for a regular army. The Spaniards, greatly assisted by English squadrons off the coast, had taken Vigo and other strong places, and were beleaguering Lugo. Romano and his colleague, the Conde Noroña, had seemed to multiply themselves; now they were at the head of an army, now in flight, now taking refuge on a British vessel to reappear elsewhere, but always eluding pursuit and fanning the flames of the insurrection.

When Soult brought his broken army to Orense, Ney had become disgusted with the desultory warfare. His soldiers were thoroughly disheartened. They had spared nothing, to the church vestments which made coverings for their *tentes d'abri,* and every sentiment and superstition of the Gallegans had been roused to ferocity. Nowhere, and not even after the guerrilla warfare first broke out, was the war carried on more mercilessly. It was said—and the southern General Barrios claimed credit for the deed, although Napier doubts the fact—that in revenge for the indiscriminate massacres of the peasantry he had drowned 500 French prisoners in cold blood. But in that ruthless war a single detail, however atrocious, signifies little. In any case, after the disastrous retreat of Soult and the mortifying failure of Ney, both Marshals were in the worst of humours. Always jealous, they now came near to an open quarrel, and that rupture, with the manoeuvres of Wellesley against Victor, not only saved the Gallegan armies from the impending catastrophe which nothing but the jealousy of the French generals could have averted, but caused the final evacuation of the province.

Wellington, when he had turned north to deal with Soult, had never lost sight of Victor. Had he failed in striking a swift and decisive blow in the north, and had Victor followed up his victory over Cuesta, the position of the English general must have been dangerous in the extreme, though he had always his base of Lisbon to fall back upon. But Providence seemed to be fighting for the English and the patriots. Lapisse had made one fatal mistake when he severed the communications between the 1st and the 2nd Corps, and the inaction of Victor is simply inexplicable. Even jealousy would scarcely have induced him to play fast and loose with his reputation, and it seems not unreasonable that Napoleon, who was frequently mistaken in the choice of his instruments, should have abused him after his Peninsular failure for a *bête, sans talents et sans tête*.

Sir Arthur, as we have seen, had been prevented from following up Soult by the condition of his army and the deficiencies of his transport and commissariat. Sorely against his will, he was paralysed for a time, when he had leisurely withdrawn with his army to Abrantes. Had he been in a position to make a swift advance, he might have placed himself between Victor and Madrid. But though he had received important reinforcements, and knew that more were on the point of disembarking, the mortality from disease had been great, and the hospitals were filled to overflowing. The men had worn out their shoes in marching, their pay was hopelessly in arrear, and when the junta at Cadiz had been literally laying by millions of British money, our own military chest was well-nigh empty. Nor was money ever more indispensable, for the Spaniards were as chary of assisting us as in the case of Moore. Most serious of all, perhaps, was the attitude of Cuesta. The old man had become more impracticable than ever, for he resented Sir Arthur having acted against Soult, contrary to his advice. To offer him a suggestion was tantamount to its rejection. His forces were scattered in face of a formidable enemy, between the Guadiana and the central passes of the Morena, and he absolutely refused to concentrate. Sir Arthur dared not move, in the apprehension that his allies might be beaten in detail, and his rear and right left uncovered.

Moreover, then—as all through the critical forthcoming campaign—he was groping in the dark, so far as trustworthy information went, and frequently acting under unfortunate misconceptions. It seems strange that among the insurgents whose cause he had espoused, and who were everywhere up in arms between the Minho and the Guadiana, he could never obtain reliable intelligence. On the one hand, he had never an idea that the alarm of Napoleon, when he found that Berthier's incapacity had compromised affairs on the Danube, had depleted his armies in Spain of 40,000 seasoned veterans. On the other, and it was more immediately important, he underrated enormously the strength of Soult. Nor had he ever given that Marshal credit for having so promptly restored the moral and replaced the equipment of his routed forces; nor did he believe that the Duke of Dalmatia had under his command the corps with which Ney had been holding Gallicia, besides 15,000 of the army of Aragon under Mortier. Had he had a suspicion that while 50,000 men were facing him in front as many more were menacing his left and his retreat as they debouched from the passes in the Northern Sierras, he would scarcely have exposed his ill-equipped men to famine and pestilence as well as the chances of battle in his daring venture in the valley of the Tagus.

Yet the situation was tempting. Victor, after a futile movement upon Alcantara in support of Soult, had re-crossed the Tagus and fallen back upon Truxillo, when he heard of the discomfiture of his brother Marshal and the return of the English. Cuesta had a nominal force of 38,000 men, had he chosen to concentrate. Sir Arthur did not believe, till despatches to Jourdan were intercepted, that Soult had more than 14,000 men, nor did he dream that nearly four times that number were mustering to cut off his retreat. Victor had advanced, assuming the offensive, but had retired again before the superior force of Cuesta joined to the British army. Following the French, and finding them in a disadvantageous position, a grand opportunity had offered for striking a decisive blow. The sullen Cuesta declined to co-operate, and Victor the cautious withdrew. At that time Victor was unsupported, for the corps of Joseph and Sebastiani were distracted by the operations of Venegas in La Mancha. A few days later, having effected his junction with the army from Madrid, Victor became the assailant in turn.

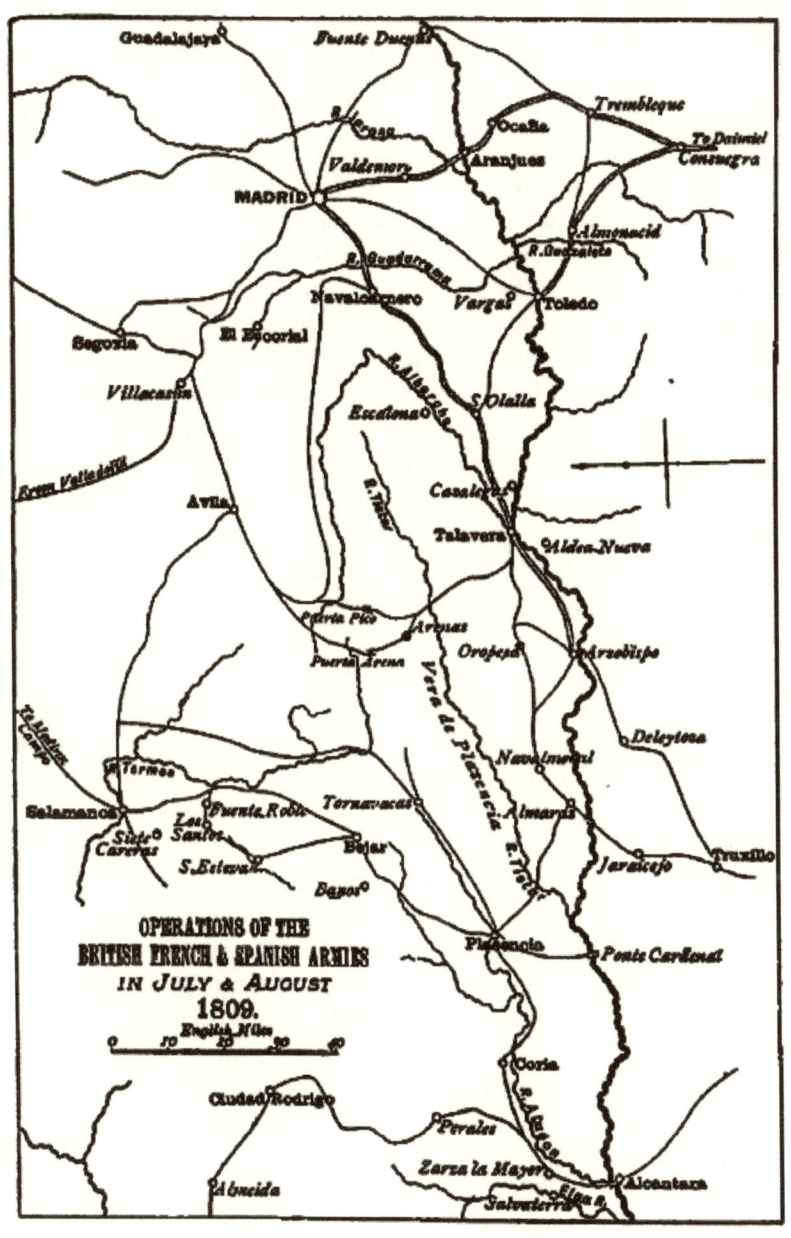

The Spanish vanguard was only saved from a rout by the gallantry of Albuquerque, and Cuesta beat a precipitate retreat to the Alberche. With difficulty Sir Arthur prevailed on him to recross that river, and the allies took up strong positions at Talavera. There, in the bloody battle of the two days, they were assailed by the united French armies. The British had 18,000 men in the field: the French numbered 48,000. The British bore the whole brunt of the fighting, for they had little more than passive aid from their allies. The Spaniards, who held the town and the heights behind heavily-armed batteries, simply secured our right like some profound ravine or precipitous mountain. Jourdan directed the chief attack on our left, but he gave timely warning of his dispositions by attempting it at first with inadequate forces. The carnage on the slopes of that flanking hill was terrible, and they were contested with fluctuating for tunes. But the critical moment came at noon on the second day, when Victor ordered a simultaneous charge along the whole of his front. The British line was nearly broken at the centre, when a fierce bayonet charge hurled the enemy down the hill.

The intoxication of that success nearly proved fatal. The Guards, following up the fugitives too fast, fell among the French reserves, between their field batteries. There was a violent recoil, and the tide came surging back again. But Sir Arthur's prescience had foreseen that possibility: a fresh battalion had been rapidly moved up, and, with the second line of Cotton's cavalry, received the shattered files of the Guards, giving them leisure to re-form. It was the enemy's last effort, and, with nightfall, he withdrew from the field. Our loss was very heavy: killed, wounded and missing numbered nearly 6000. Yet, though the victory brought no immediate results, the moral effects were perhaps commensurate with the heavy losses. For it not only confirmed the French rank and file in their convictions of the fighting qualities of the British soldier, but it assured the marshals, who had served their apprenticeship under Napoleon, that they dare take no liberties with the Sepoy-General. Nor was the influence of Talavera less appreciable with the English politicians who professed to believe in the invincibility of the Great Emperor, though for the time it added venom to their diatribes.

The victory brought no immediate results. Sir Arthur, had he wished it, could not advance. Cuesta, with a superfluity of beasts of burden, refused the slightest assistance. The townspeople of Talavera gave nothing to the starving soldiers, though, as it proved afterwards, there were provisions for three months' sustenance concealed in the city, to be unearthed by the less scrupulous French. It was then, according to Napier, that our soldiers began to nurse that hatred of their churlish allies, which led to the horrors of Badajoz and St Sebastian. A day or two were necessarily devoted to making arrangements for the wounded. The improvised hospitals were overcrowded, and numbers of the sick and mutilated were groaning on straw in the streets. A few days after the battle came intelligence that Soult had forced the northern passes, which Sir Arthur had unavoidably confided to the sole custody of the patriots. They had abandoned almost impregnable positions without firing a shot, and the leading columns of the enemy were already in the rich plains of Plasencia. When the northern army effected its junction with Jourdan and Victor, Talavera became untenable and retreat unavoidable. After the usual wearisome squabbles with Cuesta, Sir Arthur undertook to march against Soult—still estimating the strength of that general at barely 14,000 men—entrusting Talavera and his hospitals to the defence of Cuesta, and receiving the promise of the Spaniard that, in the event of his retiring, waggons would be provided for all the sick who could be moved.

Sir Arthur, reinforced since the battle, was marching with 18,000 men against, as he imagined, a far weaker force. On the 2nd August he received three sensational pieces of news. Intercepted letters told him that Soult's army must be over 30,000; that already that Marshal had interposed between him and the bridge of Almaraz, the sole passage to Portugal on the Lower Tagus; and lastly, that as Joseph was returning in force, Cuesta proposed to evacuate Talavera and to join him. Expostulations with the impracticable Spaniard proved vain, and nothing but the promptest action could save him from being crushed between the converging armies of the enemy. There was but one possible course to pursue—to withdraw behind the Tagus by the bridge of Arzobispo, a short distance below Talavera, where he could await events in an unassailable position in the Sierras which overhang the southern bank of the river. Meanwhile, Craufurd's brigade was sent off by a forced march to seize the bridge at Almaraz, if yet there were time.

As matter of fact, that passage was secured, and communications were kept up with Deleitosa, where Sir Arthur had established his headquarters. It was a commanding position, but the usual embarrassments occurred. The troops were on shorter rations than ever. Cuesta, who had posted himself to defend Arzobispo, was surprised during the noonday siesta; he saved most of his men by a hurried flight, but

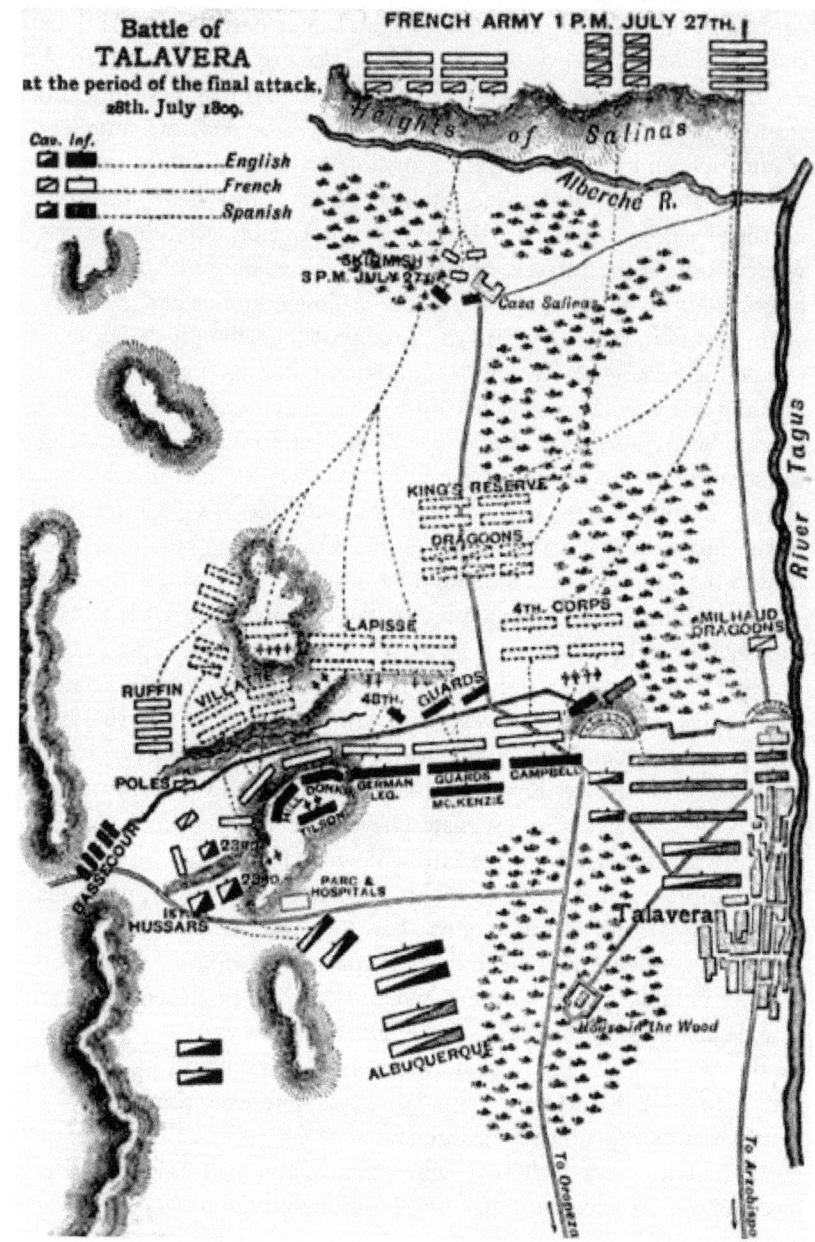

he lost the greater part of his baggage and artillery. Victor re-entered Talavera, where he behaved to our wounded with chivalrous generosity. His proceedings were in strong contrast to those of Soult, who was wasting and burning in the plain of Plasencia. Meanwhile, affairs had been going ill for the Spaniards in La Mancha, where Venegas, having been foiled in an attempt on Toledo, had concentrated in Aranjuez. With the troops at his command, he might have pushed forward to occupy Madrid, when Joseph and Jourdan had marched to the succour of Victor. But there can be little question that the Central Junta, while actually nominating civil officers to take charge of the capital, in their selfish jealousy, alike of the British and Cuesta, had given Venegas secret instructions not to be over-active, and to take care of his army.

As for Cuesta, on his side, he had deceived his brother general by assuring him that the British were to advance, when he knew they had resigned themselves to retiring. When Venegas had at last decided to attack, the French anticipated him. After for some time offering a resolute defence at Aranjuez, the favourite summer retreat of the Spanish kings on the Tagus, surrounded by enchanting gardens, adorned with noble statuary and rare exotics, he was forced to the Battle of Almonacid, and utterly routed. But the pursuit was not mercilessly followed up as at Medellin, and he rallied the wrecks of his army in the passes of the Morena.

The victor of Talavera was raised to the peerage as Viscount Wellington of Talavera and of Wellington in Somersetshire. Another incident of importance supervened. Mr Frere, for a brief space, was replaced by the Marquis Wellesley. Mr Frere's conduct has been very differently appreciated by admiring men of letters and the military critics. The former sympathise with his romantic enthusiasm for the Spanish cause, and praise him for his eagerness to advise and readiness to accept the responsibilities of his counsels. The others, and apparently with better reason, condemn the presumption which forced his advice on such soldiers as Moore and Wellesley, when writing at a distance from the seat of war and in Napoleon-like ignorance of the immediate circumstances. The Marquis believed and trusted in his brother. He also tendered military suggestions, but at once assented to his brother's decisions.

Before Talavera his brother had warned the *Junta* that as his troops were starved, and as Cuesta wantonly threw obstacles in his way, his mind was made up to fall back into Portugal. His foraging parties had actually been plundered; his magazines had been emptied to supply the Spaniards; and his ally had denied him a single mule team when he had the means of transporting a pontoon bridge from one river to another. The *Junta* had at length summoned courage to supersede Cuesta, when he anticipated destitution by resignation. Eguia, who succeeded temporarily as his second in command, was perhaps more incapable, and quite as impracticable. An agent of the Junta came with false and absurdly reassuring promises; but Sir Arthur had learned how far they were to be trusted. He announced his intention of carrying out his threats. His brother suggested that, by way of compromise, he might fall back from the heights on the Tagus to positions behind the Guadiana. The answer was that the line of the Guadiana, with its fords and shallows, was relatively indefensible; that the Spaniards, if they showed ordinary skill and resolution, were strong enough to maintain the barriers between the Upper Tagus and the Central Morena; and that, withdrawing to Badajoz and Elvas, where he could nourish his troops from the fertile Alemtejo, he could still threaten the flank or rear of any French army invading Andalusia. To Badajoz, accordingly, he withdrew.

Almost simultaneously England committed itself to the disastrous Walcheren expedition. It has been said that had that money been thrown into the scales in Spain, the turning of the balance might have been anticipated by four years. That seems questionable, although undoubtedly our limited military strength could not have been squandered to worse purpose. But the truth of the *dictum* of Henri Quatre was realised both by Napoleon and Wellington—that the strength of Spain was in the fact that weak armies were inadequate for her subjugation, and that strong armies could not be fed. While Wellington rested in observation on the Portuguese frontier, both French and Spaniards were in dire straits. The French exactions had never been more ruthless or the military edicts more atrocious than under Kellerman, the Governor-General of what the French called Northern Spain. And in Western and Northern Spain the ranks of the ill-fed and ragged Spanish regulars had been weakened by innumerable desertions. But the men only deserted to reappear in desultory bands.

Then began the guerrilla warfare, which was so potent to harass and wear out the enemy. It began in Aragon, which had been swept by Suchet, and where the convoys, carrying plunder northward to France and coming back with munitions and coin, offered the most tempting field of operations. An entire detachment might be told off to escort a single courier; letters of supreme importance were intercepted, and as the whole country, for fear or friendship, was in league with the guerrilla chiefs, the most trivial French movement, when known in advance, must be protected by a powerful military demonstration.

The successes of the guerrillas, following the defeats of the regulars in the field, should have indicated to the *Junta* the true lines for conducting the defence. Moreover, Lord Wellington before retiring had warned them against hazarding their troops in pitched battles, though his advice, acting as an irritant, had the reverse of the effect he intended. The Duke del Parque had won some creditable victories in Leon; the French had been repulsed from Astorga; they had retired from Salamanca, and it was taken as a significant confession of their discomfiture that Jourdan had been replaced by Soult as major-general of their armies. The Duke del Parque undertook to push his advantages if the *Junta* would make an effective diversion from La Mancha. Moreover the Madrileños, driven to despair by oppression, were imploring the Junta to make an energetic effort for their liberation. Consequently the *Junta* came to the insane resolution of confronting the French *en campagne ruse*, though Soult had 70,000 men at his disposal.

The number of their own troops, when collected at the foot of the Morena, fell short of 50,000. Passing over three men who, though no great strategists, had far superior credentials—Castaños, Romana and Albuquerque—they summoned Areizaga from Lerida to replace Eguia. His sole claim seems to have been that he had once been commended in despatches when serving under the gallant but incapable Blake. Having made their choice of a general, the *Junta* began by deceiving him. They assured him that he might count on an immediate British advance, and that Albuquerque had been ordered up with the army of Estremadura. But Areizaga's overweening self-confidence needed no such encouragement. Without waiting for further news of the promised support, he led his undisciplined host across the plains of La Mancha. He would listen to no warnings from foreigners in his camp, and indeed the *Junta* had given peremptory orders to fight.

Neglecting all reasonable precautions, he is said only to have realised the measure of his temerity when from the church tower of Ocaña he saw the French closing in upon him. His soldiers fought well; the artillery is said to have been excellently served; but repulse, as usual, was followed by abject panic. The fugitives from Ocaña and Alba de Tormes again sought refuge among the precipices of the Morena. As a consequence the Duke del Parque was driven from his position in the open plains of Old Castile; the French were again free to threaten Portugal alike by way of Ciudad Rodrigo and Badajoz; and Lord Wellington, withdrawing from the neighbourhood of the latter fortress, took up a new position on the Portuguese Tagus.

Meanwhile important events had been passing in Catalonia. That province, singularly defensible, with its warlike population, who took to their hills when their towns were occupied, always persisted in an independent war, with more hindrance than help from the Supreme *Junta*. Even the adjacent kingdoms of Aragon and Valencia were seldom disposed to act in unison. Had the British rendered timely or efficient assistance, had the troops that were kept idle in Sicily been embarked on a fleet under command of Lord Collingwood, the results of the struggle would have been very different. As it was, the French were everywhere hard pressed, and St Cyr, Augereau and Macdonald were successively baulked, if not absolutely baffled. The resistance of the strong places was heroic, but fortress after fortress was suffered to fall into the hands of the enemy.

On the 6th of May, the besiegers under Verdier had begun the third siege of Gerona. Not till the 11th December did the town surrender, after a defence as desperate and perhaps as skilful as that of Zaragoza, though from circumstances it was conducted more in accordance with humanity and the rules of civilised war. The great fame of Palafox may have been but ill-deserved; there can be no question as to the deserts of Alvarez. The gallant veteran, who had been constrained to give over Monjuich under the base ascendancy of the shifty Godoy, nobly effaced any stain on his reputation. Suffering from prolonged strain, he was seized by nervous fever, and delirium spared him the pain of signing the articles of surrender. The fall of Gerona assured the invaders' communications between Perpignan and their Spanish base at Barcelona.

CHAPTER 8

Fall of the Frontier Fortresses and Battle of Busaco
JANUARY—SEPTEMBER 1810

The victories of Ocaña and Alba de Tormes left the invaders at liberty to renew the designs on Andalusia which had been suspended since the capitulation of Baylen. The invading corps were replenished from the French depots. On their side, the Junta seemed paralysed. In their alarm they offered the leading of their armies to Romana, whom they had removed in their jealousy from the command in the north-west. Romana refused, although he remained with the troops in Estremadura and took timely measures for securing Badajoz. Then they recalled Blake from Catalonia, but meantime the incompetent Areizaga retained his post. It is needless to dwell in detail on their futile and feeble operations. They had men enough at their disposal—the province of Jaen furnished even more than its quota, and the barrier of the Morena might have been made impregnable.

But Areizaga's insane temerity had been succeeded by a cold fit of timidity and diffidence. The strongest positions in hill gorges are only of service when held firmly as part of an organised system. The heights were crowned; the passes were turned, and the French in several columns passed down on Andalusia. The *Junta*, in not unreasonable panic, resolved to abandon Seville and take refuge in Cadiz. The populace of Seville rose in indignation, and it was with difficulty that the members of that discredited body saved themselves. Had the direction of affairs been left to them, Cadiz would have been no place of safety. They had taken no precautions; it was weakly garrisoned and practically undefended. The French had realised the importance of occupying it, and the combined advance was swift. But at that critical moment Albuquerque came to the rescue. That general had always been under a cloud. The *Junta* is said to have been jealous of his high rank and his great popularity, both with the people in his own province of Estremadura and with his soldiers. Perhaps, too, they resented the persistency of Frere in always pressing his paramount claims. Napier avers that the real objection was a mistress known to be in relations with the French.

Wellington, questioned as to him by Lord Stanhope when they were discussing Spanish generals, was content to shake his head in significant silence. Yet it is certain that now, as on previous occasions, he acted with equal prescience and decision. Neglecting the contradictory orders of his panic-stricken civil superiors, he pushed from Cordova for Cadiz by forced marches, won the race with the enemy by a bare neck, at once bringing the men indispensable for the defence and raising the courage of the desponding garrison. Had his pursuers attacked immediately, his gallant dash might have been fruitless. Though they should have had spies enough among their many Andalusian sympathisers, it is said that they could not credit the abject incapacity of the *Junta* in neglecting the defence. Be that as it may, they had recourse to a siege, fortifying a long crescent line of circumvallation stretching from sea to sea, on the north of the isle of Leon, which is divided by a shallow channel from the mainland, and which connects itself with the sea-girt city by a narrow neck of sand. Albuquerque, appointed both military and civil chief by the Regency which replaced the *Junta*, whose scattered flight had been virtual suicide, lost not a moment in putting the island and city in a state of defence.

Batteries were shifted from the sea front to the land side, field works were thrown up along the channel, and the dilapidated forts were repaired. Albuquerque had saved Cadiz, but he was the victim of the squabbles between the Regency and the *Junta* at Cadiz. In vain he asked for food and clothes for his troops, though the magazines were filled with grain and bales of English cloth; in vain he sought to recruit his exhausted and depleted regiments from the ranks of idle citizens. In short, Wellington was never worse treated. Before the end of February he had resigned in disgust, and accepting the appointment of ambassador to England, is said to have died here of mortification and a broken heart. Meanwhile English and Portuguese troops had arrived from Lisbon; seamen had been landed from the warships, and there had been some smart affairs at outlying forts. But the siege dragged and seemed likely to be prolonged indefinitely. The fortifications had been so far strengthened that Victor declined to hazard a general attack, and the Regency never summoned energy enough to make a serious effort to break the blockade.

The operations before Cadiz languished, thanks in great measure to the British neglect of sea power. We had a commanding fleet in the Mediterranean, and the troops in Cadiz and in Sicily might have been advantageously employed in menacing the French garrisons and communications along the coasts, and, in especial, in giving effective support to the indomitable resistance of the Catalonians. Napoleon, in sanguine mood, began to hope that the struggle was well-nigh terminated, and decided on a supreme effort to expel the English from the Peninsula. Wellington was alive to the impending danger. He realised both his strength and his weakness, but he never despaired of ultimate success. He knew the numerical superiority of the veteran army opposed to him. He had learned how little confidence was to be placed in the Spanish levies still in the field. He was gravely embarrassed by the machinations and intrigues of the Council of Regency at Lisbon. On the other hand, the patriotic spirit of the Portuguese had been roused; their regulars, and even their militia, under Beresford, had been largely increased, and the English officers who had won their confidence, had brought them into tolerable discipline.

Wellington had attained an ascendancy which confirmed his high local military rank, and even the Regents and the malcontents were compelled to reckon with him. Above all, perhaps, he had now a friend in the Cabinet on whom he could count, for the Marquis Wellesley had replaced Mr Canning as Foreign Minister. Nevertheless, he was compelled to act with extreme caution, and be guided in his difficult strategy by political as well as military considerations. Busaco, for example, was to be a battle fought for political exigencies. He said repeatedly that if he seemed to throw away a single battalion, the English troops would be withdrawn from Portugal. Yet if his own moral responsibilities were weighty, and if he had a hand of most delicate cards to play, he trusted much to the jealousies of the French marshals for deranging the plans of their nominal chief; nor was he mistaken there, as events were soon to show.

Meantime he discovered the qualities of a rare military genius by conceiving a great and far-reaching plan, which foresaw all possible contingencies. And more than genius was needed to carry it out, for it demanded as well indomitable patience and inexorable will, tempered by tact and discretion. He cherished no illusions as to repelling the irresistible French advance and pushing the warfare into Spain. He simply prepared for scientific obstruction, which should culminate in forcing the enemy to fall back: and in the last resort he had arranged for a place of refuge, unsuspected by the enemy, by his allies and by his own officers.

He had retired from Badajoz, when its safety had been temporarily secured by Romana, and had taken up a position to the north of the Tagus, with his headquarters at Viseu. Necessarily in ignorance as to the French plans, he had nevertheless come to the conclusion that the advance would be made from the north, by way of Ciudad Rodrigo. General Hill, with a mixed force of English and Portuguese, was detached to the Alemtejo to watch the movements of the enemy on the side of Spanish Estremadura, though serious invasion, by way of Badajoz and Elvas, was for various reasons extremely improbable. As it happened. Hill's task was a light one, for Soult's Andalusian army was preoccupied, not only by the lingering siege of Cadiz, but by operations in Murcia and the mountains of Jaen.

The obstacles to the French advance from Salamanca, besides the numerous rivers flooded in the spring, were the fortresses of Ciudad Rodrigo and Almeida. Rodrigo, on the Spanish frontier, was but a fortress of the third rank, but it was defended by Herrasti, a determined veteran of unimpeachable patriotism, and might be expected to offer a serious resistance. Almeida, the Portuguese bulwark, with its old Moorish walls, was still weaker; but the garrison was resolute and commanded by an Englishman, Brigadier Cox. The garrisons of both places well understood that each day of protracted resistance was of importance. They knew nothing of what was being done behind the famous lines of Torres Vedras. But the proclamation of Wellington, as Captain-General, had been published, intimating his scheme of defence. It was in accordance with the ruthless principles of war and the exigencies of a situation apparently almost desperate. It exacted enormous sacrifices in the cause of patriotism, enforcing them by heavier penalties. The French advance was to be made through scenes of desertion and devastation. Mills were to be destroyed, bridges broken down, granaries emptied, homes broken up, towns and villages alike evacuated. In fact the invaders were to be starved out, or to trust for supplies to their transport. And as we know that in private life Wellington was affectionate and tender-hearted, we may conceive that the necessity for such orders seemed imperative.

In April the storm broke on the frontiers. The French had already cleared the way and covered their right flank by the recapture of Astorga and the dispersion of the patriots in Leon. Towards the end of the month they appeared before Ciudad Rodrigo and summoned it. Shortly afterwards it was announced that Masséna had been appointed general-in-chief of the army of Portugal, with supreme command of all the forces between the Tagus and the Bay of Biscay. No one of Napoleon's marshals bore a more illustrious reputation than the old revolutionary hero. But hardship and dissipation rather than years had told on the victor of Zurich and the defender of Genoa, who had been styled by his master 'the spoiled child of Fortune.' Fortune is only favourable to those who snatch at her favours. Masséna had grown sluggish if not irresolute. Afflicted with gout and rheumatism, he had directed his corps at Wagram from a carriage and four. He was grasping and sensual as Junot, without Junot's lavishness. He brought a favourite mistress into Portugal, insulted even the easy morals of his fellow marshals by her presence, and frequently regulated his movements to suit the lady's convenience. Moreover, he was regarded with jealousy by Ney, detested by Regnier, and disliked by Junot as the most favoured candidate in the running for the crown of Portugal. Once again the Emperor had made an unfortunate choice.

Under ordinary circumstances the Spanish fortress might have held out until relieved. Nothing could have been more determined than the defence; the artillery was admirably served, and the governor was ably seconded by Juan Sanchez, the dashing chief of guerrilla cavalry. When his services became useless, Sanchez saved the bulk of his horsemen by a sally, in which, not content to cut his way through, he actually charged back on the besieging squadrons. Soon afterwards the breaches were declared practicable, and surrender was inevitable unless succour came speedily.

Never, perhaps, was Wellington more sorely tried, and never did he better justify his *sobriquet* of the Iron Duke. He had advanced avowedly for the relief of the place. Romana was urging him and offering to co-operate. The Regency in Lisbon was still more pressing. Masséna, longing to bring him to battle, was taunting him in proclamations with cowardice and treachery to his allies. Indeed, his outposts on the Agueda were so near that they could hear the rattle of musketry on the ramparts. Above all, the gallant Herrasti was urging him with pathetic appeals. But his plans for Portugal's salvation must not be impaired, and his resolution was unshakable. He would not indulge

Masséna by fighting under disadvantages, where defeat was almost certain and victory would have been scarcely a gain. Herrasti capitulated on honourable terms which were broken, and the French crossing the Agueda proceeded to invest Almeida.

Previous to the fall of Rodrigo, the enemy's operations had been hampered and the spirits of the garrison raised by the near presence of Crauford with the light division and some Portuguese battalions. Availing himself of the precipitous banks and flooded condition of the Agueda, only passable at certain bridges, with a rare combination of skill and caution he had maintained a feeble line of defence, within a short league of an overwhelming hostile force whose pickets were exchanging musket shots with his own. As the river went down, his position became more dangerous, if not untenable. In prudence he should have withdrawn behind the Coa, and Lord Wellington had charged him on no account to risk an engagement beyond that river. Nevertheless he waited and an engagement was forced on him. His dispositions showed none of the skill which had characterised his protracted strategy.

The division was only saved by the courage of the men and the excellent conduct of the chiefs of battalions. As it was, the greater part of it would never have threaded the narrow passage of the solitary bridge had it not been for the abstention of Montbrun with his heavy cavalry. That general refused to take orders from Ney, when a charge would have changed retreat to a massacre. Yet jealousies were not confined to the French. Picton rode up while Crauford was in his worst difficulties; but acting, as he said, and as was certainly true, in conformity to Wellington's general orders, he declined to order up the 3rd Division.

The fall of Almeida followed that of Rodrigo in due course. It was precipitated by a catastrophe, for the great powder magazine blew up, shattering the works of defence and destroying the bulk of the ammunition. The arrangements for the inevitable capitulation were facilitated by the treachery or timidity of the Portuguese Sub-Governor. So far Masséna was still the favourite of Fortune, and the way into Portugal lay open before him, obstructed by nothing save natural obstacles.

The genius of Wellington had considered and made the most of these, but the choice of routes lay with Masséna, and Wellington's immediate plans must be regulated on those of the enemy. The first point cleared up was that nothing was to be apprehended from Andalusia; it was known certainly that Reynier after trifling with Hill, had united his corps to Masséna's main army. So the forces mustered for the concentrated attack fell little short of 70,000 men, with reserves of somewhat inferior strength scattered between Almeida and Bayonne. To these, after a junction with Hill, who had received orders to march northward immediately, Wellington could only oppose a mixed force of English and Portuguese, mustering between 50,000 and 60,000. As for reserves, they rested simply on the precarious chance of receiving reinforcements from home, and he knew that defeat falling short of disaster would be tantamount to peremptory orders for embarkation. Instead of following the direct road by the left bank of the Mondego, which would have given him the advantages of a richer and more open country, Masséna decided for turning the heights behind Celerico by way of Vizeu, and the mountainous roads to the northward.

He distributed scanty rations for fourteen days, and only French soldiers could have been trusted to husband these. Disciplined marauders as they were, they understood the necessities of self-restraint. But everything depended on prompt action, and he wasted time. The delays would have been even more serious had not Wellington's edicts of destruction been indifferently carried out. He made another mistake which might have been disastrous. He detached his artillery and transport train by the northward road, with an escort so slender as to leave it practically defenceless. Trant, with his Portuguese, attacking in a gorge, threw the head of the straggling march into dire confusion. Had he followed up his success, the invading army must have lost its guns and ammunition. The misfortune was only averted by the dashing 'bluff' of the French commander, and by Masséna's illustrious reputation. Trant could not believe that the experienced soldier would have sent his artillery train into the mountains almost absolutely unguarded.

Masséna's leading battalions pressed close upon the British rearguard, with frequent skirmishing, till brought up before the ridge of Busaco. Busaco is a range of almost precipitous heights, eight miles in length, sloping down on the south to a ford on the Mondego, and connected to the north with another *Sierra* by rugged and impracticable country. Wellington, who, as has been said, felt constrained on political grounds to offer battle, selected it as the scene of action. The allied forces, passing the Mondego, were in the act of taking up their positions when the French, under Ney and Reynier, approached the base of the mountain. Ney, with his military instinct, saw at a glance

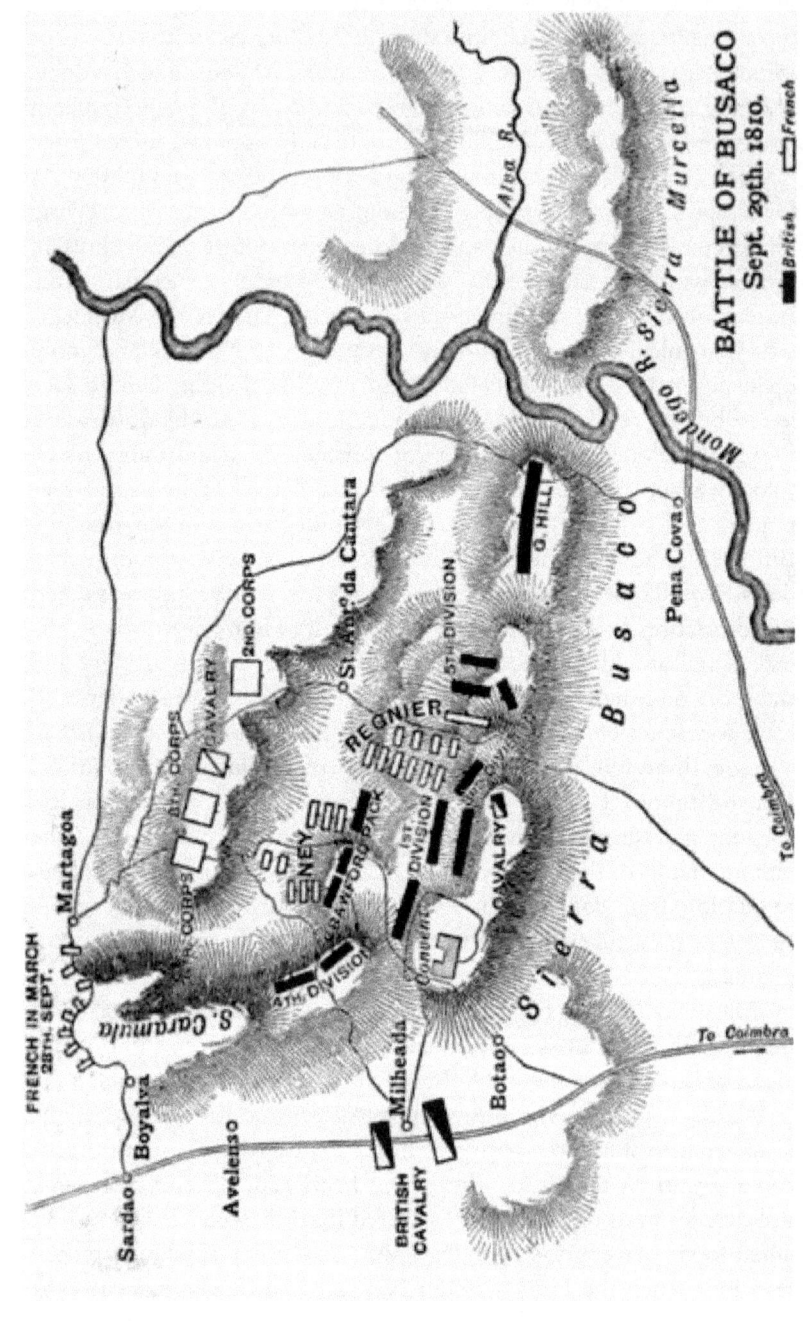

that the English preparations were only in progress. He sent to Masséna on the 26th of September to urge immediate assault. But Masséna was ten miles in the rear. He did not reach the scene of operations until mid-day, and then, after distributing the troops he had brought with slow deliberation, he proceeded to make a leisurely survey.

After hesitation and consultation he came to a resolution. Ney has been severely blamed by Marbot and others for urging Masséna to attack, and afterwards taxing him with temerity. But in fact then, as perhaps afterwards before Torres Vedras, the opportune moment had gone by. Hill with the 3rd Corps had now crossed the Mondego, and was holding the weakest position to the British right, and thence to the northward all the heights were crowned with brigades in commanding positions and batteries advantageously posted.

Nevertheless, Ney characteristically persevered, and the battle began before daybreak on the 27th September. The French formed in five columns of attack, and never did they display more dauntless courage or more wonderful agility than when scaling the steeps of that 'iron ridge.' Column after column, arriving breathless on the heights, established its broken head on the crest, to be shattered by a withering musketry fire at close range, and to be hurled downwards again by fierce bayonet charges. The combatants got inextricably mixed among the cliffs and the bushwood, till at last the British bugles sounded the recall. Had the cliffs been nearly sheer, the assailants would have been sheltered till they faced the musketry. But natural salients jutted out here and there, and on these the field batteries were established. So the scaling columns were enfiladed by storms of grape that drove along the faces of the cliffs. Even the dogged courage of Ney at last succumbed, and in the afternoon, as the fire slackened, the assailants withdrew. The loss of the French was heavy, probably amounting to nearly 5000. That of the allies was computed at 1300, and Wellington, comparatively cheaply, had won his political and material success. Perhaps one of the most important results was that it stimulated the *moral* of the Portuguese. In their first pitched battle with the enemy they had borne a creditable part in a glorious victory.

Masséna had no thought of renewing the onslaught. He could not turn Busaco on the left, for the British held the fords, and would anticipate him in crossing the river. But he had heard from a Portuguese gardener of a hill-road to his right, said to have been unknown to him and neglected by Wellington. The fact being that Wellington had entrusted its defence to Trant, and that Trant, by a stupid blunder of the Portuguese general, had been prevented from occupying it in sufficient force. Marbot declares that he had pressed his personal knowledge of it on Masséna, and that had the Marshal taken his advice in time, Busaco might have been turned and the butchery avoided. Be that as it may, Masséna tardily adopted the route, and when his army had cleared the narrow defiles, and opened out on the plain between the Sierra and the sea, its safety was ensured by its superiority in cavalry.

Wellington had fought Busaco *en parenthèse*, as it were, and now he reverted to his plan and his retreat. Evidently Masséna, though he knew nothing of the lines of Torres Vedras, should have hesitated to follow. His surest game would have been to strengthen himself on the Tagus, to occupy Oporto, the rich northern province, and maintaining communications with Spain to wait on events, with reinforcements and support from Andalusia. But feeling his reputation compromised, he was eager to retrieve his check and to hasten the embarkation of Wellington and his army.

There was no little consternation in Coimbra when the inhabitants learned that the victorious allies were still falling back, and that the consequence of the victory was to be the evacuation of their city. No time was given for preparation or lamentation. As the retreat poured through Coimbra, it was swollen by a general exodus of the panic-stricken citizens. Every beast and vehicle was pressed into the service to carry away what effects could be saved. The ranks were broken by the mob of fugitives; all discipline was relaxed, and the soldiers became riotous. When the light division had passed the bridge and entered the narrow defile of Condeixa, it was actually choked and paralysed by the crush; and for hours it was at the mercy of the French, had they charged home in earnest. But when the division had been extricated, order was restored, and Wellington's wise severity brought the riotous soldiery to reason. Thenceforth the retreat was conducted in as orderly fashion as the painful circumstances admitted, for droves of sheep and cattle still encumbered the roads.

On the other hand, Masséna, having resolved on pursuit, again neglected opportunities. Not only did he waste precious days in Coimbra, but he indulged his soldiers in licence. The stores found in the town, if carefully husbanded, might have fed his army for weeks. But they were pillaged and squandered, and when the march was resumed his commissariat was as poorly provided as before. And in the second week of October the allied army was entering the lines of Torres Vedras.

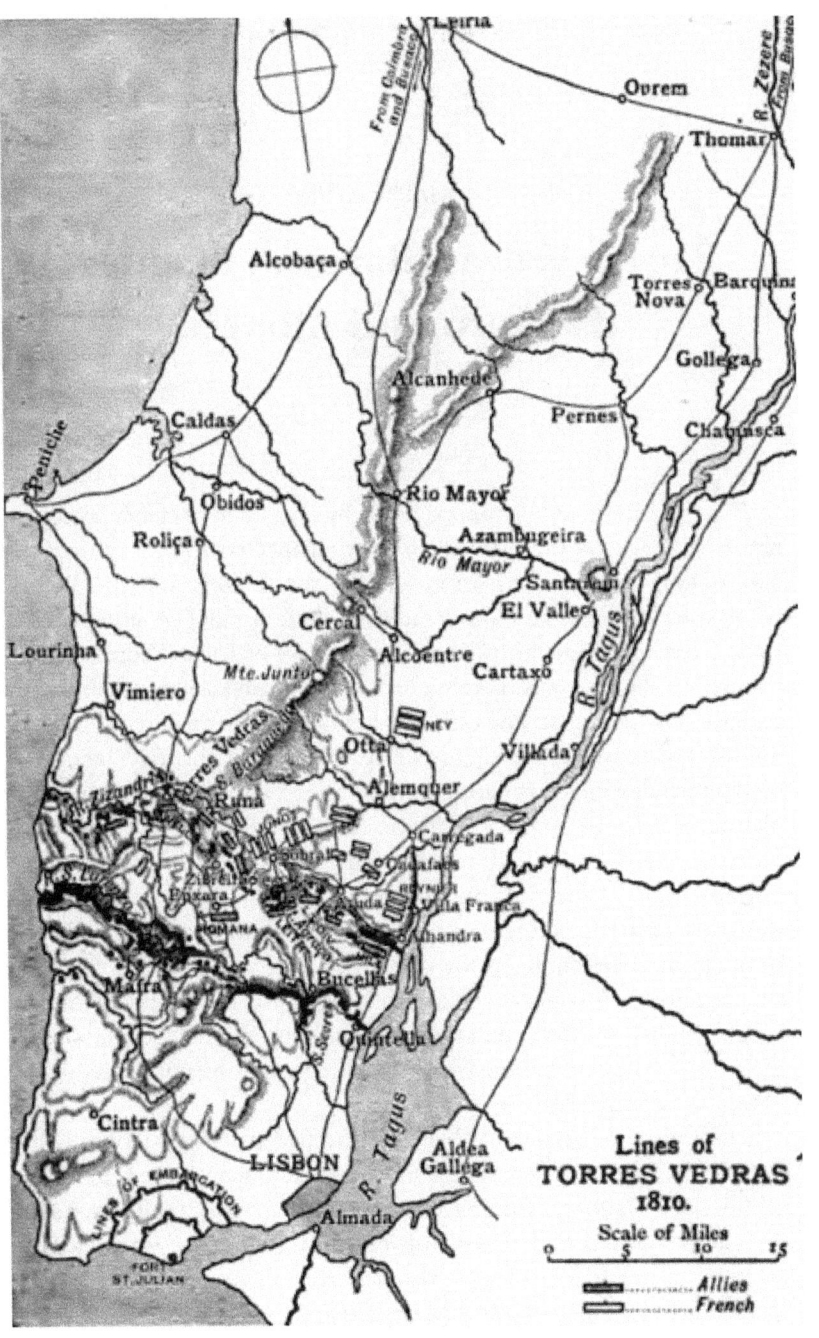

CHAPTER 9

Torres Vedras, Barossa, Fuentes d'Oñoro and Albuera
OCTOBER 1810—MAY 1811

The position had been marked out by Nature for defence, when a nation supreme on the seas was in close alliance with the Portuguese. The oblong peninsula is surrounded by the Atlantic and the Tagus, while the northern face is protected by three parallel mountain barriers. These are the famous lines—miscalled—of Torres Vedras; all are strong, but the first was merely considered an advance work, and the second is the strongest. The only weak point was on an extent of three miles to the east, where there is a level between the river and the precipitous descent of the mountains. Science and labour had assisted Nature. Sixty-nine works had been constructed along the line, and they were armed with 320 pieces of artillery. Where there seemed a possibility of the fortifications being forced, redoubts at right angles were thrown up to the rear to sweep the penetrating columns with a flanking fire. The length, as the crow flies, was twenty-five miles, and no precautions had been neglected. Hills had been scarped, streams had been diverted to submerge the low-lying country, bridges had been broken down or mined, and signalling could be conducted by a system of telegraphs.

Nothing is more remarkable than the fact that the French, with their many friends and spies in Lisbon, were left in absolute ignorance of these preparations. Nothing was known of them at headquarters in Paris, and Masséna had almost run his head against the works when he heard accidentally of their existence from a captured peasant. It is the opinion of Thiébault and Marbot that he might have attempted immediate attack with fair prospects of success. That is more than questionable. In any case, for a fortnight he waited and hesitated. Then he made up his mind for the assault. But Ney, who, as at Busaco, differed from the Marshal, flatly refused to obey both his verbal and written orders. The insubordination, for which he ought to have been promptly superseded had Masséna been more sure of his position, was reasonable, if not justifiable. Wellington had set the soldiers to work, assisted by great bodies of labourers, and each day had added to the strength of the fortifications. It is barely possible they might have been taken in the *élan* of a rush, but the French liked them less the longer they contemplated them. Their historians admit that the scare was so great, that each seam of earth turned up by the spade was assumed at once to be a trench or a battery.

Masséna's alternate hesitation and impetuosity had betrayed him into a situation which became more embarrassing day by day. He had fondly contemplated a rapid march on Lisbon, which would have given effect to the Emperor's instructions by driving the British into their ships. He found himself before a fortified camp, made impregnable to storm and never to be reduced by blockade. Meantime his own straits were severe. He had wasted the stores taken in Coimbra and Leiria. The Portuguese irregulars were pressing on his outposts everywhere, cutting his communications and capturing his convoys. Above all, Trant, by a dashing feat of arms, had seized on Coimbra, with the sick and wounded in his hospitals and the garrison left for their guard. There he lost 5000 men. Mortifying as it might be to his soldierly pride, there was nothing for it but retreat—the confession of failure—and then, as afterwards, from his next positions, the retreat was conducted in most masterly fashion. First deceiving Wellington as to his intention, then keeping him continually mystified as to his lines of march, he retired to Santarem on the Tagus, where he established his headquarters. Then the situation was reversed. Wellington, on following, found himself stopped by the river backed up by strongly-fortified heights held by a host of resolute veterans, where an attack was not to be lightly hazarded, and Masséna had no mind to throw away his advantages and come down to offer battle.

Weeks dragged away in comparative inactivity. Masséna's anxieties were in no way diminished. The connection with France was made so precarious by the guerrillas and Portuguese that Foy, who had been sent to Paris for instructions, only returned to Santarem with extreme difficulty. He brought a repetition of the Emperor's peremptory orders

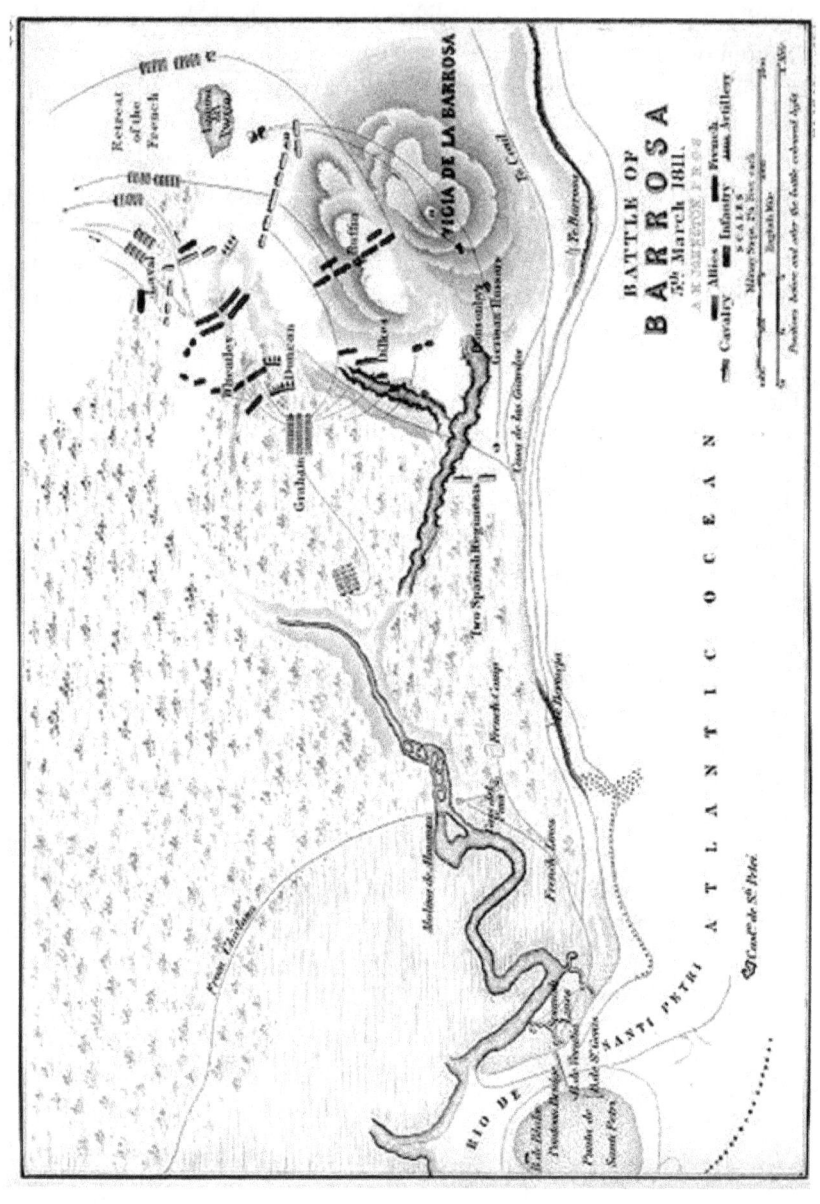

to persist in the subjugation of Portugal and the expulsion of the British. Supplies were promised. Drouet, Count d'Erlon, had been ordered forward in support with the 9th Corps, and Masséna was assured of the co-operation of the army of Andalusia, In fact a great convoy, with an escort of 5000 men, had already left Castille under General Gardanne. But communications had been so successfully interrupted that Gardanne was in absolute ignorance of where Masséna was to be found. Wandering aimlessly hither and thither, he actually retraced his steps when within a march of the Zezere River, leaving the bulk of his stores and many of his men in the hands of the Partidas.

Drouet did arrive at last, bringing half the number of troops expected. But he put forward his pretensions to independent command, which by some strange oversight were well founded; he could only be flattered into acquiescence with Masséna's plans; he was tampered with by Ney, and finally he lent his influence to the malcontents. For from Ney and the generals of division downwards the whole army was eager to return to Spain. Soult, who might have hurried forward to Torres Vedras, had been carrying out a brilliant little campaign on his own account. In the words of Napoleon, Soult won him a fortress and lost him a kingdom. At last Masséna's resolution and obstinacy gave way. Sacrificing the elaborate preparations he had been making for re-crossing the Tagus, he broke up his camp, again by his adroitness gained a start on his watchful adversary, and resumed the retreat to the Spanish frontier. His decision was probably accelerated by the news that formidable reinforcements from England were landing at Lisbon. It was on the 6th of March he commenced his movements to the rear—as it happened, on the very day after Graham had saved the battle of Barossa.

To revert to affairs in Spain. Before Masséna's retreat, his outposts had actually heard the sound of Soult's cannonading, but no help had come to him from that quarter. Consequent on the interruption of communications, it was only in the end of December that Soult had received his orders to advance to Masséna's aid. He answered that he could not spare a sufficient force to penetrate the Alemtejo; nevertheless, on the 2nd January, he had assembled an army of 20,000 men to operate against the frontier fortresses. On the 6th he had passed the bridge at Merida, Mendizabel, who commanded the Spaniards, withdrawing before him. Lord Wellington, who had foreseen Soult's movement, through Romana who was then in his camp and who was Mendizabel's superior, had warned that general to concentrate behind the Guadiana. But Mendizabel was equally headstrong and incapable. He shut up 4000 of his best soldiers in Olivença, a place of no strategical importance and incapable of defence. After a short siege the governor capitulated, giving Soult great stores of provision with many guns. He had already defeated Mendizabel at the Gebora, taking 8000 prisoners. Meantime Gazan's division had routed Ballesteros, and the Spaniards having lost 12,000 men by death, wounds, capture and desertion, at last crossed the Guadiana as a disorderly mob. Mendizabel, with several thousand fugitives, sought refuge under the guns of Badajoz, and on the 26th Soult proceeded to invest that fortress, formidable from its strength, but indifferently provisioned.

Victor, with 20,000 men, had been maintaining the blockade of Cadiz. With a garrison numerically superior, and including a strong British and Portuguese contingent, it was obvious that operations would be contemplated by the beleaguered to break the besieging lines, extending for no less than five-and-twenty miles. The British were commanded by the veteran General Graham—the Spaniards by Manuel de La Peña. The plan of the allies was to embark their forces, and, landing at Tarifa, counter-march upon Victor's covering camp at Chiclana, to the north-east of his lines. Co-operating with a corps from the city, they had hoped to take the Marshal by surprise. The expedition, though well devised, was grossly mismanaged. In the first place, Graham, to secure cordial co-operation, contrary to his instructions, ceded the chief command to the Spaniard, and was only too obedient to La Peña's insane orders. Then the elements were against the allies.

In place of landing at Tarifa they were driven on to Algesiras. When they did disembark, forgetting that the design was to effect a surprise, La Peña went out of his way to attack Medina-Sidonia, but turned back to the direct line of march on hearing that the town was entrenched. It is true that surprise was, in any case, impossible. Victor had seen the embarkation from his works, and penetrated its intention. He had gathered 10,000 of his best troops into Chiclana, and was patrolling the roads to the east. Fully expecting to find Victor prepared, Graham urged on La Peña the propriety of bringing up the troops by easy stages so that they might come fresh to the inevitable battle. La Peña brought them into presence of the enemy fagged and half-famished after a fifteen hours' march, when many stragglers had fallen out of the ranks. So they reached the Cerro de Puerco, the 'Hogback,' better known in English history as the heights of Barossa. Barossa is a low ridge, with the Atlantic cliffs on its left, overlooking a high and rolling *plateau* covered on the right by the forest of Chiclana. In front was a pine wood running up the slopes of Bermeja, which blocked the space between the sea and the Almanza creek. Under cover of the Chiclana pines Victor kept his troops, anxiously watching the movements of the allies. Graham saw at once the importance of Barossa, and would have stopped his advance there, thus occupying the key of the position.

Held by British troops, nothing could have been attempted on the Bermeja, and the allies, having given a hand to Zayas on the Santi Petri River, which flows into the Almanza River, several miles above its issue, would have been massed in assured positions on Victor's flank. But La Peña ordered him to march through the wood to the Bermeja, and Graham, against his judgment, stretched discipline so far as to obey. Still, he never doubted that these Barossa heights would be occupied in force by the Spaniards. To his intense astonishment, looking back from the wood, he saw La Peña descending from the uplands, leaving behind but two or three battalions. Victor hastened to profit by the blunder. Keeping three battalions in reserve, he launched all his available troops on the position; the heights were carried, the guns and baggage were taken; the broken Spanish regiments, mingled with the camp followers, were in headlong flight. Lautour Maubourg with his horsemen were between the British and the sea, while a column, led by Laval, was rapidly advancing on their left. The battle seemed lost, and the British sacrificed. Retreat would have been fatal.

Then the gallant veteran had what Napier defines as rather an inspiration than a resolution. He determined, with his weary troops, to storm the heights manned by soldiers who had come fresh into action. Animated by the very extremity of the peril they realised, the British wheeled about and charged up the hill. There was no attempt at regular formation. They rushed onwards in two mixed masses, one led by General Dilkes, the other by Colonel Wheatley. The musketry fire they faced was incessant and murderous. The field guns swept the ground with a storm of grape and canister. The hand-to-hand fighting was desperate, and the issue would have been doubtful had not the generals commanding the French Grenadiers fallen simultaneously, mortally wounded. The shattered columns in vain endeavoured to form again under the deadly discharges of the British artillery, and their reluctant discomfiture was completed by a charge of our handful of horsemen.

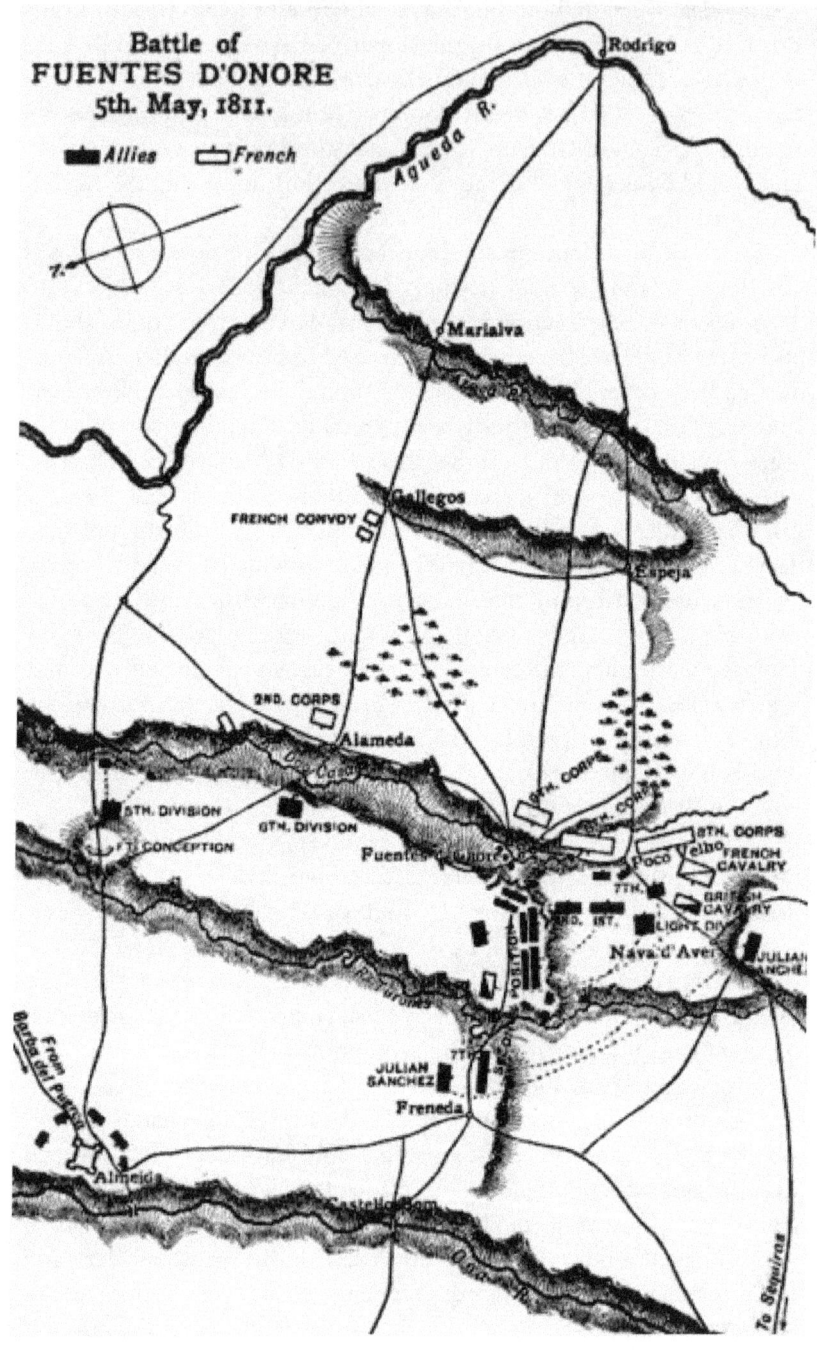

It sounds incredible, but La Peña did nothing to succour the allies who had saved him from destruction. Eight hundred Spanish cavalry—and they were led by an Englishman—never unsheathed a sabre, though Ruffin, when crossing bayonets with Dilkes, had left his flank entirely exposed. And when the battle was over, and nightfall brought temporary security, he would send no food to the famished Englishmen, and even refused assistance to bury the dead. Happily Victor made no demonstration of renewing the attack. Declining all further intercourse with his wretched commander, next day Graham collected his wounded and crossed the Almanza into the Isla. La Peña followed, and Victor resumed his positions in the lines, where he was soon afterwards joined by Soult, returning from his campaign in Estremadura. But there can be little question that, had Graham been in command, and had the Spaniards been ordinarily loyal in their co-operation, the expedition would have raised the siege of Cadiz.

The national cause was even more shamefully compromised in that Estremadura campaign, for there treachery supervened on cowardice and incapacity. After routing the armies of Mendizabel and Ballesteros, Soult had pressed the siege of Badajoz. It was bravely defended by Rafael Menacho, an old companion-in-arms of Alvarez of Gerona fame. When the place was summoned it was virtually safe, for news had just arrived of the retreat of Masséna and of the approach of a powerful relieving army. The breach was not yet practicable; there was a numerous garrison, and provisions were plentiful, while the beleaguering force was reduced to 14,000.

Unfortunately Menacho had been mortally wounded, and one, Imaz, had succeeded him in command. When the letter reached Imaz he lost not a moment in selling the fortress while it was still marketable, and he was able to make the better bargain that he was the first to communicate to Soult reliable information from Portugal. Punctilious on the point of honour, he stipulated that he should march out through the breach, but the breach had to be enlarged to give him passage. As for Soult, when he rode in at the gate, looking up at the works and frowning embrasures, he remarked dryly, 'There never was fortress so strong but that a mule load of gold could enter.' Immediately afterwards he received intelligence of the battle of Barossa. Confiding Badajoz to a strong garrison under General Phillipon, a distinguished officer of engineers who set to work at once on the dilapidated defences, he promptly returned to Seville.

Meanwhile Masséna was conducting a masterly retreat, though it was characterised by shameful atrocities. He scrupled at nothing to delay the march of Wellington who was following closely, and to cover the retreat of his rear-guard, pressed by the British columns. Towns and villages were indiscriminately fired, and the partisans when they fell into his hands were butchered. His march was facilitated by a sufficiency of provisions, whereas the pursuers were reduced to great extremities. At one time Pack's Portuguese actually went four days without food, and not a few perished of sheer starvation. He availed himself of each strong position in the passes to delay the pursuit, but these were successively and deliberately turned by Wellington, who crowned the heights and out-flanked the defenders. It should have been his object to avoid fighting, and he would have done so, had it not been for the insubordinate obstinacy of Ney, who, by loitering repeatedly, provoked engagements. Indeed, he could not count on the obedience of any one of his generals. At Miranda the troubles came to a head, and at Celerico Ney was at last deprived of the command of the 6th Corps, and replaced by Loison.

At Celerico Masséna was returned to the basis of operations, whence he had marched full of confidence for the conquest of Portugal. He was naturally unwilling to acknowledge his humiliating failure by at once re-crossing the frontier. He proposed a flank movement to Coria, which would have put his army in communication with those of the centre and the south. Moreover, it would have compelled Wellington to retrace his steps to the Tagus, and would have secured the four Spanish and Portuguese fortresses which were the fruits of the recent campaigns. In that scheme he was baffled by the opposition of Ney, who—jealousy apart—though almost unrivalled in handling troops in the field, was incapable of appreciating grand conceptions. Still Masséna had hoped to maintain himself for a time at Guarda, expecting some turn in the wheel of Fortune; but as Ney's perverseness had marred his first plan, so Wellington's celerity upset the second, and compelled him to release his hold on Portugal.

On the 1st of April the allies were again upon the Coa. The French occupied positions on the right bank on lines converging at an acute angle at Sabugal. Both flanks were covered by the Coa, for at Sabugal the river makes a sharp bend. The allies were on the opposite bank, parallel to the enemy's right. Trant and Wilson had passed below Almeida, threatening Rodrigo, as if the bulk of the army were to immediately follow. But Wellington had designed a movement from his right flank, which would have turned Reynier, separated him from

Marshal Masséna

his supporting corps to the southward, and driven him back upon the fortress. The allies passed the river at three points. Reynier was routed after a desperate conflict, but the operation proved a partial failure owing to an accident which had precipitated the attack before the combinations had been carried out. Yet the soldiers fought so well that in the despatches Lord Wellington pronounced it 'one of the most glorious actions that British troops were ever engaged in.'

Masséna withdrew to Salamanca to recruit his army, having lost from 30,000 to 40,000 men in his disastrous campaign, and Almeida was invested by the allies. Lord Wellington, having expelled the invaders from Portugal, had two alternative schemes, to be adopted according to circumstances. The more daring was to enter Spain, to occupy Madrid, to sever the northern French army from that of Andalusia, and, having taken possession of the capital with its magazines and stores, to give a hand to the Catalonians and Valencians, to strengthen himself from the English then in occupation of Sicily, and to establish a fresh base on the Mediterranean. But that depended chiefly on cordial support from home, with the prompt despatch of considerable reinforcements, and partly on such hearty co-operation from the Spaniards as he had little reason to expect. Failing that, he was to revert to the more dilatory strategy to which he was actually constrained to have recourse, although the results at which he was aiming were farther deferred by the temporising policy of Beresford. In either case the recapture of Badajoz was an indispensable preliminary, and Beresford had been detached to Estremadura with 20,000 infantry and 2000 cavalry. Having made arrangements for investing Almeida, Wellington hurried to Elvas to direct Beresford's operations.

Beresford's instructions had been to cross the Guadiana, to drive back Mortier's corps, to relieve Campo Mayor, which was besieged, and to invest Olivenza and Badajoz. The campaign opened well. Campo Mayor had been taken, though it was subsequently recovered, and Mortier's strength had been so weakened by garrisoning the fortress, and by battalions withdrawn to Andalusia by Soult, that he was in no condition to hold the line of the Guadiana. Had Beresford obeyed his orders, he would have occupied Merida, swept the country clear of the French foragers, cut off the supplies which were being poured into Badajoz, and, by at once proceeding to the investiture and bombardment of that fortress, diverted Phillipon from his elaborate preparations for defence. Yet he can hardly be fairly blamed for failing to grapple with difficulties which a general of extraordinary energy and initiative might have surmounted. The Portuguese, as usual, had broken their promises, and sent neither stores, shoes nor ammunition, land transport nor boats. He withdrew into winter quarters around Elvas, and Wellington returned to his army on the Coa. Mortier and Phillipon, who, like Wellington, were keenly alive to the supreme importance of Badajoz, spared neither energy in revictualling it nor ingenuity in rendering it impregnable.

During Wellington's brief absence, Almeida had been closely blockaded. But while ample supplies had been sent to Rodrigo, Almeida was indifferently provisioned. Unless promptly succoured, capitulation was inevitable. Masséna was already in a condition to bring relief. He had reorganised and re-equipped his army; he had received reinforcements; discipline had been restored, and on the 25th April he was before Rodrigo again determined to break the blockade. Wellington had arrived on the 28th, and immediately concentrated the main body of his army. The rivers which had hitherto protected his front were falling fast, and on the 2nd of May the French had their orders for a general advance. Rather than give up the siege, Wellington decided to offer battle.

The covering forces numbered 32,000 men, but there were only 1200 horse. They were distributed along a narrow plateau, five miles in length, defended in front by the deep and rapid Dos Casas, the left flank resting on Fort Conception, the centre opposite Almeida, the right secured by the village of Fuentes d'Oñoro, which gave its name to the sanguinary battle. As Masséna, for strategical reasons, dared not attack seriously from his right, Fuentes d'Oñoro was the key of the position.

The village lies in a valley, with hills on either side. The road to Ciudad Rodrigo passes through the main street. On one side were a morass and a wood, which made approach almost impossible. Surrounding the village were many stone enclosures offering advantageous cover for infantry; the upper village, on the edge of a steep ravine, formed a sort of citadel, and above all were a chapel and a few scattered houses, which were hastily barricaded and loopholed for musketry. On the afternoon of the 3rd May the attack began. It was vigorously repulsed, but when night fell the French were in possession of the lower hamlet, though the heights were still held by the English. On the 4th Masséna came up in person. With 45,000 men in line of battle, he made his dispositions to turn the allied right. As the onslaught was delayed till after dawn, his intention was penetrated. Wel-

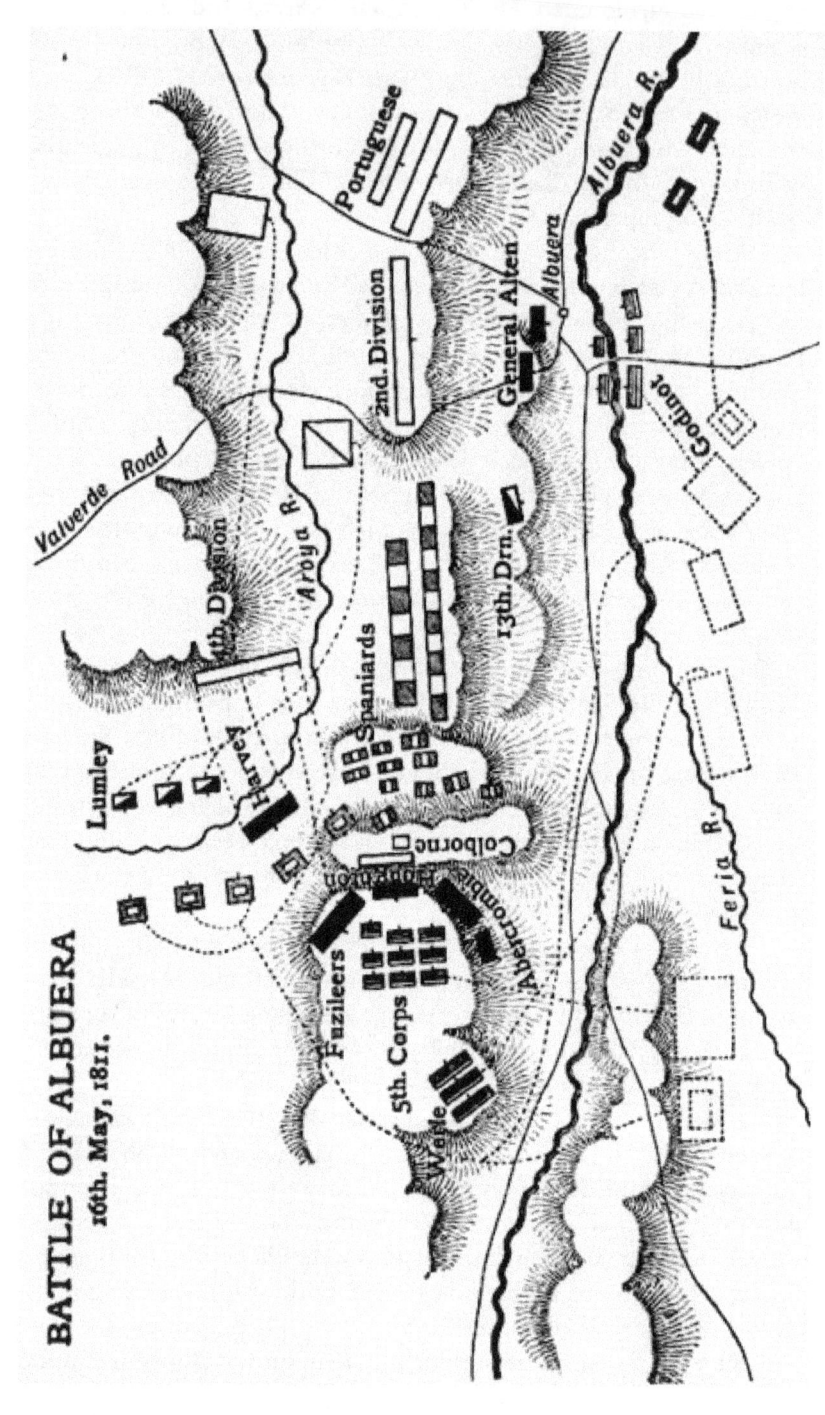

lington promptly extended his line to the right, though necessarily it was dangerously attenuated. Masséna, developing his attack, assailed it with solid columns of infantry, and availed himself of his overwhelming superiority of cavalry. The British bent and yielded.

Then Wellington saw it was necessary to concentrate again, to resume his former positions, and to crown a plateau commanding the low ground, which ran backwards towards the west, at right angles to the ridge of Fuentes d'Oñoro. Nothing could have been more delicate or perilous than the evolution, in face of an enemy numerically far superior and flushed with the conviction of victory. As a few days afterwards, at Albuera, our soldiers showed their steadiness and mutual reliance, and raw subalterns took the initiative and responsibility, behaving with the coolness of experienced veterans. The scattered and broken regiments fell into squares and small sections and mixed companies; always pressed by the enemy's infantry, charged incessantly by his *curassiers* and light cavalry, yet steadfastly persisting in the common purpose of gaining the commanding position, which stood out as a salient from the ridge of Fuentes. They fought their way to the place of vantage and held their own, while the key of Fuentes d'Oñoro was being fiercely disputed. Masséna sent forward fresh columns in support of those that were being shattered by the fire from the enclosures.

Wellington, though hard driven to maintain himself in the village, nevertheless detached the best part of his reserves to assure himself of the heights. So the carnage went on till darkness parted the combatants, and it was greatly to the relief of the exhausted British that Masséna did not renew the battle with the dawn. Both sides claimed a victory, and for several days, while the armies rested on their arms, the immediate issues remained in suspense. Doubtless the French, with their advantages, would have attempted a decisive stroke had not Marmont, at the critical moment, superseded Masséna, as Wellington was superseded by Burrard at Vimeiro. They fell back, and the siege was maintained. The place was virtually won, and the garrison seemed to have no option but surrender at discretion. Then the gallant veteran in command—General Brennier, who had been taken prisoner at Vimeiro—with a rare combination of deliberation and decision, destroyed his stores, blew up his magazines and broke through the beleaguering lines with the greater part of his force, whereupon Marmont withdrew beyond the Agueda.

  The capture of Rodrigo was the next immediate object, but the recovery of Badajoz was even more urgent. Leaving four divisions under General Spencer on the Azava River, and having learned that Soult had again invaded Estremadura, Lord Wellington hastened to the help of Beresford on the Guadiana with the 3rd and 7th Divisions.

Beresford's delays, whether inevitable or not, had given Soult time to restore affairs in Andalusia; and expecting a junction with the corps under Drouet, he was again advancing to the succour of Badajoz. In the first days of May the allies had begun the investment, but with very inadequate appliances. Phillipon kept them constantly on the alert with a heavy cannonade and well-considered *sorties*, and much blood had already been fruitlessly shed, when the approach of Soult interrupted operations. Beresford, after consultation with the Spaniards, decided to fight a battle in front of the fortress, and the position of Albuera was deliberately chosen.

It was a ridge of four miles in length, traversing the road from Seville, and commanding that to Valverde in the rear, which would be the line of retreat in case of misfortune. The Albuera river ran in front, the ravine of a hill torrent behind. Beresford had carefully concerted operations. Blake had undertaken to occupy the ground to the right on the forenoon of the 15th May. Of course he failed in his pledges. He appeared late in the day, and the last of his fagged troops were only straggling into their positions in the early morning. Soult, on his side, was acting with energy. In the afternoon the allied cavalry were forced back over the Albuera, abandoning the wooded heights in front. The possession of the woods enabled the Marshal to mask his operations. Inferior in force, but with an army of seasoned veterans, he had a great superiority in cavalry and artillery. On the morning of the 16th he rapidly developed his attack on the bridges below Albuera village, while at the same time, under cover of his cavalry, sending the mass of his infantry across the river, beyond the English right. Beresford, seeing that his flank was seriously threatened, sent an urgent message to Blake to change his front.

The Spanish general, believing that Albuera was the real point of attack, at first refused; afterwards, when his eyes were opened, he ordered the evolution. But it was carried on with pedantic deliberation, till Beresford, galloping across in hot haste, assumed the direction himself. But the situation had been gravely compromised, and indeed the battle seemed lost. His mixed army was still in the act of changing its front, and the French columns were massed on his right on a line perpendicular to the deplorable confusion. The Spaniards, everywhere in disorder, began to give way, and Soult pushed the attack on Albuera, sending forward his reserves under cover of a tremendous fire from his artillery, which had now come into play. General William Stewart made a gallant attempt to restore the battle, hurrying up his brigade by columns of companies. As they crowned the crest, facing the grape and musketry, the French cavalry, sweeping round under the dense cover of a driving shower, charged their rear with irresistible fury. The ranks were broken, and the Polish lancers followed up their success, spearing without mercy. As for the Spaniards, they kept their ground, firing indiscriminately on friend and enemy. Fortunately the 31st Regiment, which had not begun to deploy, held the hostile infantry in check, and General Lumley rode up to the rescue with the English horse. The Poles, in their turn, were ridden down by scores, and happily the rain-storm, which had concealed their deadly charge, veiled the scene of slaughter from Soult's observation. The British guns were brought up, and some Spanish regiments were moved forward.

Still the French came on again in Overwhelming force, and the British ammunition was giving out. It is said that Beresford, with sufficient reason, already despaired of the battle, and had given orders for the retreat. Then Colonel Hardinge had a daring inspiration, and accepted a grave responsibility. Without communicating with the general, he ordered up a division and a brigade, which had not yet been brought into action, and staking everything on the issue, redeemed the fortunes of the day. Leaving the broken regiments to reform in their rear, the fresh troops came steadily forward to face the French, reinforced by all their reserves. The English were staggered by the storm of grape, till they had escaped it by mingling themselves with the masses of the enemy: their volleys poured in at point-blank range opened the way for their headlong bayonet charge, and the French, clustered together on the crest of the ridge, were hurled down into the ravine in dire confusion.

Out of 6500 English, all but 2000 had been placed *hors de combat*. The loss of the French, though more doubtful, must have been far greater. The Spaniards, who looked on as judges of the lists, escaped comparatively scatheless, and Blake afterwards, like La Peña at Barossa, absolutely refused to send assistance to our wounded. It was the most bloody battle of the war and the most useless. Soult and Beresford had carelessly exposed themselves to the hottest fire in front of their soldiers. When night closed in storm and torrents of rain, the wearied survivors in the British lines could barely furnish the indispensable guards and pickets. A fresh brigade came up before morning, but their position was still precarious in the extreme as at Fuentes d'Oñoro, and it was expected that the French would renew the conflict. Probably in his ignorance of the actual state of affairs, Soult decided otherwise, and having despatched those of his wounded who could bear the transit to Seville, he fell back next morning to Solano. Wellington in public always defended Beresford, grateful for his services in drilling the Portuguese. But he wrote in private, 'Such another battle would ruin us; I am labouring hard to set all right again.' Beresford knew that Wellington was coming up in force; he knew that two of the precious British divisions were not to be risked with impunity; he knew that the blockade of Badajoz could not be maintained, and that Elvas was in no possible danger.

CHAPTER 10

The Storming of Ciudad Rodrigo and Badajoz
MAY 1811—APRIL 1812

The second siege of Badajoz was resumed with the arrival of Wellington, though foredoomed to failure. Soult had taken up a flank position at Llerena, waiting for reinforcements to resume the offensive. Their arrival was only a question of time, for Badajoz was the primary object on both sides. On the 14th June Drouet had joined Soult; the same day Marmont had arrived at Truxillo. Wellington had held on at Albuera, hoping to tempt Soult to an action before the junction with Marmont. But Soult cautiously declined battle, and after the junction, when the united French armies comprised 70,000 men, with greatly superior artillery, Wellington withdrew behind the Guadiana. Badajoz was uncovered, and supplies were freely introduced. For several weeks Marmont remained with Soult, their cavalry foraging at large behind the screen of the fortress; but the resources of Estremadura were soon exhausted, and the armies separated.

Marmont marched northward to attend to the victualling of Rodrigo, Soult returned to Seville, and Gerard, with the 5th Corps, remained at Zafra, to menace the enemy and strike on occasion. Wellington, on his side, leaving Hill to observe Gerard, turned his attention back to Rodrigo, and again shifted his headquarters to the Coa. From that central position he paralysed the far more powerful forces of the enemy. If Marmont detached troops to operate elsewhere, he left Rodrigo open to the probabilities of capture. Reduced for the time to impotence, the inaction became intolerable. He rallied the corps of Souham and Dorsenne, and, having collected large convoys of supplies, moved forward to the relief of the threatened city.

Wellington's position on the left bank of the Agueda was far extended, and consequently weak. The post of El Bodon in the centre was really not tenable against an enemy in possession of the broad plains beneath, and Marmont menaced it with 60,000 men. He was strong in artillery, and stronger in cavalry. The English general, as in the Tagus valley before Talavera, had risked his army in ignorance of the actual strength of the enemy. There could be no farther misapprehension when the troops on the heights saw the French hosts deploying beneath them. But then it was too late for Wellington to fall back without sacrificing the 3rd Division. His error in strategy, if error it was, was redeemed by a feigned display of confidence. In place of attempting to withdraw the division, under circumstances which must have led to its annihilation, he strengthened it with all the reserves he could command. The position was attacked in overwhelming force, and the assailants were repulsed with heavy loss.

It seemed to be only a brief reprieve, but to the surprise of the defenders, instead of the attack being resumed next day, Marmont merely manoeuvred his magnificent army below them, and they seemed to be assisting at a military parade on the *Champ de Mars*. Doubtless the Marshal was in some measure misled by the appearances of entrenching the ridge, as if the British were in force sufficient to hold it. But during the thirty-six hours in which Marmont held back, Wellington was busily concentrating and calling in his detachments, till he was really disposed to accept a battle. The Marshal learned afterwards, to his intense mortification, that for a day and a half the British had been at his mercy. Fortune never offered him such an opportunity again, and all that came of his overwhelming demonstration was the introduction of a convoy into the fortress.

Throughout the winter the warfare languished. The armies were kept apart by scarcity of provisions, and it was with extreme difficulty that the British could maintain themselves between the Agueda and the Coa. Moreover, it had been rumoured that Napoleon was coming to Spain in person, and bringing another army with him. The announcement that a Russian war had become almost a certainty suddenly changed the situation. Wellington, in place of retiring again to Torres Vedras, saw his way to carrying out the scheme he had ever had in contemplation. It was to seize on Ciudad Rodrigo as a stepping-stone to Badajoz. With Rodrigo again in friendly hands, he could with comparative safety assume the aggressive in Estremadura, but the capture of Badajoz was an essential preliminary. In early winter he commenced his preparations, and succeeded in thoroughly deceiving Marmont. He brought up a very inadequate siege train, giving out that he intended to repair and re-arm Almeida.

As for cannon shot, a sufficiency was found in the ruins of the fortress. On the 8th January he began the investment, but as the place had recently been revictualled, Marmont never doubted that it was safe for several weeks. Wellington knew well that time was precious; there were no positions to cover the siege to the east of the Agueda; and though the enemy's works had been but partially dismantled, and the superiority of their batteries had not been shaken, when the breaches were pronounced practicable he decided to precipitate the assault. The gallantry of the stormers failed before the main breach, but meantime the narrower side breach was forced, and the entrenchments of the defenders were taken in reverse after desperate hand-to-hand fighting. For two full days the fury of the soldiers raged unrestrained, and the inhabitants of a friendly city experienced the worst horrors of war. Not till the 26th did the news of the storming reach the French Marshal. It was a double blow, for he had not only lost the fortress but also his battering train, which prevented any speedy attempt to recover the place, and consequently left Wellington comparatively free to change the scene of operations from the Agueda to the Guadiana.

But the English general's first step was to put the battered fortress again in a position of defence. He set to work to repair the breaches, to fill up the trenches, and to gather in provisions. The place was necessarily confided to a Spanish garrison, and the governor received many wise injunctions which were duly neglected. Meantime Marmont had retired to Valladolid, and Wellington, who had been created an English earl, a Spanish duke and a Portuguese marquis, made Badajoz his immediate object. He had hoped to invest it in the early days of March, when the flooding of the northern rivers should enable him to withdraw the bulk of the British troops, leaving the observation of Marmont to his Peninsular allies. On the 5th March he handed over Rodrigo to Castaños. Within a week he was at Elvas, making his preparations for the new siege. But though the Portuguese, like the Spaniards, were lavish of compliments and honours, as usual they gave no substantial assistance.

On the contrary, the jealousy of the Regency threw serious obstructions in his way. No means of transport were provided to move the siege train and supplies from Elvas to Badajoz. Though the coun-

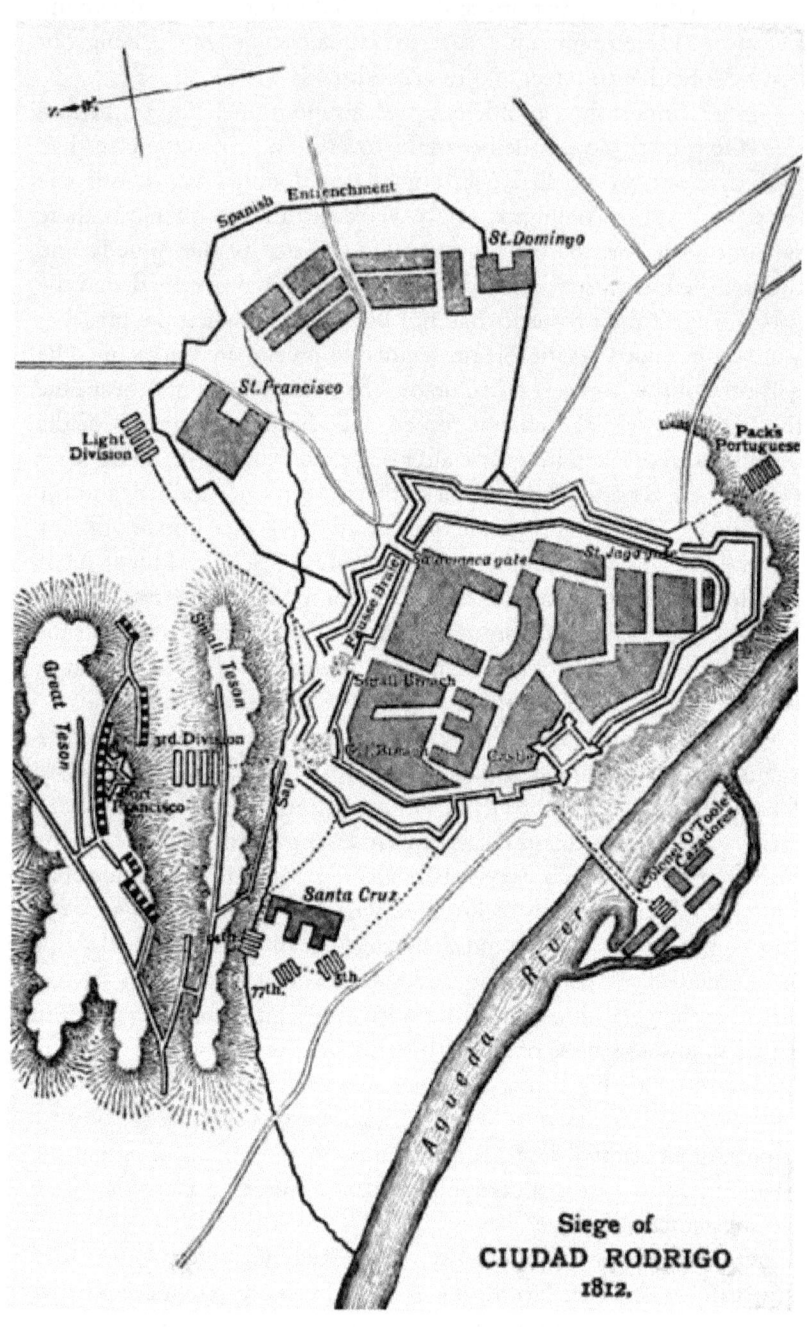

try behind him had latterly escaped ravage, neither municipality nor peasants would do anything except for ready money, and the military chest was almost exhausted. Again, as often before, he thought of renouncing his ungrateful task; for even his brother's support was failing, and Lord Wellesley was overruled in the Cabinet. Again he was spurred on by the hope that if he followed up the taking of Rodrigo by a second and more brilliant stroke, he might make himself so much master of the situation as to realise his far-reaching and far-sighted schemes. Yet the beginning of the investment was delayed for ten days, and the delay had infinitely increased the difficulties. The season of the rains had set in to flood the trenches, which had to be bottomed with sand bags; and the Guadiana, which flows between Badajoz and Elvas, by sweeping away or submerging the bridges, had nearly compelled him again to raise the siege.

Moreover, Phillipon seeing that the expected siege was imminent, had been doing all that skill could devise to perfect his masterly preparations. A fortress, scarcely of the second rank, had been made extremely formidable. Redoubts and earthworks had been repaired or thrown up, and heavily armed; the castle and town were put in a complete state of defence; ample convoys had been introduced in the previous month, and the only shortcoming was in the store of ammunition. Yet, though powder was freely expended in every shape, there should be sufficient to serve. For Soult was rapidly advancing; before the assault was delivered he had already reached Llerena, having united the divisions of Drouet and Daricau, and Wellington must again force the fighting with a politic disregard of life. Never, perhaps, in the history of sieges was there more terrible carnage in more confined space, than in the two hours which passed in fruitless efforts to storm the main breach. The broad stream of the Guadiana forms the moat of Badajoz on the rock face. It is overhung by the massive Moorish castle, crowning a precipitous eminence.

Opposite the castle on the right bank is the detached fort of St Christoval, connected by a covered way with the *tête-de-pont* of the only bridge. Elsewhere bastions, counterguards and ravelins had been constructed, with outworks on the spurs running out into the plain. Wellington, on the reports of his engineers, was compelled to set scientific rules at defiance, for there was neither a sufficiency of guns, sappers nor stores to conduct a siege in regular form. Time was pressing. It was resolved to begin by attacking the bastions on the east, where the masonry of the curtains was known to be weak. But as a preliminary, it was necessary to carry the outworks on the Picurina Hill and the battery of St Roque. On the former, the guns must be mounted which were to breach the bastions and curtains. On the night of the 17th March ground was broken. The work was carried on with infinite difficulty and heavy losses. The weather was unfavourable: sallies were made and repulsed; owing to the incomplete investment, the enemy were able to establish enfilading batteries on the right bank of the river, and these had to be taken: but, finally, at the second attempt the Picurina was stormed, after a desperate defence.

On the morning of 5th April the breaches were pronounced practicable, and on both sides the intense excitement had culminated, for Soult's advanced guard was known to be at Llerena, and his arrival might be daily expected. Yet, on close examination, Wellington decided to delay till a third breach should be opened, and Phillipon turned each moment to account with an elaboration of original and deadly precautions. The parts were distributed to the various corps for simultaneous attacks on all sides of the *enceinte*; but, while the garrison's attention was diverted to many points, it was in the breaches that, as it was believed, the contest was to be decided.

The light and fourth divisions, who had been told off for the duty, had stolen out of the trenches. At ten o'clock the stormers were crowding to the brink of the glacis, where everything was veiled in profound darkness. In the unnatural stillness, broken only by the challenges and responses of the sentinels on the ramparts, the clocks in the city struck the hour. It was the signal for lowering the ladders into what was virtually an abyss, for there had been neither time nor means for battering the counterscarp. The French, in unbroken silence, had been anxiously on the outlook. A solitary signal shot was fired from the ramparts. Then the foremost assailants had barely time to realise the almost diabolical science of Phillipon's arrangements. The glacis had been mined, and the ditch in front of the breaches had been literally paved with shells communicating with the walls by powderhoses.

At the signal the great mine was fired, and the paving of shells simultaneously exploded. The lurid glare lit up the scene, showing the French sternly massed above the breaches, while for the moment, half-dazed by the shock and surprise, the stormers were holding back in horror. The heads of their columns had been literally annihilated. But the momentary alarm changed to passionate frenzy. Rank crowded forward on rank: again the foremost were clustering like bees on the ladders, and many leaped from the parapet into the black abyss. Whether individuals willed to go onward or no, the surging mass was forced up to the breaches. In their valour or sheer desperation they must have made light of any ordinary obstacles; but Phillipon's attention to detail had effectually barred the passage. Not only had he retrenched the broken parapets with sandbags and fascines, but the breach had been closed up by *chevaux-de-frise* of sword blades, socketed in solid oak and secured by chains.

No portable explosives could have made any impression. Yet the mad impetuosity of the men behind forced forward the leading files, that the blades might be buried in quivering flesh, leaving a slope of the dead and dying to be scrambled over. The foremost endeavoured to baffle that purpose by falling on their faces, only to be trodden under foot. These breaches, moreover, were enfiladed by flanking fires of shrapnel, while all the time the storm of musket-balls rained down from the bastions and the loop-holed houses. No human resolution could withstand in passive helplessness that pitiless cross-fire—the survivors of the stormers with the supports were crowded together in the ditch, nor could any persuasions of their officers induce them to renew the assault.

It may be imagined with what impatience Wellington awaited the reports of what was really a concert of almost desperate ventures. At ten he had taken up his position on a height from which he could best direct the course of operations. Thence he could see the entire *enceinte* of the town lit up by the blaze of cannon and musketry. No reliable intelligence reached him till he was told that the assault of the breaches had failed; that almost all the officers had been shot down, and that the men were straggling about in the ditch in blind confusion. He listened with stern composure, and, in ignorance of the nature of the obstructions, ordered forward a fresh brigade. Half an hour elapsed, and then he heard from Picton that the general's feigned attack had become a real one; that the castle had been taken by escalade, and that the 3rd Division were within the walls. Very soon followed the intelligence that the bastion of San Vincente, at the other extremity of the French works, had been stormed by Walker. With the town taken and their rear exposed, after some severe desultory fighting, the garrison abandoned the defence of the breaches.

A part under the governor withdrew across the river to San Christoval, where they surrendered on the following morning. The British were in possession, but they had paid dearly for their success: the tale

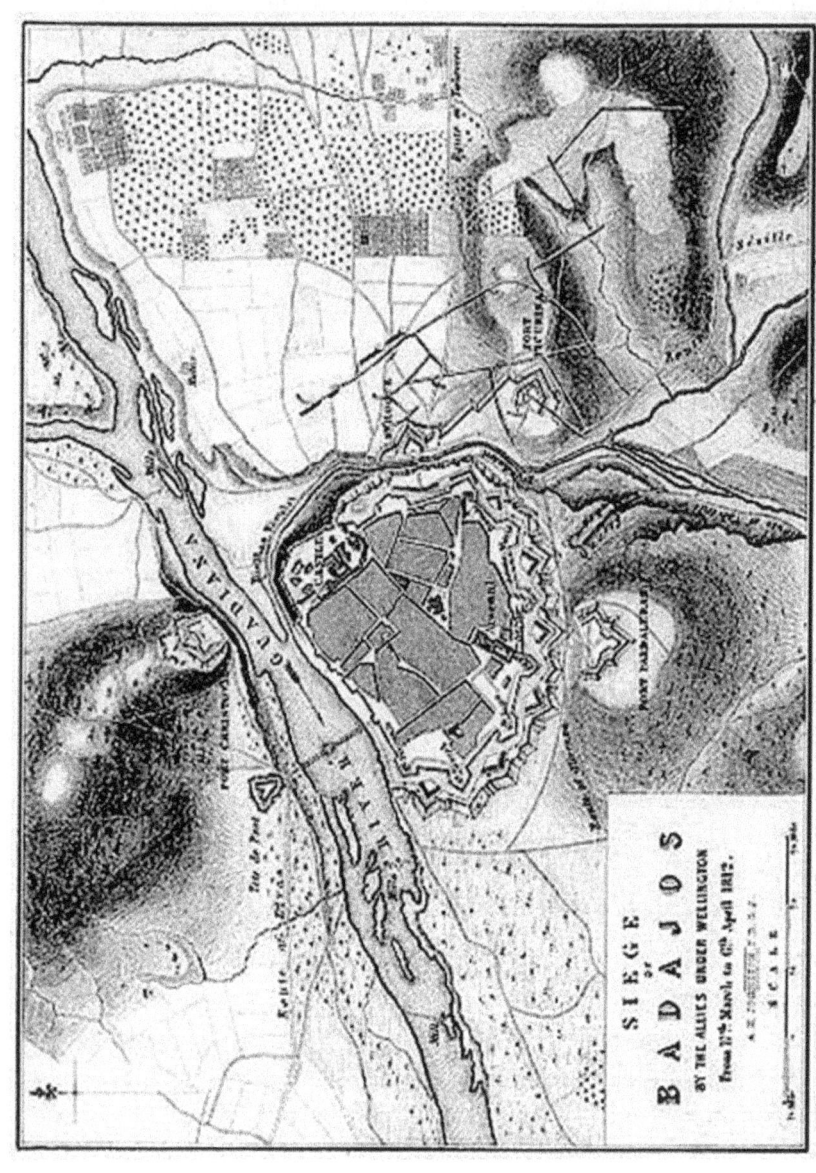

of killed and wounded was little short of 5000. Then ensued horrors and atrocities which surpassed those at Rodrigo. There was more reason for them, although no excuse, for the soldiers remembered the campaign of Talavera, when the Spaniards, concealing stores of grain, had done nothing to mitigate the sufferings of their allies. Maddened with bloodshed and afterwards with wine, the soldiery broke loose from all control, many commissioned and non-commissioned officers lost their lives in endeavouring to save the victims of drunken barbarity, and to restrain the mad impulses to incendiarism which went the length of setting matches to the powder-magazines. Even as Wellington rode through the streets the inebriates held up wine bottles, shouting, 'Old boy, will you drink? The town's our own, hurrah!' Not till the third day of the saturnalia could the provosts-marshal begin to make examples, nor were the regiments mustered and reorganised under military discipline till the intoxicated and incapable rioters had succumbed to the reaction from excess.

CHAPTER 11

Operations in Aragon And Catalonia
MAY 1810—JUNE 1811

The capture of the fortresses marked an important epoch in the war, although had it happened in the previous autumn, as Lord Wellington had hoped, the results might have been immediately decisive. If circumstances again prevented him from following up his success, a great shock had been given to French military-prestige, and that of the British soldiery had been proportionately heightened. Moreover, now that he held both the western keys of Spain, he could exercise a commanding influence on the strategy of his adversaries. For the fact must never be lost sight of, that the expulsion of the invaders was absolutely due to the action of the British armies. It has been established conclusively by the Wellington despatches and by such careful English historians as Napier; it has been confirmed indirectly by such accomplished French writers as Ségur and Thiebault, Marbot and Lejeune, and their evidence is all the more effective that it is given incidentally or reluctantly. If their statements have often to be received with mistrust, and with large allowance for mortification and *esprit de corps*, the truth is to be read between the lines; nevertheless it would be unjust not to admit that the brave but undisciplined levies of the Peninsulars played an important subsidiary part.

Like the *chulos*, who draw the bull away from the *matador* in the ring, they were perpetually distracting the French from the main attack. They could hold a fortress with heroic resolution. When their armies were scattered with terrible slaughter, they joined again next day like the pieces of the fabulous worm slashed by the sword of the knight-errant, apparently no whit the worse, and full of courage and confidence as before. Above all, the *partidas* and guerrillas swarmed like hornets around the hostile lines. Many a gallant Frenchman fell in that inglorious mountain skirmishing. Forts were surrendered because convoys were cut off. Able combinations were upset because despatches were captured, and the incessant drain and arduous service discouraged the troops, as it drove men to desertion or into the hospitals. For it must be remembered that many of Napoleon's soldiers were foreign conscripts, detesting the duties in which they were engaged; and even his veterans got weary of living by marauding, and of the monotonous revolutions in the vicious circle where cruelties provoked merciless reprisals.

So in the unwelcome suspension of activity after the storm of Badajoz, we may give a cursory glance to what had been going on elsewhere since Gerona succumbed before Christmastide in 1809. As Talavera had temporarily diverted invasion from Andalusia, so the daring though unfortunate adventure of Moore had permanently freed Gallicia from the foreigners. They never gained a footing there again, for though fresh schemes for overrunning the province were entertained, they were baulked by the activity of the British in Portugal. The Gallicians had more than their share of English money and supplies, and they were supported by our frigates and cruisers off the coast. But with Spanish selfishness, in their narrow, local patriotism they gave no effective help to the national cause. In Lower Leon, and on the plains of Old Castile, the powerful French cavalry terrorised the country. The border towns refused aid from the insurgents, in the certainty that if the garrisons were expelled they would be soon retaken.

The main lines of communication from Irun to the capital, or to Salamanca, were powerfully held by strong detachments between the garrisons, and were safe from the Spanish regulars, though ceaselessly troubled by the partisans. Through them regular correspondence was kept up between the British ships in the Bay of Biscay and the guerrillas, who were virtually masters of the wild passes through the Pyrenees where they bound Navarre and the western districts of Aragon. On the other side they were in constant intercourse with the chiefs who made their strongholds in the *Sierras* of the Guadarama and Guadalaxara, who had innumerable spies and agents within Madrid, and who, with their accurate intelligence, could be so daring in their enterprises that they once very nearly captured the usurper when feasting within a couple of leagues of his capital.

There was but a single province in the north or east where the invaders had secured a tolerably firm footing. The energies of the warlike and hardy Aragonese may have been partly exhausted by the desperate defence of Zaragoza; but if guerrillas were still numerous in the mountains, the military skill and wise administration of Suchet had brought the old kingdom of Aragon into something like submission. No doubt his exactions were severe; that was really inevitable in the circumstances; but his troops were kept thoroughly in hand. There was method in his stern *régime*, and he tolerated no gratuitous outrages. Though the passes to Pamplona and the French frontiers were held by some of the most enterprising guerrilla leaders, it is said he could trust his convoys to Spanish guards. He had mastered successively the strong places of Tortosa and Tarragona, the local centres of the national defence, and perhaps he might have given more prompt effect to the Emperor's orders by achieving at once the conquest of Valencia. The reduction of that semi-tropical province, hitherto scarcely touched by the ravages of war, would have opened up to the French rich sources of supply, making their operations comparatively independent of the dangerous transit through Catalonia But the Emperor had reckoned on his receiving assistance from the army of Catalonia, and that was what the Marshal commanding there was seldom either willing or able to give.

In fact, next to the genius of Wellington and the indomitable courage of the troops he led to victory, the Peninsula was chiefly indebted for its deliverance to the obstinate defence of the Catalonians. Gerona had surrendered in the beginning of December 1809, but the consequent discouragement had been scarcely momentary, for the patriots were enthusiastic over the heroism of the defence. A few weeks before, Augereau had superseded St Cyr, who withdrew into two years of oblivion and neglect, and who complained bitterly in his memoirs that the Emperor had withheld hearty support. Unjustly, surely, for Napoleon had the uncontrolled choice of his lieutenants, and he was not the man to sacrifice his schemes to personal animosities. The truth was that St Cyr had manoeuvred with admirable skill, and, as we have seen, his talents were so highly appreciated by his comrades-in-arms that the conspirators in northern Portugal, when plotting the autocrat's overthrow, had thought of St Cyr as his most capable successor.

St Cyr had struck heavy blows in Catalonia, but he had failed to follow them up. The irregulars, instead of being kept 'on the run,' had always time to recover heart, to rally, and to close in again. With the fire and dash of a Napoleon he might possibly have stamped out the conflagration. As it was, the fires continued to spread, and the desultory warfare, which never led to anything decisive, became more and more disheartening. St Cyr was glad to go, and Augereau was slow to come. When the imminent arrival of the former general at Perpignan at last put irresistible pressure on Augereau, he came to urge ill-considered, irregular warfare, and to meet marauding with marauding. The weakness of the French position, with its incessantly interrupted communications, was the difficulty of victualling Barcelona, the retention of which was indispensable. With its garrison and the great civil population the city was in continual straits. So much so, that even the ruthless Spanish partisans would wink occasionally at the introduction of food, in pity for their suffering country-folk.

Augereau, during his brief period of authority, did little more than maintain the defence of Barcelona. But the old '*routier*,' who was always in dire need of food, and who had to make the war support itself in a devastated country, indulged his famished soldiery in unlimited licence. The horrors of the internecine struggle were aggravated, if that were possible. Not only was no quarter given, but no tortures were spared when there was time to inflict them. The consequence was that when Macdonald replaced Augereau French operations were more paralysed than before. Macdonald was a stern disciplinarian and a man of humanity besides. Shocked at the condition in which he found his forces, and at the villainous fashion in which they were pillaging the peasants, he issued draconic orders of the day, and set the provosts-marshal to work. But he had no magazines, and the soldiers had no rations. They had to choose between undisciplined disobedience and starvation, and naturally they were still insubordinate and mutinous. While endeavouring to feed them and bring them under military control, it was all the Marshal could do to keep a hold on the province entrusted to him. He had been ordered to co-operate with Suchet and the army of Aragon in the reduction of the border strongholds.

Macdonald was more loyal to the common cause, and more free from petty jealousies than most of his brother marshals, but mainly his co-operation became a question of feeding his men. Hostalrich had fallen, and Suchet had captured the important city of Lerida when Macdonald took over the command in Catalonia in May 1810. Then Suchet's immediate object was to take Tortosa, which, as it commanded the navigation of the Lower Ebro, was a preliminary to his transporting a siege-train to undertake the investment of Tarragona. Tortosa was a place of great strength, sufficiently garrisoned and amply supplied. It kept open the communications between Valencia and

Catalonia. Consequently many efforts were made to relieve it, and the operations were protracted by the weakness of the assailants and the covering forces.

When Suchet withdrew troops from Aragon, the partisans stirred up the country he had subjugated, and he must send back detachments to suppress the risings. When Macdonald was reluctantly persuaded to lend a division to assist in the siege, or to undertake with a feeble force the indispensable duty of covering the investment, there was a course of sharp bargaining beforehand as to the magazine destined for the subsistence of either general. But Tortosa yielded at last to Suchet's skill and perseverance; the Spanish connections between Catalonia and Valencia were severed, while on the other hand the French in Aragon had secured an open passage into Catalonia. The next step was to get possession of the central fortress of Tarragona, which would open up the roads from Barcelona by the coast, from Zaragoza by the Lower Ebro, and by Lerida to Valencia.

The capture of Tarragona was a great triumph for Suchet, as it was perhaps nearly equally discreditable to its numerous native defenders, and to the British warships, which failed to lend aid at the critical moment. Moreover, undertaking the siege at all was a crucial test of Sachet's high moral courage. When the hopes of the Catalonians were at the lowest, a splendid exploit had reanimated their courage. Figueras, one of the strongest fortresses in Europe, was the gate of Perpignan, on the high road to Barcelona. The natural strength of its castle, on a hill commanding the town, its formidable batteries, its ample magazines, where stores were accumulated as a base of supply, had lulled the French into false security. The garrison in the castle was not strong; it was weakened, besides, and tired out by flying expeditions into the mountains; the commandant had become so neglectful of ordinary precautions that he had even suffered the palisades to be hewn up for firewood.

The daring partisan Roviro, who for months had been hovering around and molesting the foragers, conceived the idea of surprising the place. Some of his countrymen, acting as storekeepers in the castle, were in regular communication with him by signals or messengers. He seized the occasion when the greater part of the garrison, returning after a prolonged foray, had gone to bed exhausted. He stole down from the hills at the head of 500 men, with 3000 more following closely behind. His friends in the castle threw open a postern; most of the garrison were taken in their slumbers; with a few shots and a passing scuffle all was over. In the lower town were 500 Italians, under an Italian colonel. It seems absurd to blame them, as they have been blamed by experts, for not straightway attempting to recover the citadel. The colonel kept his head, and did the wisest thing in the circumstances. Sending off an express with the news to Gerona, he withdrew his men in good order; they rallied upon the supports that his message had brought, and the consequence was that no time was lost in laying siege to the lost fortress, Baraguay d'Hilliers, the Governor of Gerona, coming up with all his available men.

The alarm was general. Macdonald sent at once to Suchet, urging him to give up the siege of Tarragona, and to send back the 7th Corps, which had been lent. Mathieu, the Commandant of Barcelona, was as seriously preoccupied. He wrote that if Figueras were not immediately recovered, Barcelona could not be retained. Suchet, under that concerted pressure, turned a deaf ear to all appeals and remonstrances. He was a zealous soldier, an ambitious man, and he meant to win the marshal's baton, which depended on the conquest of Valencia. He did not send back to Macdonald the men he could not have spared, for as it was, with his prolonged lines of communication, the *partidas* pressing upon them from either side, the powerful Valencian army in the field, and the British squadron hovering off the harbour, his means were altogether inadequate to his object. At one time of soldiers serving in his lines barely 12,000 were fit for duty, whereas the garrison could muster nearly 17,000.

Had Contreras, who commanded, been an Alvarez, the result might have been different. He seems to have been honest and staunch, but he was jealous and hot-headed. He got rid of Sarsfield, his more talented lieutenant, actuated by malice or pure jealousy, and he was equally unreliable and inefficient in seconding any measures undertaken for his relief. On the 21st June the storming of the lower town only increased the anxieties of Suchet's position. He had failed in four successive assaults on the upper city; his communications were cut; his convoys had been captured; and what was even more serious, his base in Aragon was menaced by the combination of formidable *partidas*. He could only avert crushing disaster by achieving immediate success. He tried again, and on the 28th the upper town was stormed; excepting a few hundreds who were saved in English ships, all those of the population who escaped massacre were carried into captivity. The city was sacked and burned in scenes of horror that almost surpassed those at Rodrigo and Badajoz.

CHAPTER 12

Operations Before the Campaign of Salamanca
MAY 1812

Having possessed himself of Rodrigo and Badajoz by the skill with which he had masked his plans, and his startling audacity when they were ripe for execution, Wellington had suddenly reversed the situation. Now, in place of standing watchfully on guard, with a line enfeebled by its indispensable extension, he could impose his strategy on his enemies in the field he had opened for his operations. He would gladly have drawn Soult into a battle, but the caution of the French Marshal would not risk one where defeat must be disastrous. It might have been supposed that, striking while the iron was hot, Wellington would have followed him up into Andalusia. Officers and soldiers in our army were full of fight and eagerly expecting the order to advance. Seville must have almost certainly been retaken, and the fall of Seville would have been the signal for raising the siege of Cadiz. The Murcian army would have gained heart, the regulars and irregulars garrisoning the *Sierras* would have descended everywhere on the French communications, and the invasion must have recoiled from the southern provinces with infinite lowering of the French prestige.

It was a brilliantly enticing prospect, but unfortunately Spanish indolence and self-sufficiency had made the realisation impossible. Wellington's first consideration was to secure the fruits of his victories and maintain the advantages he had so dearly won. The breaches of Badajoz were still open, and its works had been shattered by the bombardment. There and at Elvas the magazines had been emptied, and provisions were already running short. That might have been got over, because the crippled fortresses would have been in immediate rear of the march of the army. But the northern road from Salamanca to Lisbon would have been left open to the enterprise of Marmont. Had Wellington's advice been heeded in that quarter, the road would already have been effectually closed. He had been at the pains to draw up for Castaños, who was Captain-General of Gallicia as well as of Estremadura, detailed suggestions for his action in every possible contingency, including that which actually occurred.

They were ignored by the headstrong but lethargic Spaniard; Carlos d'España neglected the bridges before Rodrigo, which he had been instructed to break down, and moreover the rivers were subsiding with the advance of the season. Little had been done to repair or re-victual the fortresses, and Marmont might easily have mastered them had the British troops been withdrawn. Already he had been busy replacing his battering train, and with Almeida practically an open place after the destruction wrought by the explosion of the magazine, he would have recovered the train he had lost, and turned the heavy guns against Rodrigo. Consequently Wellington was inevitably delayed while taking measures to remedy that culpable neglect.

Meanwhile, the time for operating hopefully in Andalusia had been slipping by. It had been the wish of the English general to march upon Seville before the early southern harvest was ripe, so that if Marmont crossed Estremadura to threaten his flank, the French might find no sustenance in the fields or granaries of the north. Now, similar reasons induced him to deliver the attack upon Marmont in place of on Soult, for the harvests of Castille are reaped a full month later than those of Andalusia or even of Estremadura; and if he should inflict a crushing defeat on Marmont's army of Portugal, it would lead infallibly to the capture of Madrid, and, indirectly, to the evacuation of Andalusia.

Although the Marquis Wellesley, succumbing to Percival and his followers, had resigned office, the political difficulties had rather increased than diminished. It is true that the tragic assassination of the prime minister had brought Lord Liverpool, instead of Lord Wellesley, into power, but the weakness of the new Cabinet was Wellington's strength. They grudged him money, they trembled before the vociferous denunciations of the Whigs, who were hopeful of storming the Treasury benches. But the lustre of Lord Wellington's achievements had already made him a power, and as mail-coaches, wreathed in laurel and placarded with flaming announcements of victory, went galloping over the length and breadth of the land, he was being idolised as the national hero.

While successful, the Cabinet did not dare to throw him over. Yet all the time he knew that his credit depended on a course of victories, and that in case of discomfiture he would be readily sacrificed. In fact, politics constantly trammelled his strategy, till in his triumphant renown he could set them at defiance. We have seen that he fought at Busaco on purely political grounds; and knowing the conditions under which he directed the warfare, we the more admire the moral courage with which he hazarded so much at Talavera, at Rodrigo and at Badajoz. But if Wellington, with his great position and fame, with an authority that was locally irresponsible, with his iron patience and indomitable force of character, was often cautious almost to timidity, and only venturesome when circumstances seemed imperative, we can understand and sympathise with the feelings of his subordinates. Next to discouragements from home, and the apathy or contumacy of his Spanish allies, his greatest anxiety was the way his generals, when in independent command, shirked their responsibilities in critical emergencies.

There was no one in whom he trusted more absolutely than in Hill; it was Hill who was detached as chief of the divisions which were to maintain communications between the Coa and the Guadiana; it was Hill who devised the dashing affair in which Gerard was routed and his forces were annihilated. Yet the Duke said afterwards, when Lord Hill was Commander-in-Chief in England, that he had always been his most valued general of division, but that his fault was the morbid fear of responsibility. All the more noteworthy was the noble action of Hardinge at Albuera, when as a simple colonel he saved the battle on the turn of the tide by boldly disobeying Beresford's orders. Men like Picton or Crauford, inclined to throw themselves gratuitously into the hottest fire, and head in person the stormers who were recoiling from a barely practicable breach, would falter before a decision that might have made their fortune when the adversary had obviously blundered. Napoleon, with all his impatient superiority, made generous allowance for daring failures, and thereby scored many of his startling successes.

But there Wellington was helpless, and we have seen how leniently he spoke of Beresford after the bloody and fruitless victory of Albuera. Yet even Wellington could not have screened him, had not Hardinge turned the day. Any general knew well that a signal reverse, in the temper of his country, would strip him of all the reputation he had won;

that he would certainly be court-martialled probably condemned; and that, in any case, as the victim of popular clamour, he would be doomed for the future to mortifying obscurity. So that, in the course of complicated operations, which were necessarily diffuse, Wellington could only reckon with confidence on the developments he actually directed in person, and he might see his plans disconcerted at any moment by his most loyal and trustworthy followers. It was fortunate that these honest, though unhappy, mistakes were counterbalanced by the inveterate jealousies of the Frenchmen. Masséna's invasion of Portugal was seriously obstructed by the insubordination of Ney, his equal in rank, and Ney was backed up by Reynier and Drouet. The battle of Fuentes d'Oñoro might have been a defeat for the British had Bessières acted cordially with Marmont when the marshes which covered our right had been crossed, and our battalions were retiring in confusion, embarrassed by the mob of non-combatants. So Soult, though perhaps with better reason, had held back from co-operating in an advance with the army of Portugal, in disobedience of Napoleon's definite instructions.

Having failed to force Soult to fight, and decided on attacking Marmont in Castille, Wellington's primary object was to force the latter Marshal to battle. Time was of essential importance, for Marmont was confidently expecting succour, and yet troops from the other corps could not undertake long marches till the reaping of the crops facilitated their commissariat arrangements. There were other inducements to immediate and offensive action in the plains. A victory would open the way to Madrid. In the event of repulse and defeat Wellington could still fall back upon the frontier fortresses. Whether he succeeded or failed, by drawing French reinforcements to Castille he would relieve the pressure on the Spaniards elsewhere, and though driven to depend chiefly on his own genius and army, facilitating distractions by their regulars and guerrilla chiefs was ever his secondary purpose.

There were other considerations which encouraged and decided him. Hitherto the French had possessed a great superiority in cavalry and field artillery; to that they owed many of their victories when the Spaniards rashly descended from the mountains into the plains. Now several regiments of horse had been ordered back to serve in the Russian campaigns; others had been used up by hard fighting and long marches. Some of the field batteries had been captured, and all were in indifferent condition. On the other hand, Wellington was stronger in the cavalry arm than he had ever been, and his well-horsed batteries left little to desire.

But to strike at Marmont effectively he must be cut off from the army of the north, and what was of far greater importance, from the army of the south. The French were as fully alive to that as the English general. Yet they dared not concentrate prematurely, for the possession of Rodrigo and Badajoz had given Wellington the incalculable advantage of threatening them all from his central position. No one of the marshals knew in what quarter the storm might burst and none with his personal advancement in view was disposed to make sacrifices to secure a comrade. Yet the French, appreciating the energy of their adversary, had taken obvious precautions. Not only the magnificent bridge of Alcantara, but other bridges over the Tagus, had been mined and blown up. Such as had been spared were old and narrow, to be approached through precipitous streets and by almost impracticable mountain roads.

Virtually the only easy passage was at Almaraz, where the Tagus was crossed by the royal road from Truxillo to Talavera, and even there for the shattered stone bridge one of pontoons had been substituted. The passage had been deliberately and scientifically fortified, and the French were so confident in the natural and artificial strength of Almaraz, that, making it a place of arms, they had stored great magazines there. The *Sierra* in front, overhanging the river, was a natural bulwark, traversed here and there by some path only used by the hillmen and shepherds. The sole practicable breach was by the defile of Mirabete, through which the road from Truxillo was carried. The crest of the Col was crowned by an ancient castle, which had been repaired and armed with heavy guns, and other works had been constructed to close the gorge beneath, which the castle commanded. At Almaraz itself, about a league distant, a *tête-de-pont* on the left bank was covered by a redoubt called Fort Napoleon. Both these works were dominated and enfiladed by Fort Ragusa on the opposite bank.

To Hill was entrusted the conduct of the daring and doubtful operation. With the facilities of defence and the difficulties of attack, all depended on surprise. Were any warning given. Hill's column would become a forlorn hope, destined to be surrounded and overwhelmed by converging enemies. Foy was in the Upper Tagus valley, D'Armagac at Talavera, and the horsemen of Drouet were so near to Merida that they could easily intercept Sir Rowland's retreat. Wellington's wise devices were intended to divert any suspicion from his real intentions.

Hill had 6000 men under his immediate command, and the covering forces under Graham and Sir William Erskine mustered about 20,000 more. Still, with all possible precautions and with good information as to the approaches, the enterprise seemed desperate enough. It must be said for Hill that in that critical emergency he faced the chances of failure like a hero. There could be no reproaching him then with shrinking from responsibility. He understood the vital importance of his instructions, and braced his resolution to act on them unflinchingly.

On the 12th of May he crossed the Guadiana with a pontoon train and some heavy howitzers as well as a dozen of light field-pieces. Three days later he was at Jaraicejo, on the southern slope of the *Sierra*, where he made his final dispositions. The advance was in three columns, which were to cross the *Sierra* in the night, and open simultaneous attacks at daybreak. The left, moving forward by side paths, was to assail the castle of Mirabete. The centre, with the cavalry and artillery, was to follow the royal road; the right column, under Hill in person, advancing by paths even more difficult than those on the left, was to carry Fort Napoleon. Difficulties and obstructions more formidable than had been anticipated upset the combinations, and there was no surprise. On a nearer examination, Hill had realised that the defences of the pass were too strong to be stormed. Taking a bold resolution, he ordered Chowne, with the left column, to feign an attack; he decided to dispense with his artillery, and leading his own column against Fort Napoleon, to take the works there by escalade.

Towards dusk on the evening of the 16th he began the descent; but though the distance to the Tagus valley was only six miles, at dawn his rear was still entangled in the passes. While he was waiting for the stragglers to come up, Chowne delivered the attack on Mirabete. As for the French in Fort Napoleon, they were not unprepared; on the previous day they had information of the enemy's presence. Still they were startled by the roar of the guns and by the clouds of cannon smoke on the *Sierra* crest, wreathing up over the passage they deemed impregnable. While crowding the ramparts as eager spectators, their attention was diverted to matters more immediate. With ringing British cheers the head of the right column had broken from under cover, and came rushing across the intervening ground. The French had their muskets ready to their hands; the British were welcomed with withering discharges from cannon and small arms, while Fort Ragusa responded to the cannon of Fort Napoleon with a heavy flanking fire.

All failed to check the rush of our soldiers, though even when they had swarmed down into the ditch and set up the ladders there was a *contretemps* that must have stopped less determined men. Nothing shows the difficulties of the undertaking more forcibly than the fact that the scaling ladders had been sawn in halves in order that they might turn the corners of the precipitous paths. Too short for their purpose, they only reached to beneath the projecting ledge of the parapet. The assailants managed to scramble over and make good a footing; then the fury of the assault became irresistible, and in fierce hand-to-hand fighting its defenders were driven out of the redoubt. The guns of Fort Ragusa were silenced, for they could not fire upon that mixed mob of friends and enemies. The fugitives rushed for the *tête-de-pont*, but there again the pursuers entered with them. In the headlong flight across the bridge some of the pontoons broke from their moorings, and many of the fugitives perished in the water.

The guns of Fort Napoleon were turned on Ragusa, and, what was rare in the war, a Frenchman entrusted with an important post lost his head and showed the white feather. The Commandant, with his garrison, joined the rout, and so nearly did the fate of these fortifications tremble in the balance that he actually met reinforcements coming up from Naval Moral. Hill had intended to bring forward his heavy artillery and breach the walls of the Castle of Mirabete, but a false report from Erskine that Soult in person was in Estremadura, induced him to change his plan and withdraw to Merida. Yet his success had been virtually complete, although Lord Wellington was much annoyed that he had not been left to put the finishing touch to his operations. Mirabete was cut off by the demolition of the bridge, although its little garrison was subsequently relieved. And before retiring. Hill destroyed the works on the river, blew up the magazines and burned the stores.

Thenceforth Marmont could only communicate with Drouet and Soult by the circuitous route of Toledo; whereas by restoring the bridge of Alcantara, Wellington shortened his own communications, enabling his right wing to communicate with his main army in almost a direct inner line. Moreover, by crossing or re-crossing the Tagus at pleasure, Hill was in a position to mystify Drouet, and consequently Soult. That restoring or rather the patching up of the superb bridge, which had been blown up to the mutual disadvantage of the belligerents, was one of the most ingenious feats of rough-and-ready military engineering. The credit was due to Colonel Sturgeon. The problem was to span a gap 90 feet in width at a height of 150 feet above the river, and to make it practicable for the passage of heavy artillery. In the arsenals of Elvas he arranged a network of strong cable, plaited in sections so as to be capable of easy transport. Cables were stretched across the abyss and secured to beams riveted in the masonry. On those hempen girders the network rested, over all was laid a flooring of planks, and the guns were drawn across without an accident.

Wellington's initial purpose had been the isolation of Marmont, and that isolation had been secured. He was favoured by the political condition of Spain and by the jealousies that prevailed among the French in high places. Marmont could hope for little from the army of the north. The activity of the guerrillas from Navarre to Biscay, the presence of flying English squadrons off the coast and demonstrations from Gallicia which he could not estimate, kept Bonnet's weakened army fully occupied, compelling him, in especial, to guard the Gallician passes into Leon. In the early spring Joseph had been appointed commander of all the armies in Spain; and the central army, which had its headquarters in the capital, was immediately under him. But the generals, doing each what seemed right in his own eyes, and looking exclusively to his own interests, paid little heed to the royal orders when they did not positively disobey. Joseph might and ought to have strengthened Marmont, when he must have suspected that the Castilles were the object of attack.

But he trembled not without reason for himself and for his hold on the capital. Madrid was mined with explosive combustibles; a spark might fire them at any moment, and he was troubled on every side by the guerrillas swarming in the mountains. Drouet's connecting corps was the pivot of the three armies, and Joseph did order Drouet to cross the Tagus and carefully observe the movements of Hill. It would have at once brought that general nearer to Madrid, and enabled him in case of need to support Marmont. Drouet was willing to obey, for he hated Soult; but when he had actually commenced his northward march, that marshal took practical measures to compel him to retrace his steps. Probably, from any point of view, Soult's dispositions were the wiser, for Drouet, when recalled to threaten Portugal and the flank of the allied advance, could still give Marmont indirect but effective assistance. Moreover, Soult seems to have believed to the last that Wellington held to his original plan and contemplated the invasion of Soult's own province, and Wellington, being aware of that false impression, did all in his power to confirm him in it.

So, thanks to skilful strategy and shrewd diplomacy, Marmont and

Wellington were face to face on the eve of a campaign of which both appreciated the supreme importance. The adversaries were not unequally matched. Inferior in genius and flexible decision to Wellington, the French Marshal was no mean master of the art of war, and he seldom showed more strategical science than in the manoeuvres which ended in his defeat at Salamanca. The armies were nearly equal in numbers. Marmont had 52,000 men, and although Wellington's strength was somewhat greater, about two-fifths of his army were Portuguese. It was universally admitted that the Portuguese fought well, nevertheless they could not be relied upon like the British. But one most gratuitous difficulty was thrown in Wellington's way. Again, when the ministry at home were squandering subsidies on the juntas, his military chest was as empty as that of Moore when Moore marched upon Sahagun, or as his own when he fought the battle of Talavera. He must buy meat, as he insisted, for his soldiers in Spain with ready money. Of money he had next to none, and the Treasury would not even back his bills. As he wrote to the Premier in emphatic words, 'I cannot think without shuddering upon the probability that we shall be distressed; nor upon the consequences which may result from our wanting money in the interior of Spain.'

CHAPTER 13

Campaign of Salamanca
JUNE, JULY, 1812

Nevertheless his resolution was not to be shaken, and on the 13th June he crossed the Agueda. The troops were in the highest spirits, the weather was glorious, and for days the march was through a richly-wooded country, backed up by the snowy peaks of the *Sierras*. There was no sign of an enemy till at last the German horse who headed the advance came upon one of the French pickets. Then the hostile cavalry showed in some force, careering over the plain and hovering along the heights on either flank. Sundry sharp skirmishes ensued. With evening the enemy withdrew behind the Tormes, and the allies lit their bivouac fires in front of Salamanca, with its piles of ecclesiastical buildings hanging over the shallow river, all crowned by the great dome of the cathedral. Marmont had evacuated the city on the preceding day, retreating towards Fuente el Sauco.

No city had suffered like Salamanca from the French occupation. Even more than Zaragoza, the venerable seat of learning was an agglomeration of massive convents, churches and colleges capable of indefinite defence. The French had never contemplated holding all the city with its rambling suburbs, but they had spared no pains and certainly shown no consideration for sentimental associations or for the citizens in constructing a fortress that should be virtually impregnable. The site chosen was the suburb of San Bias, where precipitous cliffs rise sheer out of the river. It is said that some thirty convents and colleges had been razed to furnish the blocks of masonry for the stupendous forts. A crowded quarter had been swept away to clear ground for the broad glacis, the casemates, the scarps and the counterscarps. Ever since the English landed at Lisbon the French had been industri-

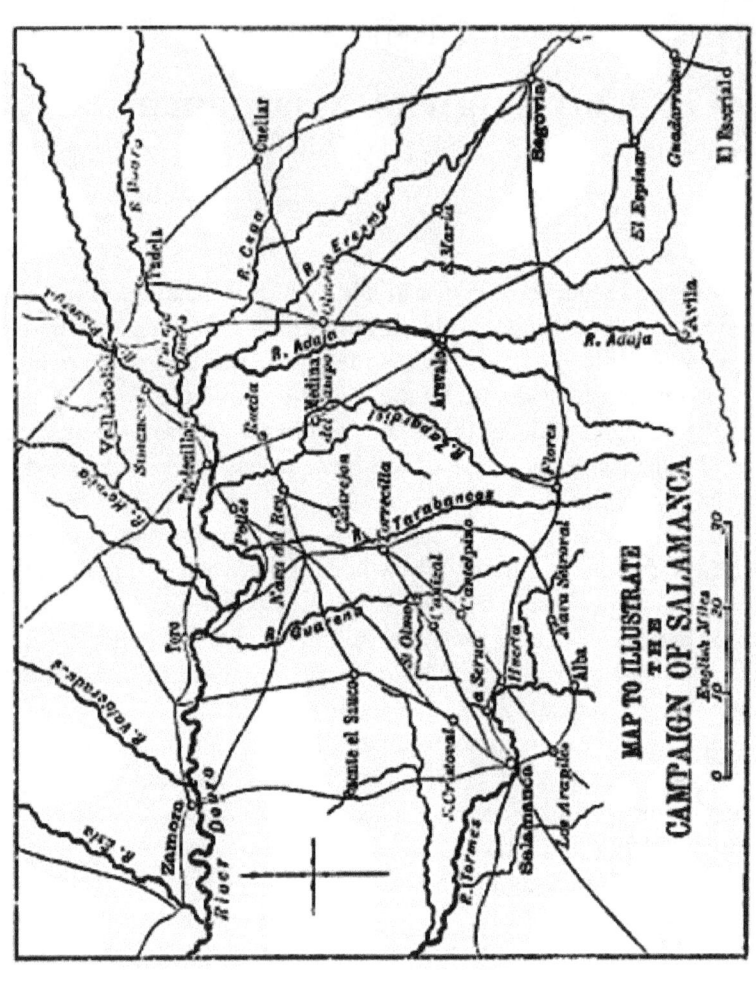

ously wrecking and reconstructing, and now the approaches had been mined. So Marmont, in the full assurance that three weeks to a month must elapse before his forts could possibly surrender, retired with the intention of returning for their relief.

Wellington was welcomed with passionate demonstrations. The streets and spacious *plazas* were decorated with flags and flowers, and illuminated after nightfall. He rode to his quarters amid the shouts of the crowd, and the women, falling on their knees, were pressing their lips on his stirrups. He would not have been human had he not been touched. Probably the dread of giving over the joyous and grateful city to the vengeance of the enemy may have influenced his determination to offer immediate battle, even under disadvantages. Yet it was essential to his plans that he should possess himself of the forts, and hold them with the only bridge which had been left standing. By that bridge was the only passage on his line of retreat to Rodrigo. But the Tormes was shallow when not in flood, and now his army passed it on the 17th June, by fords above and below the town. General Clinton, with the 6th Division, invested the forts, and Wellington, after his enthusiastic reception, took up his position with the army on the ridge of San Christoval, a natural bulwark four miles long, protecting the city to the north five miles in advance.

Thenceforth the strategy of either general was directed to attack and to defend a line of communications. Marmont was bound to guard against being cut off from Valladolid and Burgos, while to Wellington it was of even more vital importance to maintain his communications with his fortresses. Had he been beaten and thrown back upon Eastern Castille, between the armies of Marmont and Joseph, his case would have been well-nigh desperate. As for Marmont, in the event of defeat, he would undoubtedly have left the way open to Madrid, a sufficiently serious consideration. But for himself, as his talents must have almost infallibly saved him from a rout, he would be merely pressed back upon his supports. Already, now that Joseph had awakened to the real state of affairs, Caffarelli was coming up in considerable force, and Bonnet was making a demonstration from Leon, although he was recalled by an unlooked-for burst of activity on the side of Gallicia.

Yet the issues depending on a battle were so grave that Marmont had no desire to fight. What he did wish was, by outflanking the allies on their right, and threatening with his own left the road to Rodrigo, to save the Salamancan forts, and manoeuvre Wellington into a retrograde movement. Indeed he succeeded in forcing his great opponent to the perilous tactics of showing a front to the enemy parallel to a line of retreat. And for once Wellington's genius made an exception prove the rule, by extricating himself triumphantly from an embarrassing situation, and being only prevented by the almost invincible Spanish *laches* from inflicting a crushing defeat on his adversary.

Wellington had underrated, as Marmont had overestimated, the strength of the Salamanca forts, and the siege was far more tedious and formidable than he had expected. The ruins covering the rocky soil prevented excavation, and earth for the approaches had to be carried up under cover of night. The bombardment began on the 17th, but it was not till the 20th that the heavy iron howitzers arrived from Almeida. Then the old masonry of the Convent of San Vincente, solid as it was, collapsed; there was a stone-slip, bringing the roof along with it, which crushed many of the defenders. A yawning chasm was opened into the heart of the place. Shells and carcasses fell in showers; the timbers were fired, and there was a widespread conflagration. Nevertheless, the brave garrison under heavy fire succeeded in extinguishing the flames. On the 23rd the siege operations were suspended from lack of ammunition. A previous attempt at escalade had been repulsed with considerable loss. Three days later an ammunition train arrived; the batteries reopened, and again San Vincente was set on fire. On the 27th the white flag was hung out. The forts had held out for ten days; they would have surrendered several days before, had not the British batteries been compelled to suspend their fire, and so Marmont had made a grave miscalculation, when timely action was of supreme importance.

Time, as he believed, had been on his side. Each day was bringing him reinforcements from the north, and more than once he had countermanded his marching orders, as expected succours were delayed. In one respect he was master of the game, for prudence compelled Wellington to act strictly on the defensive. He had determined not to provoke an action unless he could strike with deadly effect. A drawn battle would have been tantamount to defeat, and a barren victory would scarcely have improved the situation. For Marmont had a safe retreat to Valladolid; he would have fallen back on the French forces of the north, and Joseph had now set the central army in motion. It was known, besides, from intercepted despatches, that the intrusive King had repeatedly sent peremptory orders to Soult to detach Drouet to Marmont's assistance. It was known also that Soult had as often declined; but it was notorious that Drouet made no secret of his insubordination, and was more disposed to take orders from Madrid than from Seville. It is true that, so far as that very independent general was concerned, Hill, who commanded the allies in Estremadura, thanks to the capture of Mirabete and the restoration of the bridge of Alcantara, could unite himself to Wellington by a direct march, whereas Drouet could only join Marmont by a difficult and circuitous route.

But if either army were forced to an orderly retreat, everything was in Marmont's favour, and, moreover, his reputation was seriously at stake in preventing the fall of fortified Salamanca. The loss of the stupendous works over which the invaders had expended infinite labour, would be regarded by the Emperor—as indeed it was—as a visible sign of the Marshal's incapacity. He was watching his opportunity to compel Wellington to fight at a disadvantage, and on a field where he could avail himself of his numerical superiority. Failing that, he sought to inflict a moral defeat and gain a substantial advantage, by compelling the British to raise the siege and to abandon the city which had received them with patriotic jubilation. To that end he directed the manoeuvres, which, by turning Wellington's left flank, would have barred his only line of retreat.

As for Wellington, his mind was made up to the practice of that patience which had often before served him so well. He would not be provoked to fight, except upon his own terms. If he must again fall back upon the Portuguese frontier, he would rather do so than risk disaster. Seldom was his resolution more sorely tried, and more than once it seemed that circumstances and the undeniable science of his adversary would prove too strong for him.

Never, perhaps, have there been more dramatic operations than those directed by Marmont for the relief of the forts, and those others a month later, which, when the former had failed, preceded the fiercely-contested battle. On the 17th June, when Wellington entered the town and General Clinton invested the forts, the allied main army had taken up its covering position on San Christoval, while Marmont, with two divisions, withdrew to Fuente el Sauco, on the road to Toro on the Douro. Relying on the resistance of the forts, he had only withdrawn to return. He had rallied to him 25,000 men, when on the 20th he marched southward again. The whole country to the north and east of Salamanca was wild and open, without enclosures. Marching troops had unlimited liberty of action, but every movement could be discerned from afar. The British battering-train was immediately placed in safety across the river, and the army remained ranged in battle order on San Christoval.

The position was favourable and very strong. The summit was a broad flat on which the battalions could deploy. The steep front was traversed by deep, hollow lanes and dotted over with defensible stone enclosures. At the base were sundry villages which were occupied. The concave amphitheatre of heights was flanked on the right by the upper Tormes, with its fords; on the left it sank down into marshes on the lower river, which sweeps round the back of the position. From those commanding heights everything could be seen for miles which was passing on the plain below, and they were practically safe from direct attack. The sole drawback was that the heat was intense, and there was neither shade nor water, nor fuel for cooking.

Towards evening the enemy's horse made a demonstration, as if to turn the left flank by the lower Tormes. The light division was detached in support of our light cavalry, and the demonstration was checked; but meantime it had become clear that the real attack was developing on the right. Massed at the base of the hills, their mortars began shelling the ridge, and even after the night had settled down the flights of shells still illuminated the darkness. The allied outposts were driven in, and the French established their own within gunshot of our batteries. Both armies were on the alert with the dawn, in full expectation of a battle; but the 21st was passed in inactivity. Wellington, who had slept on the ground, was looking out for an offensive movement by Marmont, but Marmont was awaiting the arrival of reinforcements. They came on the 22nd—three divisions with a brigade of cavalry, and there being 40,000 men at his command, he extended his line to the left and seized upon some heights from whence he could threaten the allied right. Moreover, the movements of the allies were no longer masked, and so far he was on equal terms with his adversary.

But what he saw did not encourage him to maintain an exposed position; towards evening his extended left was attacked and driven back before supports could be brought up, and in the night he cautiously withdrew to a range of parallel heights, six miles in the rear. Lord Wellington has been sharply criticised for not availing himself of the rash move of the enemy on the 20th, when Marmont pushed forward to the base of the allied position with forces visibly very inferior. Nor does it seem clear why he did not then hurl down his masses, to overwhelm the enemy with a serried shock, as when he began the battle of Salamanca. He may have made a mistake then and again on the next day, when even partial historians are inclined to blame him. But the explanation evidently is that the calculated inactivity was part of the system which had determined to risk nothing needlessly. He would have welcomed an attack on his strongly-defended heights, but he would not go down to the plain to deliver one, when the descent of the difficult face of the hill might have thrown his columns into confusion. Besides, the circumstances were distinctly different: Marmont's forces might be the weaker, but his divisions were well ordered and all in close touch. There was no such tempting opportunity to strike as on the day of the battle, nor had it become imperative to force an engagement, in order to save the only line of retreat.

Marmont's new position was well chosen, and it was needful that he should be more carefully observed than ever. Still hanging about anxiously for the relief of the forts, it was apparent that he meant to send his left wing across the Tormes. But the allies could baffle him by operating on a shorter line, and the fords of Santa Marta and Huerta were guarded—the one by General Graham with two divisions, the other by the heavy German horse. The 23rd was again a quiet day, but on the following morning shots were heard from the dense mist which veiled the lower ground. As the fog lifted, the Germans were seen in retreat before massive columns of infantry, preceded by field batteries, which opened fire periodically. Graham and his divisions thereupon were ordered across the river, with Le Marchant's English cavalry. The rest of the army was concentrated in readiness between the villages of Cabrerizos and Moresco. The French advanced till, as their skirmishers crowned an eminence, they saw Graham deploying in order of battle, and perpendicular to the Tormes. With him were eighteen guns in position.

While on the eminences to the right were the masses of our main army, and the light division below was prepared either to cross in support of Graham, or to join in the attack on the French who were posted on the right bank. The French general had timely warning of the danger into which he was rushing. He promptly turned back, recrossed the Tormes, and resumed his former ground. Then came in the hesitation induced by the knowledge that further reinforcements were on their way. He would have fought on the 23rd, when he had rallied his forces, but he had learned that Caffarelli was on the march. Consequently he had fallen back to await the arrival. On the 26th he felt that time was pressing, for the forts had signalled that they could only hold out for three days. He had again made up his mind to fight on the 28th, but the evening before he learned to his mortification that they had surrendered. Thus there was no longer a reason for hazarding a battle, with the advantages of position against him. He broke up his encampments and retired in the night towards the Douro.

He was suffered to pass in peace to the northern bank. Wellington, acting on doubtful and imperfect information, had scattered his troops, and was in no condition to attack at Tordesillas, the only place where a bridge was still standing. From Toro on the west, to Simancas on the east, all the other bridges had been broken down. Toro, on which Marmont's right was rested, was a strongly- fortified post; so was Simancas, on the Pisuerga which was unfordable; and at Valladolid the bridges and *têtes-de-pont* were fortified and efficiently defended. There were various fords, but they were doubtful and treacherous, and even in July subject to freshets in sudden rain-storms. It was a long-extended line which Marmont had to defend; but his operations were effectually masked by the river, and as the Douro takes a wide sweep to the south, he could act upon a direct line, while the allies had to circle round an arc.

Nor had Wellington accurate information from his spies as to any point where he might pass to resume the offensive. With numbers altogether inadequate to the work to be done, he had looked for assistance from Castaños, who was laying siege to Astorga. It was his desire that the Spaniard should place himself in communication with Silveira, and that they should unite an army behind the Esla strong enough to check the foraging of the French, and throw them back upon their magazines. But experience had taught him to expect little nor was he disappointed, for Spanish procrastination, as usual, disconcerted the plan. Then ensued a weary time of waiting. Neither general cared to fight. Marmont knew that he would be reinforced from the armies of the north, or the reserves which Napoleon had established in Burgos and elsewhere. Meantime he had lost touch with the army of the centre, for Joseph, on hearing of his unexpected retreat, had withdrawn the garrison from Arica, and the King's headquarters at Segovia were isolated by the activity of the guerrillas. And with possession of the bridge at the central point of Tordesillas he was safe from attack; for Wellington dare not attempt the passage of the river, when the enemy might fall on his flank and cut communications he had abandoned.

On the 8th July Bonnet brought up 6000 men, and Marmont thereupon showed signs of activity. He began to repair the bridge at Toro. Three parallel tributaries flow into the Douro from the south.

Wellington's headquarters were on the Trabancos, the central stream, and his right at Rueda, to the east of the easterly Zapardiel. Now, in response to Marmont's movement, he extended his left to the Guarena. Some considerable time was passed in inaction; and the careless interlude is an example of the amenities that soften war, when brave men are professionally pitted against each other. The pickets on either side crossed the river and freely intermingled, interchanging wine flasks and tobacco-pouches. If they could not speak they could communicate by signs and gestures.

But on the right there was demoralisation in the British ranks, nor was it possible to restrain the soldiers from brutish debauchery. There were similar scenes, with more leisure for indulgence than in those which had disgraced the retreat of Sir John Moore. Rueda is the capital of a rich wine district. Vast quantities of the strong red vintages were stored in the famous labyrinth of wine-cellars, where the pick-axe has aided Nature in excavating the soft limestone rock. The British privates offered hospitality to their French comrades, and many drunkards of both armies got lost in these labyrinths, to die miserable deaths. Even the men who showed more self-restraint were seldom altogether sober, and it was almost impossible to enforce ordinary discipline. What was even more serious, both officers and men, living in plenty or luxury, had leisure to grumble; full of fighting ardour, they blamed the general for having evaded battle at San Christoval; and then was generated that dangerous spirit of insubordination which showed itself under graver aspects in the retreats from Badajoz and Madrid. Perhaps it is a questionable compliment to say that they were less discontented at the pay of all ranks being lamentably in arrear.

Wellington's situation at that time is a striking example of the anxieties and responsibilities that may weigh upon a general, charged with great and complicated operations, yet dependent upon others for their satisfactory execution. Napoleon was supreme master; what he ordered he had the means of carrying out. The English general was at the mercy of ministers at home, with whom the means of correspondence were slow and precarious. As we have seen, when it was inconvenient to assist or impossible to answer him, they simply ignored his applications and left him to himself. Now the army, disgusted at what seemed cowardly caution, was verging on open mutiny; even officers high in rank made no allowance for his difficulties; the Spaniards were failing him, and he was equally worried by dilatoriness in the north, and apprehensions of the rashness of those who should have relieved him from pressure from the south and east. The Portuguese were reasonably clamorous for promised subsidies which had been long withheld; and finally, his military reputation was being imperilled by causes altogether beyond his control.

The immediate necessity was a supply of money, and no money was forthcoming. He wrote a despatch on the 15th June, and when we remember the position after Talavera we may understand the force of his protest.

> I have never been in such distress as at present, and some serious misfortune must happen if the Government do not attend seriously to the subject and supply us regularly with money. The arrears and distresses of the Portuguese Government are a joke to ours, and if our credit was not better than theirs we should certainly starve. As it is, if we don't find means to pay our bills for butcher's meat there will be an end to the war at once.

With extreme reluctance he had almost made up his mind again to fall back upon Portugal, when Marmont, of all men, came to his relief

Marmont, secure in his positions behind the Douro, had only in policy to play the waiting game. For some inscrutable reason he decided to assume the offensive. No doubt the discomfiture in his attempts at saving Salamanca had been fretting him. The fear of being superseded for that failure was always before his eyes. The prospect of being joined by the King with the central army should have been an argument for sitting fast. Yet the arrival of Joseph might rob him of future laurels; and it has been suggested that Wellington's backwardness at San Christoval had led him to underrate the talents of the adversary. Be that as it may, Wellington learned on the 16th, to his delight and relief, that Marmont had suddenly marched upon Toro, and was passing his troops across the river. Immediately he took his precautions to meet the move by concentrating his centre and left at Canizal. He had welcomed the movement as a relief, nevertheless it gravely endangered him. His left was actually turned; the French Marshal had got a fair start for Salamanca, and by persisting in a direct march on that city, anticipating the allies, he would seize upon the road from Salamanca to Rodrigo.

Wellington would consequently be forced to fight, and everything must be staked on the battle. Both armies, ranged parallel to the road to Salamanca, would be in a flank position. To either, defeat would be almost irremediable disaster. Yet the French would probably fare the worse, for an English victory would cut them off from their crossing place, and throw them back on the Lower Douro, among the Spanish and Portuguese irregulars who were swarming forward to the mountain passes. But Marmont had no mind to push matters to so desperate an issue. The movement from Toro had been merely a feint to leave the passages over the upper river open. Wellington, although inclined to believe the feint an actuality, had nevertheless always misdoubted it, and while concentrating his main forces to the left, had left his right on guard on the Trabancos, watching Polios and Tordesillas. And Marmont, counter-marching on the 17th, had crossed the river at those two passages, concentrating his whole army that evening at Nava del Rey. The allied right was much in the air and very critically situated.

At midnight Wellington learned at Toro that it was confronting the whole hostile army. There was no time to move his left and centre to its support. He therefore decided to concentrate on an inter- mediate line of defence. At seven o'clock on the 18th he was on the Trabancos, where General Cotton, who had maintained his dangerous position through the night, had been resisting a formidable attack since daybreak. Meantime Marmont had learned that only a part of the English army was before him. He crossed the Trabancos in two columns, marching at best pace for the Guarena, over open country and rolling downs. The British infantry, retreating on a parallel line, made a sharp race of it, protected by the cavalry on flank and rear. The day was oppressively hot, and the air was loaded with dust. That was one of the strangest spectacles in the story of wars. When the clouds of dust thinned or lifted, the parched and fagged soldiers could be seen pressing forward, often within short musket-range, with no thought but that of arriving the first at the goal.

Now and again, when there was some momentary halt, there came a rapid exchange of bullets, and invariably a field gun opened fire, provoking a quick response to the challenge. The British won the race for the river by a bare neck, for as the Light Division stooped to drink in fording it, the French batteries, galloping up to the ridge, rained down a shower of shot upon them. But the right had already crossed the river and was resting upon the main body; an attempt of the French to force the passage was repelled, and the armies remained quietly in presence throughout the 19th.

The armies again faced each other on their respective lines of retreat. From Wellington's right there were roads leading to the bridge of

Salamanca and the fords over the Tormes; nor did he expect that Marmont would attempt to turn it. Had he known that Carlos d'España had neglected his instructions to garrison the castle at Alba, which commanded the uppermost crossing, his dispositions would have been different. His immediate object was the protection of Salamanca, for should the French recover it they would be strongly posted behind the river, with control of the bridge; the fruits of the recent sieges would have been lost and his way barred once more for a further advance.

Marmont knew—what Wellington did not—that Alba was unoccupied. Therefore on the 20th he concentrated to the left, moved his columns up the Guarena, crossed the river and marched for Alba. To parry the stroke at his communications, the English general was constrained to follow. Then the race recommenced under identical conditions and over open country as before. Nor could it have been conducted without precipitating an encounter undesired by both, unless directed on either side by consummate tacticians. But the French justified their reputation as the best marchers in Europe. At Contalpino the allies had been outmarched and outflanked. Marmont had reached Huerta on the Tormes.

Wellington, inclining to the south-west, took position on the heights to his right. He was back at his old position on San Christoval, which he had quitted in triumph a month before. He was gravely disquieted that night and full of anxious forebodings. Marmont had fairly outmarched him, exhibiting excellent strategy and familiar knowledge of the ground. Were the race to be resumed on the morrow he must be outpaced again, and again the enemy would anticipate him by seizing the road to Rodrigo. He had, apparently, nothing but a choice of dangers. A battle under disadvantages was less advisable than ever, for Caffarelli's cavalry were known to be on the march, and Joseph was coming up with the army of the centre. If he remained where he was, his communications would be severed; if he decided for retreat, he lost Salamanca.

On the 21st Marmont was crossing at Alba and Huerta. He threw a strong garrison into the castle at the former place, and his leading divisions took ground at Calvariza-Arriba. That village was on the outskirts of a forest covering the ground to the river. Wellington hastened to meet the movement by sending troops across at the lower fords. Meantime he could only wait, but it became evident that the decisive battle was impending. Hitherto everything had gone in favour of the French, but unless Wellington were actually defeated their previous gains must go for nothing. And if Marmont were suffered to have his way to the south of the Tormes, the allied communications with their base would be effectually intercepted. The morning of the 22nd relieved Wellington from his dilemmas; for the second time Marmont made a mistake, and it was a more fatal blunder than the former.

If the night of the 20th had been an anxious one for the English general, that of the 21st was more disquieting to his army. When the light division descended to the ford of Aldea Lengua it was enveloped in premature and pitchy darkness. One of the sudden summer storms had been brooding, and now it burst. The men could hardly hold their own in passing the swollen Tormes; the incessant roar of the thunder was deafening, and the lightning, drawn down by the bristling bayonets, caused many casualties. The 5th Dragoon Guards had picketed their horses on the left bank. The startled animals broke loose from their fastenings, and as they galloped to and fro in the darkness it was believed that the French cavalry were charging. Nevertheless, through darkness, difficulties and alarms, the infantry moved forward in unbroken order, bivouacking upon the ground assigned to it in circumstances as miserable as could well be conceived.

With break of day Marmont occupied the ridge of Calvariza-Arriba in greater strength, and his intentions became unmistakable. A little to the left of the position were two isolated hills named the Arapiles, and had Marmont succeeded in securing both he might have formed across his adversary's right and fought the battle with everything in his favour. But as Wellington described what occurred, with his racy and inimitable succinctness, we can do no better than quote him. Thus he wrote to Graham,—

> I took up the ground which you were to have taken during the siege of Salamanca. We had a race for the large Arapiles, which is the more distant of the two detached heights. This race the French won, and they were too strong to be dislodged without a general action. I knew that the French were to be forced by the cavalry of the army of the north on the 22nd or 23rd, and that the army of the centre was likely to be in motion. Marmont ought to have given me a *pont d'or*, and he would have made a handsome operation of it; but, instead of that, after manoeuvring all the morning in the usual French style—nobody knew with what object—he at last pressed upon my right in such a manner, at the same time without engaging, that he

would have carried our Arapiles, or would have confined us entirely to our position. This was not to be endured, and we fell upon him, turning his left flank, and I never saw an army receive such a beating. I had desired the Spaniards to continue to occupy the castle of Alba de Tormes. Don Carlos d'España had evacuated it, I believe, before he knew my wishes, and he was afraid to let me know that he had done so, and I did not know it till I found no enemy at the fords of the Tormes. When I lost sight of them I marched upon Huerta and Encinas. If I had known there had been no garrison in Alba I should have marched there and should probably have had them all.

Chapter 14

Salamanca and Burgos
July—September 1812

Marmont 'had been manoeuvring all the morning,' and Wellington began to believe that the manoeuvring meant nothing. He had retired accordingly from the English Arapiles, when a report was brought him that the French were at last in rapid motion and advancing fast to the Rodrigo road. He galloped back to his former position and eagerly scanned the plain below. Then a light broke over his stern features, and those who observed them might read in the intensity of his relief the anxiety he had concealed beneath an air of impenetrable composure. The French left, hurrying too fast, had entirely lost touch with the centre. His enemy had delivered himself into his hands. 'Egad, I have them now!' he exclaimed, in triumphant jubilation. The orders came quick and brief, and in a few minutes the avalanche of serried columns was launched in the gap that had opened so opportunely. The English rushed down under a tremendous fire which opened on the heads of their columns from the French Arapiles.

Marmont, looking down from behind the batteries, lost not a moment in taking steps to retrieve his error. He sent back to hasten the advance of his centre; he sent forward to check the advance of his left wing. He saw everything but the approach of our 3rd Division, which was hidden from him by the hills. He hoped that with the terrible fire directed on them he could hold the British in check till he had brought up his supports and restored the battle. But then he saw the 3rd Division break forth from behind the heights and throw themselves across the advance of his left. The left was led by Thomières, whose courage was as undeniable as the rapacity which distinguished him among the plundering generals who served in Portugal under Junot. Thomières deemed that he was carrying all before him, and had expected to see the allies in full retreat along the ridge, closely pressed by forces of the Marshal. On the contrary, Pakenham, one of the most dashing and impetuous of soldiers, had flung himself in the hot ardour of onset across his path, and simultaneously he was arrested by the orders of recall.

At the same time, *pour surcroît de malheur*, the French lost their leader. Marmont, hurrying to the front, was struck down by a shell, which shattered an arm and inflicted grievous body wounds. Bonnet, succeeding by seniority, almost immediately met a somewhat similar fate, and then the command devolved on Clausel, one of Napoleon's latest creation of marshals, whom he always held in exceptional consideration. Nor did he ever show his qualities with more distinguished brilliancy than when he withdrew his army from the rout of Salamanca, after heroic efforts to redeem the day, which were very nearly successful.

The day was drawing on, and the decision must be speedy. It was at five o'clock that Pakenham assailed Thomières. The French, though disappointed and disheartened, offered an obstinate defence; but there was no denying the British rush, and no resisting the persistent tactics which worked round steadily to the left. Thomières, fighting fiercely, fell back on the Arapiles, where the British centre was making good the ground in face of the storm of shot and shell. The 4th and 5th Divisions kept pushing forward, and between their attack and that of Pakenham, the cavalry, light and heavy, were coming to the front. Clausel had by this time effected his junction with Thomières, and was showing a gallant front to the impetuous advance. But the troops were in disorder; the sun was beating in their eyes, and through the dense clouds of dust they could only fire at random. Then from behind the impenetrable veil they heard the rush and trampling of horses in masses.

It was Le Marchant charging at the head of the English heavy cavalry on disordered squares and broken lines, and the light dragoons were flanking the heavies. The ranks broke, and there was a *sauve qui peut*, the fugitives scattering in the dark confusion, and even seeking refuge, in their bewilderment, in the British squares. The horsemen used their sabres unsparingly, and the carnage was terrible. Le Marchant had fallen, but Cotton replaced him, and the rout of the French left was complete. The victors closed up in a formidable line, and Pakenham, upon the French left, was still pressing onward.

The battle had been won on the allied right, and all was going well on the other wing, in spite of a most determined resistance, for several of the French divisions had only now come into action. Our 4th and 5th Divisions, passing the village of Arapiles, were steadily pressing Bonnet back. Then an unfortunate mistake jeopardised the day. Pack and his Portuguese, acting apparently without orders, in their onset assailed the French Arapiles. Though admirably led, and fighting with the greatest gallantry, they were hurled down again with heavy loss. Consequently the right of the British infantry was left exposed to a flanking attack which threatened to succeed.

Clausel saw his opportunity, and skilfully availed himself of it. His fresh troops were still coming up from the forest on his right, and he formed them behind his shattered battalions. The tide of battle ebbed backwards, and for the moment it seemed as if the 4th Division would be repulsed and the allied right-centre broken, for Maucune, left at liberty now the French Arapiles hill was secure, was menacing the 4th Division on flank and in rear. The English generals were falling as the French had fallen before. Cole and Leith, and lastly Beresford, were successively carried off the field. The fortunes of the battle hung in suspense, and a trifle might turn them either way.

Happily Wellington, who had been almost omnipresent, was on the spot, and his prudence had held back a strong reserve. Clinton, with the 6th Division, was ordered up, and the charge of 6000 fresh combatants, infuriated by impatient waiting, was not to be denied. Wellington followed up that hard-won success by an order to cut the faltering line of the French with the advance of the 1st Division. That order, for some reason, was not executed, and to that mistake, with the French occupation of the castle of Alba, their army owed its escape from practical annihilation. Clausel, when his noble attempt at retrieving the day had failed, turned his attention promptly to securing his retreat. He was admirably seconded by Foy, and above all by Maucune. It was Maucune who covered the retiring of Foy, till that general had withdrawn to the shelter of the woods. But the most effectual protectors of the orderly withdrawal were the falling shades of night. Wellington, watching the pursuit, could only gather what was going forward by the fitful flashing of the musketry and occasional blazes from the batteries.

At length the last fires died out in the darkness, and he knew that for the time the enemy was beyond his reach. He cared the less, for he believed that Clausel was effectively trapped. For, as will be remembered, he was still in the belief that Alba and its passage were guarded.

He fancied that in the morning he would find the French crowded up at the fords of Huerta, and thither, with the first light, he pressed forward, personally directing the march of the light division. All his strategy had been directed to strengthening his left, that he might follow up the action with a decisive stroke. But Clausel, knowing that his retreat was open by Alba, had skilfully availed himself of his adversary's misapprehension and of the short night. His army was passed across the Tormes by the narrow bridge and the fords, and daylight found him in swift retreat, having already organised a formidable rearguard. Never did the French prove their marching powers in more marvellous fashion. His rearguard was engaged in sharp skirmishing, but his next night halt was at Flores de Avila, forty miles from Salamanca. Moreover, his line of retreat to the eastward was well chosen, for Wellington naturally expected he would have returned to Tordesillas and the former positions behind the Douro.

The victory threw the game into the victor's hands, and again left him master of the future operations. Nor should it be forgotten that the effects were not limited to the Peninsula. The rude shock of Salamanca was felt on the banks of the Moskowa. It was on the very eve of the bloody battle of the Borodino that Marmont's *aide-de-camp*, bearing the disheartening tidings, arrived at the headquarters of the Grand Army. Though the Emperor read the despatches with apparent indifference, and, strange to say, made no harsh comments, the effect was stunning. The officer who entered his tent in the morning found him with his head buried in his hands. Forgetful of appearances, he loudly bewailed the inconstancy of fortune.

While the battle with the Russians which he had so ardently longed for was raging, he wandered aimlessly about on a hillock, his head sunk on his breast. No doubt grief was aggravating the bodily ailment that troubled him, and his thoughts were wandering to Spain. Murat and Ney sent to demand reinforcements. Then, says Ségur, 'Napoleon was seized with unwonted hesitation.' In place of the prompt decision of old, he was plunged in painful deliberation. He issued orders, only to countermand them, and finally refused the supports. Murat declared that on that eventful day he had seen nothing of the genius of his brother-in-law; and the Viceroy of Italy as plainly avowed that he could not understand the Emperor's indecision. In fact, at that most critical moment, it was to Wellington that Kutusoff was indebted for the reprieve by which he profited, and for which he had never dared to hope.

After a night passed at Flores de Avila, Clausel crossed the Zapardiel and retired on Valladolid. The pursuit was slack, for our troops were exhausted; nevertheless, the light cavalry harassed his rear, and numerous stragglers fell into the hands of the peasants, from whom they had no mercy to expect. He made no stand at Valladolid, retreating upon Burgos, and abandoning the former city with its guns and magazines. His garrisons on the Douro were also sacrificed, and the Gallicians, after their long delays, at last came down in force. Wellington entered Valladolid on the 30th, but he lost no time, and made no stay there. Strengthening his left, and leaving it to follow Clausel up the valleys of the Pisuerga and Arlanzon Rivers, on the following day he had re-crossed the Douro, and established his headquarters at Cuellar. For himself, he had decided to march upon Madrid, in consideration of the moral consequences of occupying the capital.

The defeat of Marmont and the discomfiture of the army of Portugal had thrown Joseph into extreme perplexity. He had been advancing leisurely to Marmont's support, and now he was confronting the main forces of the victorious allies. He decided not to defend the passes of the Guadarama, as they might be turned by the valley of the Tagus. Clearly he was in no condition to hold Madrid, and the only question was how and whither to conduct the evacuation. Soult had, as usual, disobeyed his orders, which were to send 10,000 men to Toledo. But Soult in Andalusia was his most reliable resource, and accordingly he resolved to move thither by La Mancha.

In fact it was flight far more than retreat. The troops of the escort had broken loose from all restraint, and plundered those they were supposed to be protecting. They would have broken into open mutiny had it not been for the presence and authority of Marshal Jourdan. Including soldiers, there was a mixed multitude of 20,000, of every age, sex and condition. In their train were 2000 or 3000 carriages loaded with baggage and booty. Provisions were scarce, and were seized by the soldiers, who dragged the women and children from the beasts which were carrying them. No sort of order was restored till the mob was on the southern side of the Tagus, where it was joined by the garrisons of Aranjuez and Toledo. But nothing is so bad that it may not be worse, and Wellington might have launched his cavalry on the panic-stricken fugitives. Napier suggests that he withheld the order in mercy, because he knew that the soldiers would probably have escaped, and that the blow would have fallen on the weak and the helpless.

On the 13th of August he entered Madrid. The reception of the deliverer rather resembled the adoration of a god than any welcome of a mortal. He and the members of his staff scarcely dared to venture abroad. In vain they dressed themselves in civilian clothes and went out for exercise in the dark. Invariably they were recognised and followed with acclamations. That the conqueror never lost his head for a moment is shown in his despatches. He appreciated those very sincere proofs of his popularity at their true value, and declared from sad experience that they would have no practical effect on the Spanish allies, as was demonstrated only too soon by the sluggish movements of the Gallician army, and by the resentful insubordination of Ballesteros, which left Soult and King Joseph free to resume the offensive operations which might have been defeated or delayed by a demonstration on their left flank. Wellington was constrained to remain in the capital till it had been decided whether Soult should abandon Andalusia.

Joseph had again sent peremptory orders that Soult should join him with his united forces, falling back either through Murcia or Valencia. Soult, who had disobeyed all the previous instructions, and who had a soldier's contempt for the monarch's military talents, naturally hesitated and remonstrated. Moreover, he and the King mutually misunderstood each other. Evidently Soult honestly believed that Joseph meant to throw the Emperor over, and endeavour to make such terms with the Spaniards as might save his throne. Undoubtedly all his thoughts were directed to the recovery of his capital. Soult's confidential despatches to his master were intercepted and opened by Joseph, who was naturally embittered against the Marshal by a perusal of the contents. But he was himself writing to his brother at the same time, charging Soult with aspiring to a crown in Andalusia.

There was even less ground for that charge than for the earlier accusations of a similar character. But the King and the Marshal firmly believed their respective charges, which was fatal to acting in concert as joint leaders. Joseph had set his heart on recovering Madrid, and Soult had conceived a daring and original scheme, which was beyond the King's timid comprehension. Yet it commended itself so forcibly to the genius of Napoleon, that it was then he declared, with hasty injustice to Suchet, Clausel, St Cyr and others, that Soult was the only military head in Spain. Soult was naturally loath to relinquish all the advantages he had gained by three years of able military operations and sagacious civil administration in the south. He had acted so ably, indeed, that it seemed certain that the French sympathisers would soon have the ascendency in Andalusian councils.

Briefly, his scheme was this. He would sacrifice communications, if necessary, with France by the western roads, leaving them to be guarded by the armies of Portugal and the north, which in case of reverses might retreat upon the frontiers. He would still hold Andalusia, press the siege of Cadiz, and keep open the more circuitous communications by the east, Joseph should retreat through La Mancha upon Despeñas Perros, and the army of occupation would concentrate behind the Morena. If possible, Joseph should bring with him the army of Portugal. Then, if Spain north of the Morena were to be abandoned, nevertheless 80,000 or 100,000 French, resting on the magazines and strong places in Andalusia, would have changed the theatre of war. Wellington must turn his attention to the safety of Lisbon, or force the formidable passes of the Morena. Meantime the French could afford to wait, till succours came by way of the north from the Emperor, and everything was to be gained by activity in delay. But when Joseph decided to rally Suchet to him on the Valencian roads, Soult had no option but to comply.

Wellington's genius had either suspected the conceptions of Soult, or he had some actual indications of his intentions. Hence he remained at Madrid till he should have information of the abandonment of Andalusia, which was not until Soult, recalling his garrisons, had concentrated the retiring army upon Granada. The protracted siege of Cadiz was raised on the 24th August with a great destruction of guns and the loss of the gunboats. Meantime Joseph, by another blunder, had needlessly weakened his force by leaving a garrison to occupy the Retiro, a fortified palace to the east of Madrid, containing vast stores and munitions. Necessarily the Retiro surrendered, and its defenders were sacrificed. Then the capital saw a strange situation. The markets were overflowing with provisions, but there was no money to buy. The population of all ranks was absolutely penniless. The tyranny of the intrusive Government had squeezed it dry. When taxes had been remitted by edicts the imposts had been made heavier. When the *octroi* duties had been nominally repealed in response to the cries of distress, they had in reality been increased. Forced loans were wrung from the citizens; the poorest artisans were compelled to take out licences to entitle them to work.

The Government 'cornered' the grain, to sell it at arbitrary prices. The hospitals were overcrowded with the sick and starving, and of the deaths in the spring of 1812 two-thirds were attributed to misery and hunger. When the allies entered Madrid, the pay of all ranks was in arrears. Yet the first thing some of the charitable officers did was to establish subscription soup-kitchens for the relief of the famishing. Nor were political animosities much less embarrassing. The sorely-oppressed patriots, driven to desperation, naturally were eager to wreak their vengeance on their weaker countrymen, who had reluctantly acquiesced in the foreign domination. But the well-balanced judgment of Wellington recognised that there was no little excuse for many of those *Juramentados*, and that if the wounds of bleeding Spain were to be stanched much must be forgiven and forgotten. He set an excellent example of toleration and oblivion by inviting *Afrancesados* and *Juramentados* to his official receptions, and in his wise liberality he was well seconded by Carlos D'España, who had been appointed to the captain-generalship of the city and province of Madrid. D'España was a poor leader, and he had lost Wellington the best fruits of Salamanca, but he was a sincere patriot and a fair administrator. The capital began to calm down as money began to flow back to it, yet it was ever oppressed by the well- grounded fear of Wellington's withdrawal and Joseph's return.

In fact the omens were all unfavourable, and the withdrawal was soon seen to be inevitable. The blame must be shared between the Spanish allies who, as always, were backward, and the British ministry, who starved the military chest and sent inadequate help to the Eastern coasts from Sicily, in place of cordially co-operating with the commander-in-chief. If Wellington's comprehensive plans broke down for the time, and if the French evacuation of the Peninsula was deferred, it was because the divisions in the north, but chiefly on the east, were inefficient, and because his freedom of action was paralysed by insuperable difficulties of transport. He had hoped for 12,000 men from Sicily to support the Catalonians and Valencians, and give occupation to Suchet.

Barely half that number was sent. Maitland, who was in command, was a gallant soldier, but no Wellington; moreover, he was in wretched health and anxious to be relieved. He arrived off the coast on the 1st of August, and had he been more firm of purpose he might well have been puzzled by the conflicting information he received from the Spanish chiefs. Each spoke according to his hopes or wishes. One absurdly magnified the forces of the French, another more gratuitously underrated them. One said that the *partidas* and the peasants of the mountains were eager to be summoned to arms; another declared that they were profoundly discouraged. But all agreed that the native levies must be paid and fed from the British squadron. Maitland, after exciting false hopes elsewhere on the coast, disembarked at Alicante, much in the dark, and conducted desultory operations with the languor of a confirmed invalid. The rash ignorance of the Spanish generals provoked a crushing defeat at Castallo, and the upshot of the expedition was simply to weaken Suchet, till he was joined by Jourdan with Joseph, and subsequently by Soult.

The best that can be said is, that Alicante did not fall to him—a very negative gain. On the north-east Sir Home Popham's squadron which had detained troops from joining Marmont before Salamanca, had now compelled the able Caffarelli to withdraw the garrisons from Santander and other places. But the Gallician army under Santocildes, from which Wellington had hoped for efficient support, and which figured on paper for 30,000 men, could only furnish a third of that number, and these were undisciplined and wretchedly equipped.

Joseph, Soult and Suchet had united nearly 100,000 men. Clausel, who had been reorganising his routed army, had 25,000; he was gathering in the fugitives who had scattered after the defeat, and was being strengthened by the reserves wisely provided by Napoleon against the chance of a disaster to Marmont. Clinton, who had been left to hold Clausel in check, was menaced by Foy as well. Nor in the south had Wellington's carefully-considered dispositions gone more smoothly. He had instructed Ballesteros to advance to join Maitland and threaten the flank of the French, should Joseph and Soult counter-march on the capital. But the Cortes, in an outburst of gratitude after Salamanca, had appointed the English conqueror commander-in-chief of all their armies. To which Ballesteros, in a fit of peevish resentment, responded by a violent protest, throwing up his command. So far as his forces were concerned, the French could operate in absolute immunity from danger. Knowing their dispositions, Wellington decided to reinforce his divisions on the Douro with those he had scattered, from considerations of coolness and health, through the mountains to the north and west of Madrid; to drive back Clausel; to take the castle of Burgos, and to leave Hill to hold the enemy in check till he should hasten southward again to take the initiative in person after the capture. But the obstinate resistance of that fortress upset those calculations.

On the 1st of September he departed from Madrid, leaving two divisions in garrison. Hill was to cover the capital on the side of the Xarama, and Ballesteros had been requested to reinforce him. The troops were mustered at Arevallo, and on the 6th they passed the fords of the Douro. Thereupon the enemy evacuated Valladolid, crossed the Pisuerga, and withdrew along the right bank. Wellington, following, occupied Palencia, and there he received despatches from Santocildes. Little as he had expected from Spanish assistance, he learned then, to his surprise and disappointment, that he could have no effective assistance from Gallicia. The musters on paper were even more illusory than usual; he was only joined by 11,000 men, indifferently equipped and disciplined; and so he was compelled to abandon the idea of leaving the Spaniards to hold Burgos, while he returned to Madrid to provide against eventualities.

Meantime he had followed the retiring French up the fertile valleys of the Pisuerga and Arlanzon. Hitherto both districts had almost escaped ravage; there was a sufficiency of provisions and a superabundance of heady wine; already our soldiers, breaking into the wine shops and cellars, began to indulge in the excesses which demoralised the subsequent retreat. Clausel exhibited the genius which had asserted itself at Salamanca by again conducting a retreat in masterly fashion. He had the choice of a succession of formidable positions, and each morning found him offering the battle which Wellington did not care to accept as he could only attack in front. Clausel entered Burgos on the 17th; Marmont, who was suffering from his wounds, had left it a few days before. Thither Caffarelli hurried to confer with him, and after a council of war it was decided that Burgos must in turn be evacuated: no time was lost in recommencing the retreat, and by the following forenoon the city was abandoned.

The city had been abandoned, but the historic castle had been garrisoned by 1800 staunch soldiers under Dubreton, a general of rare skill and determination. The allies, treading on the heels of the French, found the town in a blaze and the conflagration spreading. The garrison, to clear the surrounding space, had fired the houses adjoining the castle. The bands of *partidas* breaking in, took advantage of the confusion to plunder as if they had been sacking a hostile city. Burgos, for the time, was a veritable pandemonium, and it was only by the strenuous exertions of Alava, whose unfailing co-operation won the lasting friendship of Wellington, that some sort of order was restored.

The English general had reasonably supposed that the castle could not long hold out. It was scarcely a fortress of the third order; and it was commanded by some heights to the eastward, within short gun-range. But then began one of the most remarkable sieges of modern times, for both French and English were miserably deficient in all the scientific appliances of modern war. The French had swept the country of mules, horses and cattle; and Wellington could find no transport to bring up his siege-train. For his batteries he had only three 18-pounders and five antiquated iron howitzers. Repeatedly the supply of powder ran low, nor did he dare to expend it utterly, lest Clausel should return and challenge a battle. Repeatedly the feeble bombardment was suspended, till fresh supplies were brought up from the ships on the coast. Finally, when he fell back upon difficult and tedious sapping and mining, he had only four engineer officers to direct operations, and no regular sappers. When three of these officers had been killed or crippled, the last was carefully kept in the rear as his life was too precious to be rashly exposed.

The castle crowned a rugged hill, overhanging the town and the river beyond it. It was surrounded by triple lines of hasty construction. The first line of defence consisted of an old wall, with a new parapet and flanking works. The second was of earth and palisaded. The innermost was likewise of earth, embracing the two commanding points of the hill, one surmounted by an old church which was entrenched, and the other by the massive keep of the castle. So solid was the ancient masonry that it bore the super-structure of a casemated work, armed with heavy guns. The battery on the keep dominated everything except the hill of San Miguel to the east, one of the eminences already mentioned. San Miguel was defended by a horn-work, as yet unfinished and only closed by palisades, but commanded by the heavy guns on the keep, and flanked besides by the other defences. The French batteries opposed to Wellington's antiquated battering train were armed with nine heavy guns, eleven light field pieces and half a dozen of howitzers, and as the reserve artillery of the army of Portugal was in the fortress, they had the means of remedying any casualties. Where they came short was in powder and projectiles.

Four assaults were successively delivered on the fortress. The first was directed on the heights of San Miguel. It was admirably planned, but indifferently executed. The covering party, advancing on the front, began to fire far too soon; when they reached the ditch, many had fallen and the rest were demoralised. The simultaneous attacks on the flanking bastions failed, owing to the shortness of the scaling ladders. But Major Cocks, although he had lost half his stormers, found the gorge of the work undefended; with the survivors he clambered over the stockade, and the French, suddenly stricken by panic, fled back into the castle.

The works had been won 'by a fluke,' but the confidence of the allies had been dashed. Moreover, San Miguel, though raking the castle from its narrowest point, was commanded and out-flanked by the castle terrace. The assailants had lost 400 men, the defenders little more than a third of that number. But Wellington could now study the defences. They were weak, but his means of assault were yet more feeble, and his best hopes were in the current report that the garrison was short of water and provisions. He resolved to press the siege by the slower approaches of sap and mine. When the first mine was completed, his batteries on San Miguel were to open, and an assault was to be delivered on the foremost line; if successful, it was to be followed up by another on the second.

On the 22nd he had changed his plan. He determined to attempt an escalade on the first line, without waiting for the breaching. For some unexplained reason the Portuguese were told off to lead, and they fell back in utter confusion before the desultory fire of the common guard. The British scrambled down into the ditch and planted the ladders, but the officers who mounted were unsupported by their men. The French, manning the parapets, poured down a deadly fire on the soldiers crowding in the ditch; and the commander-in-chief, who had been watching the attack from San Miguel, with the bullets from the castle flying all around him, had the signals sounded for retreat. Altogether, it was a discreditable affair and indifferently planned; the British were infected by the panic of the Portuguese, and both were humiliated and discouraged by their failure.

Again Wellington fell back upon his former plan of sapping up to the walls and mining them. As he had neither sappers nor pioneers, his four engineer officers were compelled to face the hot fire of the enemy while personally directing the unskilled soldiers. Then it was that three of the four were killed or placed *hors de combat*. On the evening of the 29th the mine was sprung and the wall breached. The leading party of twenty stormers mounted without meeting opposition, for the French were taken by surprise, but as the handful of assailants was left unsupported, the defenders rallied and hurled them down. The leader of the supporting company had missed the breach in the black night; he returned to report the failure. In consequence of his mistake the stormers were withdrawn, and Wellington determined to risk no more night attacks.

Yet the fourth assault, undertaken in daylight, was no more successful than its predecessors. The preparations had been delayed owing to the lack of powder, but were resumed when a supply was sent up from the fleet. On the 4th October the batteries on San Miguel had cleared away the obstructions on the old breach. A second and more formidable mine was ready for explosion, and orders were issued for a double assault. The explosion of that mine was tremendous. It blew many of the garrison into the air, and crumbled thirty yards of the solid wall into fragments. While the report was still echoing between the castle and San Miguel, one column of the 24th had rushed up through the clouds of smoke and stone dust, while another had scaled the debris encumbering the old breach.

Both points were carried and so far secured by imperfect lodgements formed in the darkness. But the success, such as it was, was of no long duration. The French, with indomitable courage, had only been waiting for their revenge. On the afternoon of next day they charged down the hill with irresistible force, and sweeping labourers and guards from the old breach, recovered the works and carried off the tools. They did not attempt the second breach, but the advantage encouraged them and disheartened the besiegers. Officers and soldiers began to feel that they were contending against exceptional disadvantages, with means entirely inadequate. Moreover, not a few of the most intelligent were inclined to suspect that for once the general did not know his own mind. Then the rain had fallen in torrents, swamping the trenches and parallels.

Meantime the garrison had been indefatigably active, breaking out besides in furious sorties, which were only repulsed with severe loss. The batteries on San Miguel were silenced by the overwhelming fire from the fortress. And the death of Major Cocks was no slight loss, for he was one of the most able of the British officers, with a long and distinguished record of service. After the defences had been breached in a third place, the fifth and final assault came off. It was also delivered in the daytime, but was as unfortunate as all the others. And then Lord Wellington's tenacity yielded to circumstances which compelled him to think of securing his retreat.

CHAPTER 15

The Allies Fall Back on the Portuguese Frontier
OCTOBER—NOVEMBER 1812

Masséna had been offered the supreme command, but had declined. Had he been younger and less indolent, he might have been more eager to retrieve the reputation he had seriously impaired by his failure in Portugal. Souham had been preferred to various claimants, although Clausel might have naturally been retained as the chief of the army he had handled so well. In Clausel, Maucune and Foy he had admirable lieutenants, and the discomfited army of Portugal, reinforced by 12,000 men from France, now mustered 35,000 under arms. Burgos was within the command of Caffarelli, and that general had assembled at Vittoria 9000 men for its succour. Caffarelli urged Souham to fight, and Souham would have willingly consented, had he not greatly overrated Wellington's strength. As matter of fact, Wellington had barely 20,000 English and Portuguese, for the 11,000 of the Gallician levies could not be reckoned on seriously for a pitched battle. Souham, on better information, had at last made up his mind to a grand effort for the relief of the castle. The chances were in his favour, and if he were worsted, he could lose but little, for his positions were good he was strong in artillery and an easy line of retreat lay behind him.

But on the 19th, when on the eve of setting his forces in motion, important despatches reached him. Hitherto they had been delayed or intercepted by the guerrillas. Joseph announced that he was advancing on the Tagus with 70,000 men. He ordered Souham to co-operate, and forbade him in the meantime to engage the enemy. Souham, though on the spot and acquainted with the circumstances, reluctantly and, perhaps, weakly obeyed. On that very same day Hill had communicated with Wellington. He sent similar intelligence; he announced the untimely defection of Ballesteros, and said he was forced to fall back on the Tagus, when that river was becoming everywhere fordable, after weeks of drought. Consequently Wellington's position had become untenable, and though loath to abandon a siege which had cost him such heavy losses, he was constrained to withdraw without hazarding battle when defeat would have been ruinous.

The movement was executed in a manner as masterly as the passage of the Douro when Oporto was surprised. He had a choice of roads and of two bridges, but he determined to retire by that of Burgos, for time was of supreme importance. But Burgos bridge was beneath the castle, and enfiladed by the fire of the batteries. The operation resembled that of Napoleon when taking his cannon past the fort of Bard in his passage of the St Bernard. The army quitted its positions after dark, leaving the camp fires burning, and stole away in absolute silence. The wheels of the cannon had been muffled. All would have passed off well, for Dubreton suspected nothing, had not the guerrillas lost their heads and set spurs to their horses. Then the castle batteries opened, and the first discharge was murderous. But the artillerymen seem immediately to have lost the range, and the rest of the allied troops crossed without further casualties. Souham did not begin the pursuit till late on the next day, and the time gained by the more direct passage was turned to good account. That same afternoon the allies were over the Pisuerga, and on the 24th the march was continued towards the Carrion.

Behind the Carrion Wellington halted in a strong position, where he was joined by a regiment of the Guards and other detachments. The delay was needful to restore discipline. On the advance the army had indulged freely in wine; on the retreat they set all discipline at defiance. The hill country was undermined by caves, and these cellars were overstocked. The soldiers broke into them during the night, and in the morning it was almost impossible to withdraw the drunkards. Napier asserts that at one time 12,000 men were to be seen in a state of helpless inebriety. Measures were taken to check the pursuit. At Palencia they failed, owing to the promptitude of the pursuing French, but elsewhere the bridges were mined and blown up.

The passage of the enemy at Palencia compelled Wellington to change his front, and threatened seriously to aggravate the danger of the situation. Consequently an attack was made on those who had crossed, and they were driven back with considerable loss. On the 26th the retreat was resumed, and the allies passed the Pisuerga at Cabezon del Campo, where they rested be- hind the bridge, which was hastily mined and barricaded. When the mists cleared next morning, Souham with his whole army was seen encamped on the slopes of the opposite bank. Wellington, surveying them from a rising ground, could realise how greatly he was outnumbered, and had good reason to congratulate himself on having avoided a battle at Burgos. Souham made no attempt on our front, but extended his army for flanking operations on the right.

It then became a race for the bridges of the Douro at Simancas, Valladolid and Tordesillas. Colonel Halkett blew up the bridge at Simancas, and that at Valladolid was held by Lord Dalhousie. At Tordesillas the enemy, thanks to a feat of daring gallantry, were more successful. It is true that the bridge there had been broken down in time, and was held by a regiment of Brunswickers; but sixty of the French constructed a raft, on which they placed their arms and accoutrements, and swimming across the broad and rapid river, scrambled ashore under cover of the fire of their field guns. They surprised and stormed the tower commanding the bridge, and compelled the Brunswickers to abandon their positions.

It was a gallant exploit, but it led to nothing, except, indeed, that it inspired the sharp counter-stroke of Wellington. He had destroyed the bridges at Cabezon and Valladolid, and now, having learned the loss of the passage at Tordesillas, with amazing rapidity he marched by his left, resuming his former positions between Rueda and Tordesillas, where, confronting the French right, he anticipated the arrival of their main body. There he remained till the 6th of November, having destroyed all the bridges down to Zamora, giving much-needed rest to his own army, and leaving time for Hill to carry out his instructions. For now that he was aware of the strength of Souham, it became urgent to bring that General back from the Xarama in order to assure his own safety.

Hill, with his 40,000 men, had withdrawn his whole forces behind the Tagus. His own right was resting on Toledo, and with the Spanish and Portuguese he commanded the course of the river from Talavera down to Fuente Dueñas. But as the fords were falling, he became anxious about his position, and, as it chanced, on the very day on which he received Wellington's last orders, Soult's columns showed on the banks of the river. He was ignorant of the numbers of the advancing armies, but, in fact, he was confronted by nearly 60,000 seasoned veterans. He had received his orders on the 29th, and would have marched on the following morning, but was delayed till evening by the failure of a mine, which enabled the French to pass the Xarama and attack his posts there. The attack was repulsed by Colonel Skerrett, who had joined him with a Portuguese corps, and no further attempts were made to molest him, for Soult, who was always at issue with Joseph, was conducting the campaign with almost excessive caution. He said that a defeat meant the French evacuation of Spain, whereas a victory would only throw the English back upon Portugal somewhat sooner.

Hill pressed his march through the night, and reached Madrid in the morning. He found the capital in excitement bordering on despair, for it was known he would only make it a halting place. What the inhabitants dreaded most was the temporary occupation by the guerrilla bands, whom they feared even more than the French. By what appears to have been a culpable oversight, no precautions had been taken for emptying the great magazines of provisions which had been collected, although the populace was starving, and Hill's army on its march to the Tormes had to live on the fallen acorns, or maraud among the herds of swine. The municipality asked that the stores should be sold, but red tape interfered. Some say that the people were permitted to help themselves; others that there were scenes of violence, and that the magazines were sacked by the mobs. Be that as it may, all bear testimony to the admirable bearing of the better classes of the populace in circumstances which tried them to the uttermost.

Napier's description of the scenes—and the stern military historian has no great tenderness for the Spaniards—is touching and pathetic. He tells of men, women and children crowding round the troops, bewailing their departure. For more than two miles they followed them, leaving their houses empty, while the French scouts were already at the eastern gates. Many of the English partisans, who had committed themselves too deeply, were compelled to accompany the retreat, as the *Afrancesados* had fled south with King Joseph. The works at the Retiro had been destroyed and the guns spiked; on the 1st November the French entered.

On the 6th Hill was at Arevalo. His march had been delayed by the incompetence of the staff officers and the miserable mismanagement of the commissariat, from which Wellington was to suffer equally.

There he found himself in communication with the commander-in-chief, and received orders to march on Alba de Tormes. Wellington had been impatiently expecting him, in the hope of attacking Soult with their united forces. But now that hope had failed. For Souham, having seized Toro and Tordesillas, was menacing his rear, while he dare not bring up Hill to the Douro lest Soult, in their absence, should establish himself on the Tormes. So, directing Hill to occupy Alba, he fell back himself, on the 6th, upon Salamanca.

For the third time he was in position on the familiar heights of San Christoval. What his sagacity had foreseen had come to pass. As the victory of Salamanca had forced the French to evacuate Andalusia, that evacuation had now brought their united armies upon him, for Spanish co-operation had failed him again. Allowing for deductions for garrisons, etc., the French still numbered 90,000; all were reliable soldiers, and they were exceptionally strong in horse. Wellington, with Spanish and Portuguese had barely 70,000. Again he was reduced to the old choice between abandoning Salamanca and making sure of his communication. Trusting in the strong positions from San Christoval to the Arapiles, which he knew so well, he would willingly have fought, with circumstances in his favour. But these did not depend upon him, and, as usual, there was disunion in the hostile camp.

Drouet, always a favourite with Joseph, had superseded Souham in command of the army of Portugal, and that did not tend to smooth matters over with Soult, who had ever found Drouet insubordinate. Joseph, strongly supported by the veteran Jourdan, and relying, with reason, on the quality of his superior forces, was eager to bring the English to a battle. But his dispositions included the disruption of the army of the south, and that Soult resolutely opposed. He had brought his fighting machine into perfect order and would not consent to break it up. Moreover, he still held to his opinion that it would be folly to risk a defeat which might be fatal. He had his way, because without his hearty concurrence no scheme of strategy could have succeeded. Then began on a greater scale, and with more guarded caution, the manoeuvres which had preceded the battle of Salamanca. Marmont had carelessly attempted his turning movement with an unsupported column at the very bases of the heights held by the British. Soult swept round in a far wider semi-circle, and left Wellington time to withdraw, after his position had been compromised.

The French Marshal has been reproached for undue timidity, and it has been said that Wellington might have struck vigorously, as before, between the French main army and its left in the air. So far as Wellington was concerned, his habitual prudence was surely not out of place, with such vast and decisive issues at stake. As for Soult, that able general probably knew his own mind and congratulated himself on his strategy. Always averse to lighting, except with everything in his favour, he nevertheless forced the enemy to retreat, and, retaining the prestige of a successful advance, left them a golden bridge to Portugal. At the same time he had in view the other alternative of bringing on a battle with every advantage. For Wellington had waited dangerously long, and apparently was only saved from disaster by some of the innumerable chances of war.

On the afternoon of the 15th, feeling himself too weak to attack, and seeing that the French cavalry were threatening his communications, he had resolved on retreat. The decision once taken, it was carried out with brilliant promptitude. The army was formed into three columns; the left flank was covered by the cavalry and guns. His movements were masked by a dense fog; he marched by the high roads, while heavy rain made the country and by-lanes well-nigh impracticable for Soult's corps; in turn, with his massed forces, he worked round the French left, and before nightfall had crossed the Vamusa River, one of the smaller affluents of the Tormes. Then began the miseries of that pitiful retreat. The men were exhausted and dispirited. The rains which had delayed the French had turned fields and olive gardens into swamps. There was no sort of shelter, nor was there a possibility of lighting fires. There was little food for the men and no forage for the horses. The horses snatched at the boughs of trees, or cropped the bushes of wild brier. Had the French pressed the pursuit, the safety of the army might have been imperilled. But they contented themselves with harassing it with their light cavalry, and picking up the numerous stragglers.

The rains continued through the next two days. The ground was a morass, and the country was thickly wooded. As in Hill's retreat on Madrid, the famished soldiers fed greedily on the acorns, and, breaking their ranks, kept up a continual running fire on the herds of swine they found ranging the forests. Even Wellington's personal authority was set at defiance, nor could the provost-marshal and summary hanging make head against hunger. But again the French failed to urge the pursuit, as they would undoubtedly have done in the earlier days of the war. Yet even the smaller rivers and gullies were so flooded that, in one instance, the men had to pass in single file over the single tree trunk bridging an abyss.

There was one somewhat serious attack on the 17th, when Sir Edward Paget, who commanded the central column, riding to the rear to ascertain the cause of a delay, was taken prisoner. The troops were halted, and formed on the heights; Lord Wellington himself rode up, and there seemed some probability of an action. But the dense fog befriended a retreat, and again the French failed to seize an opportunity. Again the men bivouacked on the soaking ground, without rations; but they had left their bivouac long before dawn, and next night their headquarters were safely established at Ciudad Rodrigo. Southey gives the total losses in the retreat—killed, wounded and missing—as about 1300. Napier ridicules the estimate, and puts it, with much more probability, approximately at 9000, including the soldiers who had fallen at Burgos.

CHAPTER 16

In Winter Quarters
November—December 1812

Don José de Miranda had been left in charge of the castle of Alba. Though the garrison was weak, he maintained the place with great gallantry, making frequent and successful sorties. After defiantly answering repeated summonses to surrender a post that was no longer tenable, on the 24th November he withdrew in the night, leaving his lieutenant to give over the fortress, with the sick and prisoners. The sick were well treated, for the enemy chivalrously recognised the spirit of the defence. Thereupon the French fell back from the Tormes, and when Wellington was assured of that, and had dismissed the fear of an invasion of Portugal by way of the Tagus valley, he distributed his troops in winter quarters. Hill on the right held the passes of the mountains, with the bulk of his men at Baños and Bejar. The light division remained on the Agueda. Carlos d'España, who, notwithstanding his unfortunate blunder at Alba, was the most reliable of the Spaniards immediately under Wellington's direction, was left to garrison Ciudad Rodrigo, and the rest of the infantry were scattered along the Douro.

The greater part of the British cavalry were in the fertile valley of the Mondego. But, indeed, all those winter arrangements were dictated by facilities for feeding the troops, as supplies could be sent to the cantonments by the Tagus, Douro, and Mondego. Neither side was anxious to resume operations, for Wellington's troops were worn out, and a third of the men were in hospital. As for the French, they were in worse condition. They had lost artillery, arsenals and magazines in the preceding campaign. Harassed by the guerrillas, they found extreme difficulties in feeding their armies, and though they could operate upon more direct lines, the wretched roads through the *Sierras* were obstructed by snow. It is significant of the apprehensive attitude of both armies that they vied in destroying all boats on the Tagus.

The disorders on the advance to Burgos and in the retreat were matters of grave anxiety to Lord Wellington. His first act, after having made his dispositions for the winter, was to issue a circular addressed to the commanding officers of battalions. He spoke with his habitual courage and candour, nor did political considerations induce him to soften his language. Admitting that discipline must necessarily be relaxed after a long and exhausting campaign, he added that 'the army under my command has fallen off in this respect in a greater degree than any army with which I have ever served, or of which I have ever read.' The officers had lost all control of their men. Outrages of every kind had been committed with impunity. Yet the army had made a leisurely retreat, and met with no disaster. He went on to say, 'I have no hesitation in attributing these evils to the habitual inattention of regimental officers to their duty.' And as an army marches proverbially as much on the stomach as on the legs, he proceeded to condemn the system of cookery, or rather the want of system. He told the regimental officers that it was not the least of their duties to overlook the comforts of the men; that there should be organised arrangements for fetching fuel and water, and serving the meals, such as they were, with the punctuality of parade. 'So that the soldiers should not be exposed to privations at the moment when the army may be engaged in operations.'

The circular had its effect on those to whom it was addressed, but it created no little surprise and sensation at home. Yet its severity was not unjustified. The retreat had been effected with admirable skill, but the fighting reputation of the disorderly troops had only saved them from a catastrophe. It was fortunate that the French cautiously held back when the men were gathering acorns and beech mast, or had broken loose for the slaughter of the swine. It shows, besides, that the British soldier, when discipline was relaxed, was neither better nor worse than the much-abused Frenchman. Nothing could be more disgraceful than the drunken confusion on the retreat to Corunna; nothing more shocking than the atrocities at the storming of Badajoz. The difference between the armies was, that in the one pillage and rapine were too often a part of the strategy condoned by the chiefs; in the other, the criminal excesses were violations of orders from headquarters, and visited, when proved, with summary punishment. The

French generals, with but few exceptions, from the intrusive King and Soult downwards, compromised their fair fame by greed and plunder; but no breath of scandal brought a reproach on Wellington or any one of his lieutenants.

The circular which sent a thrill through the Peninsular cantonments strengthened the hands of the Parliamentary Opposition at home. We mark with astonishment now the tone of some of the speeches delivered by men who were sincerely patriotic, however much they might have been mistaken. Those pessimistic speeches were a tribute at once to the panic established by the unscrupulous genius of Napoleon, and to the self-denying determination which bore Lord Wellington up when he knew he was misrepresented at home, as he was being criticised and maligned by subordinates. Repeatedly he had to turn back and bide his time at the risk of supersession or an abandonment of the war. A change of ministry might have resulted in either. Fortunately he had a powerful and intelligent advocate in the Upper Chamber.

The Marquis Wellesley, with his personal knowledge of Spanish affairs, struck the true note, and indicated the wise and safe course. After all, he addressed, on the whole, a sympathetic audience. The enthusiasm of the country had been somewhat chilled by the check at Burgos and the damnatory circular. But the nation had followed with pride and satisfaction the glorious course of the Peninsular victories, and had rejoiced in the qualities of its soldiers being rehabilitated. The Marquis demonstrated with fervid eloquence the brilliant work that had been done in face of unexampled difficulties; as fervently he vindicated the genius of his brother. He showed conclusively that any shortcomings were due to misplaced economy and ministerial hesitation. The war had been starved both in men and money; for even if the men had sufficed, the military chests were left empty, and no general could move in a friendly country when he could pay neither for transport nor provisions. The eloquent appeals of the one brother seconding the successes of the other saved England from the possibility of a humiliating surrender; both reinforcements and money were forwarded to Portugal, and the campaign was to be reopened in the spring with more encouraging prospects than ever.

Meantime the French armies were being weakened by the withdrawal of good soldiers to the frontiers of Russia. Twelve thousand had been recalled from Aragon and Catalonia. Their best officers in Spain began to misdoubt the upshot, as was learned from their interrupted despatches. While Marmont was being beaten and Madrid abandoned, the *partidas* had been more or less active in all quarters, aided by our ships and flying squadrons, which perpetually menaced the enemy's flanks. When Caffarelli returned to his command in the north, Souham had in turn been replaced by Reille as head of the army of Portugal; and those rapid changes, showing irresolution and distrust at headquarters, could not fail to be demoralising. Caffarelli had found a desultory littoral warfare going on all along the coast, from Corunna to Santander. Sir Home Popham's squadron furnished the *partidas* with speedy means of transport, and with arms and accoutrements as well. From Biscay to the Catalonian borders of Aragon, the whole country was up, and the most daring of the guerrilla chiefs were exceptionally busy. Mina had absolutely cut the communications with France, through the 'ports' of the Pyrenees in the north of Aragon.

Further to the east in that province, Villa Campos did good service by harassing Suchet's rear, and preventing him from sending supports to the army of the centre. When these irregular bands were defeated, they only scattered to rally again. In New Castille, when the French armies of the south and centre followed in pursuit of Hill, Elio, Bassecour and the Empecinado had come down in force on Madrid. The apprehensions of the *Madrileños* were fully realised, for they were mercilessly pillaged by their own countrymen. But the miserable citizens, who had learned to endure, cared the less, as the reoccupation of the capital by their French oppressors could only be a question of time. Suchet, with his outposts continually attacked, in apprehension for his communications with the coast, and doubtful of the King's plans, had remained passively on the defensive. Then the Duke del Parque with the army of Ballesteros entered La Mancha from the south, where he established communications with Alicante, through Elio and Bassecour, who had marched from Madrid to Albacete.

But on the 3rd December things were changed, when the French, in turn, had decided on the distribution of their forces for the winter. Joseph, retiring to Madrid, expelled the remaining guerrillas, and Soult established his quarters in Toledo. Sending out his cavalry to scout on the plains, he obliged Del Parque prudently to re-cross the Morena. Elio was simultaneously compelled to retire; thus Suchet, relieved from pressure, was again left free to act.

Elio had some reason to complain, for he seems to have been somewhat shabbily treated by the commanders of the British auxiliary forces, detached from Sicily to Murcia and Valencia. For there the changes in the command had been as quick and as frequent as in the French army of Portugal. Mackenzie had succeeded Maitland, to be superseded by General William Clinton, and when General Campbell came with 4000 men from Sicily to relieve Clinton, he intimated that he was but the precursor of Lord William Bentinck, who was speedily to follow with another reinforcement of similar strength. Elio had urged Clinton to co-operate in an attack on Suchet. Clinton had 12,000 men, and nearly a half were British. Elio could support him with 10,000 Spaniards, and yet nothing was attempted.

Campbell arrived in the beginning of December with the reinforcements. Elio again urged the propriety of active operations, but Campbell declined to move till the arrival of Lord William Bentinck. Suchet, naturally expecting an attack, had withdrawn his outposts and concentrated at Xativa, but when he found to his surprise that no attack was contemplated, he resumed his aggressive attitude. Soult's detachments were already overrunning La Mancha; the Duke del Parque, retiring, had re-crossed the Morena; and then Elio, finding his position dangerous or untenable, withdrew into Murcia. The British soldiery found it hard to bear the sneers of the Spaniards they had so inefficiently supported; and the sickness, incompetency or timidity of the generals who had so rapidly relieved each other, irritated and discouraged the patriots who had been making head against Suchet. Yet that able leader, like his *confrères*, had begun to apprehend that the evacuation of the Peninsula by his countrymen was but a question of brief time. His sagacious and resolute administration of Aragon had hitherto been tempered by leniency and self-restraint.

It was significant now that he changed his methods, and making the most of the short space that might remain to him, began to enrich himself by exactions and the pillage of church plate and pictures. Meantime there had been little activity in Catalonia. After General Maitland had gone, the regular warfare had almost ceased. The Catalonians had lost faith in their leaders; the generals of the regulars were quarrelling among themselves and with the guerrilla chiefs; no combinations were possible, and little was undertaken; and the French, who formerly must escort their smallest convoys with formidable columns, could now guard the sea-line and harbours with handfuls of men, and land supplies for their garrisons almost with impunity. British ships were still hovering off the coast; but if the enemy eluded the blockaders they were safe. Nevertheless the French knew well the character of the country and the temper of the mountaineers. It was only owing to temporary causes that the fires were smouldering, and a disastrous conflagration might break out at any moment, on what would be their only line of communication, should Wellington, as seemed probable enough, in the coming campaign, master the western road to Bayonne and Paris. So the French action was paralysed for months to come, and though their armies still mustered 140,000 excellent troops, that formidable garrison was practically invested.

Such being the situation, Wellington had leisure to turn his attention from war to diplomacy. He went to Cadiz towards the end of the year to come to an understanding with the Spanish ministers as to the co-operation of their armies. If these armies had generally failed him in the hour of need, he had no cause to complain of his reception when it was a question of speech, state and ceremony. The Spaniard who courteously places his house and its contents at the disposal of any stranger has always been a master of meaningless magniloquence, and is more lavish of honours and titles than of things more necessary to existence. The English *generalissimo* of all the Spanish armies was welcomed by a deputation from the Cortes, and was subsequently complimented by the President in high-flown language, which compared him to the Cid, to St James and to the Archangel Michael. The President looked forward in full assurance to the Duque de Ciudad Rodrigo driving the hosts of his enemy across the Pyrenees, and, if necessary, following them up to the Seine. What was more to the purpose, should the promises now be kept, 50,000 soldiers were placed at his disposal. Castaños was to take the field in conjunction with him, as Captain-General of Old Castile and the adjacent provinces, with armies in reserve in Andalusia and in Gallicia. Three other armies were to act on the east under Copons, the Conde de Abispal and Elio.

From Cadiz Wellington proceeded to Lisbon. After he had passed the frontier at Elvas, his journey was one long triumphal procession. Arches were erected in all the towns, and everywhere his arrival was acclaimed by shouting mobs. The peasants crowded from their villages to see the conqueror pass. Nowhere was he received with greater honours than in the capital, though the authorities had given him infinite trouble, nor had their murmurs been without reasonable justification. But for these grievances the great captain was known to be in no way responsible, and the enthusiasm of the citizens was unbounded. For three successive nights Lisbon was voluntarily illuminated. A drama, specially composed in celebration of his victories, was brought out with brilliant *éclat* at the theatre of San Carlos, where the boxes were decorated with crowns of victory.

But in all these displays of pageantry and pomp, the business of the war was never neglected, nor did compliments and flattery disarm criticism. The circular of censure addressed to the British was followed by another equally severe, in which Marshal Beresford reprimanded the Portuguese for the same faults. The Marshal could speak with the more authority, that he could honestly praise the troops under his command for gallantry in presence of the enemy as great as that of their British allies. If they had sometimes been unfortunate, as at the battle of Salamanca, it was because they had been asked to storm impregnable positions. But, as in the British army, the regimental officers had been negligent of duty and discipline, and they had been dispirited and demoralised in retreat or by reverses. Severe examples were made, for some of the more notorious culprits were court-martialled and suspended. Lord Wellington returned to his headquarters on the frontier, to find his men in worse conditions as to health, looks and equipment than the Portuguese he had recently inspected. But from the beginning of the new year things began to brighten; with rest in good quarters the sick were reviving, and reinforcements with supplies of all kinds were continually arriving from home.

CHAPTER 17

Joseph Abandons Madrid, and Suchet is Checked in Valencia
January—April 1813

The year 1813 opened with some considerable Spanish successes. In the north, in the closing days of December, when Caffarelli marched to the relief of Santona, the energetic Longa had surprised General Frimont when returning to Burgos with requisitions and hostages. Seven hundred Frenchmen had fallen, and nearly as many more had been taken prisoners. He followed up that stroke by the surprise of Bilbao, and then he seized on Salinas de Anaña, which led to the abandonment of other fortresses. Caffarelli was compelled to send strong detachments against him, and he only retreated in good order when threatened by greatly superior forces.

Things were going still worse for the French in Biscay, Navarre and Aragon. In these provinces Mina was the directing spirit—as admirable a master of irregular war as Wellington was in comprehensive and scientific strategy. Seemingly omnipresent, generally eluding serious attack, always minimising defeat or repulse, the genius of the guerrilla chief resembled instinct. He had trained cautious yet dashing lieutenants in his school, and his exploits and example had set the country on fire. The state of matters had greatly changed since Moore fell back to Corunna, after relieving Andalusia like Wellington. Then the rest of Spain was left at the mercy of the enemy, directed by Napoleon in person, with absolute freedom of action. The Spaniards only resented their wrongs or indicated their patriotism in spasmodic fits of frenzy and frequent assassinations. Now the *partidas* had everywhere become a power to be reckoned with. They were well-equipped and not badly disciplined; they had learned to co-operate, and were organised for combined aggression.

On all the coasts they were in communication with British squadrons, which supplied them as they everywhere menaced the French, who were in ignorance where the next descent might come off. Mina had been gazetted a general in the regular army, and nothing is more suggestive of the new position he had asserted than the fact that Suchet and Suchet's subordinates had changed the system of ruthless repression for the usages of civilised war. When Mina made prisoners, as he did not unfrequently, their lives were spared, and they were kept for exchange. When his hospital fell into the hands of the French, the sick were kindly treated in place of being butchered. And the guerrillas of Navarre and Biscay had been reinforced in another way. Insurrectional juntas had been organised in every district, and volunteers, familiar with each nook and corner of the country, were enrolled under men of birth or position. These new corps were the more formidable to the enemy, that they were seldom guilty of violence, and assured the goodwill of their country-folk by repressing the outrages of the partisans.

Early in January Mina took the strong place of Taffalla, having repulsed a relieving expedition from Pamplona; and then, in concert with other chiefs and the volunteers, both banks of the Ebro were occupied below Calahora and Guardia with a force of 19,000 men. Napoleon's instructions to Joseph, when he was withdrawing from Spain many veterans and good officers for service in Germany, were to hold Madrid only as a post of observation, to transfer the military headquarters to Valladolid, and to crush revolt to the north of the Ebro, employing, if necessary, the army of Portugal as well as that of the north. Thus his rear and the communications with France would be secured. But Joseph had been stiff in his own opinions, hesitating in his movements and at strife with his generals. So Napoleon's able schemes had been baffled, and the invaders were beset by the dangers which his presence would have guarded against.

Joseph was at variance with his generals; with the exception of Jourdan, a special favourite, there was none with whom he was in really cordial relations. But Soult, although after their meeting at Valencia they had established apparently friendly relations, was the object of his particular aversion. Soult had never heeded his orders. Joseph was honest, and doubtless he honestly believed that Soult was actuated by personal ambition and a traitor to the master who had made him.

Be that as it may, Joseph got rid of his ablest assistant when Soult's services were most indispensable. On his return to Paris from Russia, the Emperor found letters accusing the Marshal of all manner of turpitude, and even taxing him with cowardice in his conduct on the Tormes. Napoleon valued Soult, nor did he give credence to the absurd charges. But he felt that, in consequence of the friction between them, either he or Joseph ought to leave Spain, and as it did not suit his plans to withdraw his brother's candidature, Soult was ordered to Germany. He was destined to return to the Peninsula when Joseph had been expelled, and in the meantime, to show that he had lost no favour, he was placed in command of the Imperial Guard.

In fact, Joseph's position was becoming impossible for a man of humanity and sensitive conscience. He would have gladly conciliated his Spanish subjects, but that was out of the question while the invading armies were living at free quarters, and yet these armies were the support of his throne. Had it not been for Lord Wellington and the British assistance, the tenacity of the resistance might have been worn out, and the country bridled by garrisons. Many of the democratic members of the Cortes would have accepted peace and a free constitution even from the usurper. Napier more than suggests, though admitting that there is no written evidence, that at one time the armies of Elio and Del Parque had actually offered to go over, when a brilliant British victory made them hesitate and then draw back. He adds that, had the traitorous negotiations been carried out, Joseph might have recovered Andalusia with his Spanish troops.

At least the usurper's relations with Spaniards encouraged him to hope that, with patience and leniency, he might win their toleration. But when he wrote to his imperious brother as King of Spain, he was reminded that he was a Frenchman, and a mere puppet, who must dance as military exigencies pulled the strings. So the generals knew that they had the support of their real master, and that the armies of occupation must be fed and kept contented, before any revenues were remitted to Madrid. Joseph was reduced to extreme straits, and his unpopularity increased every day. The people were excited to fury under exactions he had forbidden. The starving citizens of Madrid were oppressed with forced loans and excessive taxes and *octroi* duties. His court could only be kept up on credit, and the nobles who had attached themselves to him were reduced to penury, with nothing to hope. Their worst fears were realised when the intrusive King, early in April, transferred his headquarters to Valladolid.

On the 11th, General Hugo, the Commandant of Madrid, informed the municipality of the immediate departure of the troops. Art treasures and other objects of value were hastily packed up; arrears of contributions were rigorously exacted, and all the remaining horses and mules were impressed to drag the commissariat waggons and carry off the plunder.

Meantime Suchet had been hard pressed in the east, and had he been opposed by Wellington, or even by Hill, his discomfiture would have been complete, and his forces would have been driven back on the Catalonian seaboard. In the end of February, Sir John Murray came from Sicily to supersede Campbell. This fifth change of the generals in a few months was not a fortunate one. Murray was no mean strategist, but irresolute to an extreme and morally timid almost to cowardice. Suchet seems quickly to have taken the measure of the man, for he showed a contemptuously audacious front, and acted in indifference to the caution which generally guided his movements. Murray, who was in touch with Elio, was superior in numbers, and only weak in cavalry. But that inferiority was comparatively of slight importance, considering the nature of the country in which they were manoeuvring. Ranges of rugged and precipitous mountains ran in parallel Sierras from La Mancha to the sea.

On one of these ridges, beyond the River Xucar, Suchet had formed a rudely-entrenched camp, covering the rich city of Valencia with its fertile *huerta* and the fortress of Murviedro behind it. Murviedro was really his place of arms, though Murray was deceived into the belief that his base was Valencia. But though Suchet could dispose of 30,000 men, they were distributed over a wide extent of country. He was watching the sea fortresses, observing the roads to Zaragoza and Madrid; and guarding specially against his right flank being turned by Elio, who might be joined by armies from La Mancha. Yet, in order to assure the subsistence of his troops, he had thrown out other detachments to occupy Alcoy and the outlying towns which covered a variety of fertile valleys. That arrangement was, doubtless, advisable or indispensable, but it invited, as it facilitated, attack. The resources of Alcoy and the produce of the neighbourhood were as desirable for the allies as for the French.

Accordingly Murray, who had done much to restore the *moral* of his troops, at length determined to force the positions of the French Marshal. On the 6th of March he moved forward in four columns. The allies took possession of Alcoy, and the French who held it were driven back on their main body; but the combinations, though well devised, partially failed, and Murray faltered when he might have pressed his advantages. Nothing of import happened for more than a fortnight, save that Murray was weakened by the recall of 2000 of his best soldiers to Sicily. But Suchet, on his side, was growing anxious and impatient. The definite withdrawal of Soult from the south had set the Spaniards in Andalusia and La Mancha at liberty. Apprehending that they would come to the assistance of Elio, Suchet resolved to take the initiative and strike. Perhaps he was confirmed in a somewhat hazardous determination by the inaction of Murray after the occupation of Alcoy. For the character of the ground was all in favour of the defenders, and the English general was posted even more strongly than himself In fact, as it proved, the allied positions on the right were virtually impregnable; the left was likewise situated on a precipitous Sierra, and the centre could only be approached by the narrow pass of Biar. Away to the left were Elio and his Spaniards, and owing to that general's obstinacy a mishap occurred which sacrificed the best of his battalions. He refused to listen to the advice of Murray, who urged the withdrawal of the garrison of Villena. He only consented when too late, for meanwhile Suchet had taken the place by storm.

The Battle of Castalla was fought on the 13th. When it came to the point, neither general was eager to engage. Suchet, when he had forced the pass of Biar, recognised the strength of the allied positions, and yet Murray actually desired to abandon them, and is said thrice to have given orders for retiring. But the hands of both generals were forced by their skirmishers coming into lively conflict; the supports hurried up on either side, and the battle was engaged. Suchet had seen that our right was unassailable, so while opening heavy artillery fire on the allied right and centre, he directed his serious onslaught in several columns on the left. There the struggle was decided by the gallantry of the 27th Regiment. The French, notwithstanding obstinate resistance, had topped the hill, and were firing and recovering breath behind a natural breastwork. The moment was critical when the 27th dashed at them, and they were literally hurled back again to the bottom of the steep.

The repulse was felt all along their line; the enemy had been everywhere discouraged by the obstacles to be surmounted, and simultaneously they began to retreat. The converging columns with guns and tumbrils in a mixed mob got choked in the defile. The rear-guard told off to defend the entrance was fiercely pressed by Mackenzie, and it was on the point of being thrown back to confound the confusion, when Murray, in place of supporting the movement, sent order after order to recall the troops, and Suchet succeeded in holding the defile, to withdraw in the night to Fuente de la Higuera. Suchet deserved his defeat for the rash attempt to storm precipitous rocks with one narrow pass behind him, but Murray's timid abstention seems inexplicable. He risked nothing in supporting Mackenzie, and had everything to gain, for he might have changed the repulse into an irretrievable catastrophe. Yet the indirect effects of the battle were very considerable. Not only did the prestige of the French Marshal suffer seriously, but thenceforth ample occupation was found for him, as the Spanish armies were swelled from the south; and Wellington was relieved of all apprehension that Suchet could send to strengthen the enemy in the north.

CHAPTER 18

The Rout of Vittoria
MAY, JUNE 1813

The spring saw the opening of the crowning campaign of such a series of victories won against odds, or apparently insurmountable difficulties, as is scarcely paralleled in the history of war. The more we study them the more are we persuaded that all was due to the extraordinary qualities of one who was veritably 'the man of destiny.' Secondary causes had undoubtedly come into play, and greatly favoured the final operations which swept the French out of the Peninsula. The fate of Spain was to a considerable extent decided in Russia. The destruction of the Grand Army, the defection of Prussia, the wavering of Austria, had all conspired to weaken the position of the invaders. But had it not been for the iron self-restraint and indomitable patience of Wellington, no time could have been given for those causes to come into play. It is safe to say that no other man could have kept ministers at home firm to their Peninsular policy, as perhaps no other general could have risked his reputation and faced obloquy and calumny in the trust that he would yet have opportunity to finish his work. His victories had roused the national enthusiasm, as they won him the confidence of the troops, except when demoralised by retreat and wine-vaults; and yet a single defeat, whatever the cause, would have compromised him alike with the nation and the army.

But the responsibility perpetually weighing upon him was but one source of his anxieties. He was hampered by the Portuguese Regency and their Council of Administration; he had to spur the sluggish but susceptible Spaniards to tardy co-operation; he had to smooth over the financial difficulties of both nations, while the pay of his troops was in arrear and the military chest almost empty; he had to solve the problem of feeding and moving an army when short of money and with doubtful credit. He combined a temperament of rare energy with the most imperturbable coolness, and his mind in moments the most exciting was under perfect command. There is no more striking proof of that than the fact that when in grave anxiety on the heights of San Christoval he wrote a masterly paper on the intricacies of Portuguese finance. It reminds us of Napoleon's memorable despatch on the Grand Opera at Paris, hastily dashed off during the conflagration of Moscow. For Napoleon in critical emergencies would divert his mind to trivial digressions, whereas Lord Wellington's was essentially concentrative, and never lost grasp of the business in hand. He might have to fight for existence on the Tormes on the morrow, but his future was based on Portuguese finance as much as on the fortresses of Rodrigo and Almeida. In another point he had the advantage of his great rival, inasmuch as his health had never failed, and he could always snatch an undisturbed sleep, waking up, in his own words, with five o'clock courage and coolness.

Now the vast and comprehensive schemes which even the ablest of his enemies had but vaguely penetrated, were on the verge of being brought to maturity. They embraced the whole compass of the Peninsula, and each detail had been carefully thought out. Even allowing for the backwardness, jealousy, or over-impetuosity of the Spanish allies, they could scarcely fail of success. To the last he had been harassed by the intrigues at Lisbon; and the Portuguese levies, not without reasonable excuse, had been on the point of mutinying for the long arrears of pay. By tact and firmness, and an appeal to the patriotism of the soldiers, these troubles had been tided over and all was in readiness for taking the field. In May 200,000 combatants were under arms, and the general dispositions were as follows:—

Copons, with 6000 men, was in Catalonia; Elio had 20,000 in Murcia, and the Anglo-Sicilians under Murray numbered 16,000. Del Parque with 12,000 was in the Morena. There was an army of reserve of 15,000 in Andalusia. The troops in the northern command under Castaños—which extended from Southern Estremadura to Gallicia—were estimated at 40,000. Besides these there were the detached bands of guerrillas. The force directly under Wellington himself amounted to 70,000 English and Portuguese. Beresford's severe discipline had borne excellent fruits; the Portuguese were almost as reliable as our own countrymen, and animated by a similar spirit. Either flank of the land forces was covered by the British fleets. Ample occupation was to be given to Suchet by menacing the harbours and fortresses on the eastern coast and his lines of communication with the north along the shore, while Wellington, in co-operation with the Gallicians, was left to deal with the four other French armies, the remainder of the Spaniards closing in upon flank and rear. The effective fighting force of the united French armies was estimated at about 110,000 men.

The French forces were loosely distributed from Toledo on the Tagus to Toro on the Douro, partly from difficulties of provisioning them, for Napoleon's instructions as to forming magazines had been neglected, but chiefly because their generals were in doubt as to the line of Wellington's advance. He might either move on the central provinces or direct his attack on the north. For various satisfactory reasons he had decided against the former course. When making his dispositions for the winter, his plan had been already settled, but the enemy, to the last, was kept in profound ignorance. Nothing seemed more natural than that he should establish his cantonments in the undevastated districts of Portugal, or that he should send his cavalry to find forage in the rich valley of the Mondego.

Now all the movements of Hill's divisions and the guerrillas were arranged so as to seem significant of an advance on Toledo. He had resolved to take the direct road to the Bidassoa, and to carry the war beyond the Pyrenees into France. But what was actually the shortest road bristled with obstacles. Already he had studied the ground when advancing to Burgos and returning from it; he had himself destroyed the bridges and burned the boats, thereby inspiring the defenders with false confidence. The conclusion he had come to was to turn defences which were too formidable to be cheaply forced; and while the French were fixing their attention on their right and the Tagus, the storm was gathering on their other front and their left flank, and was to burst in its violence on the Esla and Tormes.

The troops quartered in Northern Portugal were quietly directed to the Tras os Montes. The plan was to pass the Douro on Portuguese territory, beyond the observation of the French; to ascend the right bank; to cross the Esla, and to rally the Gallicians. That left wing, forming the bulk of the army, was led by Sir Thomas Graham. Meanwhile the centre, under Wellington himself, meeting the right under Hill before Salamanca, was to force the passages of the Tormes and unite in turn with Graham. So the concentrated host, having turned the Douro and Pisuerga, would force the enemy to fall back upon Valladolid.

The concerted movement, when three armies were advancing from points widely apart, through hilly country, by wretched roads and with the rivers in flood, involved the most delicate combinations. On the 26th May Lord Wellington was looking down on Salamanca from the opposite heights. Turning his eyes to the right, beyond the familiar cones of the Arapiles, he saw the heads of Hill's two columns appearing on parallel roads. Salamanca was held by Villatte, with three battalions and some squadrons of horse. That skilful officer had taken every precaution; he had blocked the bridge, barricaded the streets and sent back his baggage. But he could do nothing against the overwhelming forces opposed to him, and his error was that he tarried too long. When he withdrew, he was sharply pressed and suffered considerable loss. Yet, if he erred, he amply redeemed the mistake by the gallantry of the well-managed retreat, when, with a relative handful of men, he repelled all the charges of the allied cavalry, and safely rejoined his supports.

On the two following days the allies marched onward with the right towards Toro and the left inclining to Zamora. But no news had come from Graham, and Wellington was uneasy. On the 28th, leaving Hill in command, he hurried off to the left bank of the Esla. Above Zamora all the bridges had been destroyed. The Douro was down in flood; at Miranda it is 100 yards in width, and it was raging between its precipitous banks. The ordinary ferry was impracticable, and Wellington was swung across in a cradle worked by a rope, suspended 30 feet above the water. He found, as he feared, that Graham's march had been delayed by a succession of difficulties. In the rugged Tras os Montes the roads were generally so narrow that guns and waggons could barely pass between the mountain walls, and in many places they were intersected by the beds of torrents.

Now the troops were confronted by the Esla, which ought to have been passed on the 29th. Had the French realised their danger, the crossing must have been impossible. As it was, they had been more utterly taken by surprise than on the Tormes, and their preparations for obstruction were even more feeble. On the 31st the river was forded by some squadrons of light cavalry, with infantry holding on to their stirrups. The enemy's pickets and outposts were driven in; the pontoon bridges were thrown across, and the columns were passing over. On the 1st of June the allies entered Zamora. After evacuating it, the French had retired on Toro, and, destroying the bridge there, again fell back. They left the allies united on the Douro, for on the upper waters the river could be forded.

But now they were brought to the conviction that they had been out-manoeuvred, and began to understand Lord Wellington's plan. It was known through our spies that they were actively concentrating, and it was possible they might force on a battle. Consequently Wellington paused and took his precautions. He halted on the 3rd June for the Gallicians to come up with the rear of the left wing, which had been delayed on the Esla. The right wing passed the Douro by the bridge and the fords of Toro; and the whole army, by consummate strategy, with little fighting, could show front to the enemy's flank on the northern bank of the river. The French had concentrated behind the Pisuerga, but when Wellington manoeuvred to threaten their right they withdrew to strong positions behind the Carrion. Joseph hastily quitted Palencia, to be followed by his troops on the next day. Treading closely on his heels, Lord Wellington entered the town amid showers of flowers and shouts of welcome.

Even on the 30th, Joseph, in false security, was indulging in a fool's dream. Assuming that he had ample leisure, he wrote to his brother, suggesting sage schemes for administering the provinces to the north of the Ebro, and for the invasion of Portugal after the repulse of the allies. The slight delay of Graham's advance contributed to deceive him. Yet then he was in the meshes of the net which was fatally closing around him. Wellington was in his front and on his flanks with 70,000 men under British colours. The *partidas* and the Spanish reserves drawing in from all sides numbered 30,000 more. For himself, his army had been gradually swelled from 35,000 with the eagles to nearly twice that number. But when at last he took serious alarm, and ordered Foy, Sarrut and Clausel to join immediately, these summonses were sent too late. He was strong in cavalry, though scarcely more so than the allies, and as for guns, he had 100 in the field, with any number more in the arsenals of Vittoria. For in Vittoria, to his subsequent embarrassment and discomfiture, were collected all the baggage of three entire armies, with the cannon, ammunition and stores withdrawn from Madrid, Valladolid and Burgos. Moreover, there were the trains heavily laden with the loot of the King, his generals and their officers.

On the 7th June the allied army crossed the Carrion. On the 12th Lord Wellington gave some repose to his left, worn out by incessant marching, while his right felt the French positions before Burgos. These were sufficiently strong, but both their flanks being menaced, they beat a retreat with some sharp skirmishing. Burgos was protected by two swollen rivers, but in the night Joseph retreated again by the highway to Pancorbo. Not only had the castle, repaired and strengthened after the siege, been mined, but many quarters of the city. Happily the trains had been hastily laid, or were prematurely exploded. The castle blew up with a terrific report, burying some companies of the retiring troops under its ruins, and the glorious Gothic cathedral, malignantly doomed to similar destruction, only escaped through the failure of the fuses.

Now the enemy hoped to make a stand on the line of the Ebro, blocking the royal road to Bayonne by garrisoning Pancorbo, and calling in their detached corps from Biscay and Navarre. But Napoleon's plans of crushing at any cost the revolt in Navarre and Aragon had not been carried out, and Wellington was ever persevering in his turning manoeuvres on the left. Simultaneously with the recovery of Burgos, by a conception as daring as the execution was determined, he had turned the head waters of the Ebro, and Graham was marching eastward down the left bank. Graham, who had always the lion's share of difficulties to surmount, had been contending for six successive days with the natural obstacles on roads the French had deemed impracticable and left out of their account. Defiles were penetrated which a few men could have easily defended; guns were hauled up or lowered over precipices, and let down by ropes into flooded watercourses where a squadron or a company might have barred the passage. As the allied forces toiled along, in each side valley they were joined by guerrillas following the mountain rills rushing to the Ebro, and it was only when bursting down on the broad plain of Vittoria that they felt the enemy for the first time.

Intelligence of Reille's first encounter with the allies reached Joseph at Pancorbo on the night of the 18th, yet neither the King nor the general had awakened to the scope of the movements which were forcing them irresistibly to destruction. Nevertheless, it was clear that their rear and right, as well as the road to Irun, were probably threatened, and no time was lost in withdrawing from Pancorbo. That night, again, the army retreated. But it was a delicate operation to pass the long and narrow defile, which was the direct access to what Napier describes as the basin of Vittoria, and Reille had orders in the meantime to maintain his positions vigorously. These orders he executed with equal science and gallantry, and the French army was formed for the final stand on heights that cross the plain and cover the town.

Further retreat was impossible for strategical, political, or material

Battle of Vitoria

reasons, and the question of the French hold on Spain must be settled by a decisive battle. For at Vittoria converge the three great roads, leading respectively from Bilbao, Bayonne and Pamplona. It is the centre of communications. In Vittoria were crowded the trains and stores, the sick and wounded, the women and children, and all the plunder. In fact the hopeless block of waggons and carriages, tumbrils and guns, put an orderly retreat out of consideration. The French were formed in three lines, behind the Zadora, which was passable by sundry narrow bridges, and again the King sent an urgent summons to Clausal at Logroño, which is eleven leagues distant. Before Clausel could come up, the battle was decided.

Apparently Jourdan, who really commanded, had little chance, but his positions were dangerously extended. His left rested on heights facing or flanking the entrance to the defile of Puebla; the centre of his first line stretched along the hills overhanging the Zadora, and these were heavily armed with batteries, enfilading the bridges. His right was fronting the river, to defend the passage of Abechuco. But the rocks and tangled undergrowth on the south bank of the stream offered safe cover to the assailants. Above all, it was of supreme importance that Reille on the far right should hold his own, for Graham was already advancing by the highway from Bilbao, and threatening the only road for retreat. Yet Reille, though reinforced before the battle, was virtually out of touch with the centre, and the long and somewhat attenuated line offered a skilful enemy favourable points of attack. To understand the battle the ground must be studied. To the west of Vittoria, the Zadora runs south, but subsequently it turns at a sharp right angle and, roughly forming two sides of a square, takes a course but slightly to the south of due east. D'Erlon with the army of the centre, was in the second line behind Gazan, and the great body of the cavalry, with the royal guards, were held in reserve at the village of Gomecha, situated in the valley at about half-way between the Zadora and Vittoria.

With daybreak on the 21st, in a dense mist, the allied columns were in motion. Hill, on the right, first came into action, and a Spanish corps, led by Morillo, rushed to the storm of the heights of Puebla. There the tide of battle ebbed to and fro, as supports were sent up on either side. The defence was as stubborn as the attack was resolute, and for a time there was little lost or gained, till at last Hill, with the remainder of his corps, forced the defile of Puebla and, emerging on the plain, reunited himself to the troops on the heights, and asserted a forward position at Subijana de Alava, a village at the foot of the Eastern *Sierras*, and in the south-eastern corner of the basin.

Meanwhile Wellington was directing the attack on the centre in person. From the camp and villages on the Bayas he had brought the 4th and light divisions, with the cavalry, down to the Zadora. Each division was fronting a bridge, and a hot fire was exchanged between the skirmishers. But it would have been rash to send those divisions across to take ground beyond the gorge of the Puebla, for nothing had as yet been seen of the 3rd and 7th Divisions. They had been told off to attack the centre and right of the enemy, but their march had been delayed by natural obstructions. While Wellington was impatiently expecting them, he was informed by a peasant that one of the upper bridges had been left unguarded. A brigade of the light division was immediately pushed across; it took up ground under cover behind the enemy's advanced posts, and later it came into the close action with decisive effect.

Towards one o'clock Joseph became seriously alarmed. Hill, on his left, was forcing the fighting at Subijana, and away to the north, on his right, the sound of guns and the smoke told that Graham was pressing the attack on Reille. Hurrying back his reserves from Gomecha to the town, Joseph gave orders to Gazan to follow. Had Gazan been inclined to obey, compliance had become impossible. For at that critical moment, Picton and Lord Dalhousie were seen coming down at last on the bridge of Mendoza. They were received with a storm of shot and musketry fire as the French cavalry approached to oppose them. But then the light brigade, which, as we have seen, had been thrown forward, interposing between the cavalry and the river, took the enemy's infantry and batteries in flank. Under cover of the fire of the British guns, the 3rd and 7th Divisions passed over by the bridge and an upper ford.

To their right the French were so closely engaged that no regular retreat was possible. To our right, Hill had been urging his attack, and the French centre had been already weakened by detaching troops to the assistance of their left. As at Salamanca, Wellington saw his opportunity. He carried Picton, with all of the 3rd Division that were not engaged, across the front of the hostile line to assail the denuded positions. At the same time the 4th Division moved forward on the right, supported by the masses of heavy cavalry. The French were weak in men there, but strong in guns. They opened such a deadly fire as threatened to repel the advance, but batteries on the British side were brought up to quell it. The French withdrew in the thick vapours of smoke, but they formed again on the heights before Gomecha, which had been abandoned by their reserves. Yet they still held the advanced village of Arinez on the main road, and there was desperate fighting before it was won.

They had maintained themselves at Subijana on their left with even greater obstinacy. But now that position was turned by troops descending into the plains from the eastern Sierra, and their whole army fell back, crowding together in confusion, and striving to get out of the broken country and gain the only high road. Never was there a more sudden collapse from resolute defence to panic. Gun after gun was abandoned, and the mob went surging wildly into the city, while the shot from the English field batteries lent wings to the flight. Still Reille was manfully holding his own, and the safety of the shattered wreck depended on him, for he was fighting for the sole lines of retreat; and the artillery of the armies of the south and centre were still belching out their fire from eighty pieces on the eastern range of heights before Vittoria.

For a time the allied advance was checked, but then the hills held by the French on their left were turned. Reille was now isolated, and in great danger. For Joseph had given orders for the flight, and he had little option as to the line by which he should save himself. The road to Irun was blocked by waggons and fugitives, and accordingly the flight was directed on Pamplona. The cavalry did something to protect it, but the very excess of the panic was more effective. For the road to Pamplona lay through a swamp, skirted on either side by deep ditches, and it was obstructed besides by broken-down carriages, dead horses and the encumbrances the fugitives had flung away. Then two days of heavy rain succeeded, which, though they added to the miseries of the rabble, delayed the pursuit of our light cavalry, which followed up to within gun-range of the works of Pamplona. There the governor refused admission to the runaways; he had no mind that they should either demoralise his garrison or devour his provisions. So soldiers, women and camp-followers bivouacked together on the saturated grass of the glacis, under cover of his guns.

Never, perhaps, after a battle, were the material gains more important. Three armies, perfectly equipped, had concentrated everything and lost all; 450 pieces of ordnance were taken; only two guns were carried away, and one of these was captured on the road to Pamplona. All the stores and ammunition fell into the hands of the allies. All the plunder, so rapaciously amassed, was recovered. Some of the masterpieces of Spanish pictorial art were presented to Wellington and are now at Apsley House. By the way, when he understood their value, the Duke afterwards offered to return them to Ferdinand, an offer which the King declined. Five millions of dollars were in the intruder's military chest. All were looted; some fell to the soldiers, though these, for the most part, were too busily engaged to pick them up. The greater portion were picked up by the camp followers, enriching suttlers and Jewish traders; and the townsfolk of Vittoria, generally French in their sympathies, had excellent bargains of valuable goods.

For several days an auction was held in the town, at which rich silks and valuable plate were sold for a trifle. The cumbrous dollars were at a heavy discount, and were exchanged at a premium for more portable gold coins. For once Wellington relaxed his discipline, and declined to make any of the fortunate soldiers disgorge. 'They have earned the money well,' he said, 'and they ought to keep it.' Joseph, after narrowly escaping the musket balls, had to sacrifice his coach with its precious contents. Among the trophies was the leading staff of Marshal Jourdan. It was sent by Wellington to the Prince Regent, who gracefully presented him in return with the *bâton* of a Field-Marshal of Great Britain.

CHAPTER 19

Operations in the East and Siege of San Sebastian
JUNE, JULY 1813

Reille, by skilful manoeuvring, had rallied his troops at Betonio, on the left bank of the Zadora, to the north-west of Vittoria. From thence, though threatened on all sides, he had fought his way to Metanco, on the Pamplona road, always covering the retreat. On the 22nd June the allies followed the convoy which had moved off towards Bayonne on the previous morning. A sufficient force was left in Vittoria, and the rest of the army went in pursuit of Joseph. On the morning of the 22nd Reille had thrown himself across their line in front of Salvatierra. There he had halted till the fugitives had gone on, and then he continued his march as the rear-guard. Joseph had sent orders to France to make arrangements for the reception of the beaten army, and then Reille had orders to march on the Bidassoa with part of the army of Portugal. The rest of it was under Clausel. For himself, with the armies of the south and the centre, the King was to cross the Pyrenees by the defiles of St Jean Pied de Port.

Foy, who then had his quarters at Bilbao, was left isolated and endangered. When the news of the disaster reached him, he took his decisions promptly. He was a good general, though a ruthless administrator. Graham, with Longa and the Gallicians under Giron, was racing to cut off his retreat into France. But Graham had to cross various parallel ridges, whereas Foy had the advantage of the high road. Yet he barely saved himself by the skin of his teeth where the two lines of march intersected. Knowing that the passes of Guipuzcoa were undefended, he had called in the garrisons of Biscay and pressed forward for Tolosa, on the Bayonne road, whither the convoys that had escaped from Vittoria were hastening. Uniting himself to Maucune's escort before Tolosa, he boldly offered battle, but was slowly forced back by superior numbers. Again he offered battle in front of the town, but when his flank was turned he again retired, and Tolosa was taken. That happened on the 25th, and on the 1st of July he had gone over the Bidassoa, his rearguard being sharply engaged with Giron's Gallicians at the bridge of Belchite. There he was brought into touch with Reille. Guns and ammunition had been sent forward from Bayonne, and so 25,000 good men were in position behind the line of the Bidassoa.

Clausel, on the other flank of the French, was in a somewhat less perilous position. In case of the worst, he had Suchet and the army of Aragon to fall back upon. He had been advancing to the help of Joseph when the tidings of Vittoria reached him. He withdrew to Logroño, where he halted till the 25th. Then he made a forced march to Tudela, whence he had hoped to escape into France. But a friendly *alcalde* having warned him that he was intercepted, he re-crossed the Ebro and marched on Zaragoza, sending Suchet intelligence of his arrival there with 15,000 men. As it happened, that message only misled Suchet, for Clausel was gone again before their armies could be united. Meanwhile Hill had been pressing the main body, and had seized the passes from Roncesvalles to St Estevan. Wellington proposed to besiege Pamplona, and had actually landed stores and siege-trains at Deba, a small port to the west of San Sebastian. For the victory of Vittoria was followed by the strategic evolution which changed his base from the Bay of Lisbon to the more accessible Bay of Biscay, where there were excellent harbours from Corunna to Passages. But when the guns had been landed, news came from the east coast which induced him to re-embark them and postpone the siege of Pamplona.

Suchet, generally successful alike in warfare and administration, and sanguine of the future as his imperial master, had held on to his command with indomitable firmness. It might have been better for him ultimately had he complied with the wishes of the usurper and added his army to the others before the decisive battle. Holding to Valencia, Wellington's plans had provided him ample occupation, and if Murray had had anything of the best qualities of his chief, the campaign in the east would have had a different issue. Murray had been instructed to attack Tarragona. Towards the end of May an expedition sailed from Alicante, numbering nearly 15,000 men. The French had sighted it from Valencia as it sailed by, but on the 3rd June the disembarkation was effected. The siege was begun and fire opened on the outworks.

The French outside were not inactive. Suchet, breaking up his camp on the Xucar, made forced marches to Tortosa, sending at the same time orders to Decaen to advance to the relief of Tarragona from Barcelona. Murray did not want a wise counsellor. Whittingham, who commanded a Spanish brigade, urged him to leave the Catalans to cover the siege while he crushed Decaen with superior forces. Murray did not accept the suggestion, but continued to dally with the siege as if time were of little value. When he heard that Suchet was approaching with 12,000 men on the one side, and Decaen with 8000 on the other, he showed exceptional promptitude, but in the wrong direction, and not only abandoned the siege operations, but all his heavy artillery and stores.

Moreover, he acted in the face of strong protests from Admiral Halliwell. Sir John was court-martialled for the proceeding, but leniently reprimanded for a simple error of judgement. The consequence of that precipitate embarkation was to cause the retreat of Copons and his Catalonians to their mountains, while Decaen countermarched on Barcelona. The campaign thenceforth resolved itself into a dilatory game of cross-purposes. Murray re-landed part of his infantry to cover the uncompleted embarkation of his cavalry and field guns. Then, taking alarm again at the menace of Suchet's movements, and learning or suspecting that Decaen had withdrawn, he landed once more to fight the Marshal. But Suchet, hearing in turn of Decaen's withdrawal, had no mind to risk anything for a barren victory. Again Sir John decided to re-embark after consulting a council of war.

That very day, as it chanced, Lord William Bentinck arrived from Sicily. He accepted the council's decision; and the blowing up of the coast fort at the Col de Balaguer told Suchet, to his great relief, that the immediate danger was over. He and Lord William received almost simultaneously the news of Vittoria. That battle relieved Valencia from the invasion, as Salamanca had liberated Andalusia. Suchet, picking up or calling in his scattered garrisons, prudently determined on retiring to Zaragoza, where he expected to find Clausel. It was the apprehension of that junction which had constrained Wellington to defer the attack on Pamplona. But events in Aragon were soon to restore his freedom of action.

Clausel had made no long stay at Zaragoza. Mina, indefatigable as ever, was menacing his communications. It was said, besides, that he was swayed by the desire to place his vast booty in safety. If that were

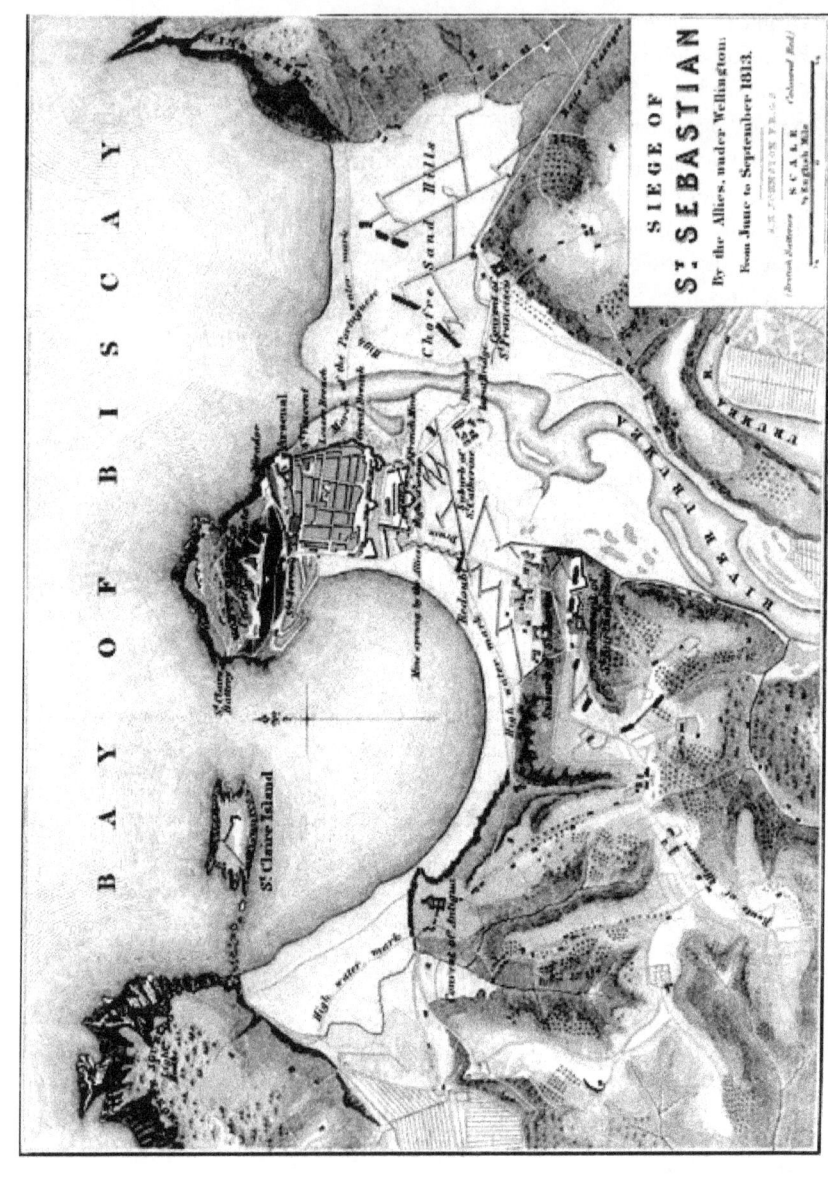

so, his hopes were disappointed. Leaving his guns behind, he hurried off to France by way of Jaca, and as the guerrillas swarmed down upon him while threading the passes, the bulk of the plunder had likewise to be abandoned.

Mina united his forces to those of General Duran, the commandant of Lower Aragon, for the deliverance of the faithful Zaragoza. The battered fortifications had been in some measure restored, and it was strongly garrisoned under General Paris; nevertheless, the long *enceinte* and ill-repaired breaches laid it open to assault, and it was said that the citizens to a man were ready to rise in aid of the liberators. Mina for once counselled caution; the veteran Duran was eager and impatient. There was sharp fighting, with sundry sorties. At last, in the second week of July, Paris, despairing of succour from Suchet, and having booty of his own to secure, blew up the bridge and moved off in the night. His orders had been to join the Marshal if he were driven to evacuate. But finding the road to Mequinenza impracticable, he was compelled to follow Clausel's line of retreat by Huesca and Jaca.

So Suchet lost a second body of auxiliaries on which he had confidently relied, and Zaragoza, after four years of oppression, though shorn of its splendour and laid in ruins, passed back into the hands of the Spaniards. Suchet, resigning himself to the sacrifice of Aragon, withdrew with his remaining garrisons into Catalonia, the last stronghold of the invaders. He had lost the line of the Lower Ebro, nor could he support his troops in the barren neighbourhood of Tortosa, which was open besides to descents from the sea. There could no longer be any apprehension that the siege of Pamplona would be interrupted by efforts from the east. Nor were considerations of time of much importance, so the blockade of the place was entrusted to the Spaniards, while Lord Wellington turned his attention to the capture of San Sebastian.

San Sebastian has been termed the Gibraltar of the north; it is accessible only by a sandy isthmus resembling 'the Spanish lines.' To the west is the harbour; on the other side flows the tidal estuary of the Urumea. The town is commanded by the castle hill, and behind the citadel is the eminence of Orgullo, which was to play an important part in the defence. Foy, on his retreat, had strengthened the garrison, and now it numbered nearly 4000, commanded by Emmanuel Rey. The place had stood sundry sieges in its time, but the fortifications had been neglected, for the invaders had never dreamed of being driven back upon it. Rey lost not a moment in repairing the defences, and when the Spaniards came in sight of them, the hillside and the town walls were seen to be swarming with workmen. The Spaniards had no siege-train, and could only establish a blockade, till Graham came up with the 5th Division. The 1st Division, under General Howard, were covering the great road from Irun, and supporting a Spanish corps which watched the Lower Bidassoa.

Operations were commenced with promptitude, for time was rightly considered so precious that Graham defeated his purpose by neglecting due precautions. An indispensable preliminary to the reduction of the fortresses was to drive the defenders from their post of St Bartolomeo, advanced some 700 yards before the town. There was a massive convent there, with an unfinished redoubt. A feigned attack was pushed too far, and the assailants were repulsed with serious loss. After sundry unsuccessful attempts, the convent was fired with red-hot shot, but the flames were extinguished as often as they broke out, and the French still made good the position, covered by a storm of shot and shell from their batteries. Finally recourse was had to the bayonet. The defenders were driven out and followed up to the glacis, the pursuers suffering severely on their return.

The possession of St Bartolomeo was a great step gained. The weakest point of the defence was at the works confronting the isthmus. They could be enfiladed from the low range of the Chofre sandhills on the right bank of the river. There batteries had been thrown up on the night of the 17th, so as to take the town defences in reverse. One of the two was established in a crowded cemetery; the coffins and corpses were used in the construction; the sights were revolting as the stench was intolerable. Nevertheless, we are reminded of the proverb, *à la guerre comme à la guerre,* for the soldiers did their cooking over fires made of coffin wood. The scheme of attack was inspired by Major Smith, who had distinguished himself by the defence of Tarifa. Sir Richard Fletcher, the veteran of Torres Vedras, who was in command of the engineers, heartily concurred. It was approved by Lord Wellington, and should have succeeded had not Graham, irresolute in council as he was bold in action, got perplexed amidst a multitude of conflicting advisers.

There were two attacks: one was directed on the front, the other from the batteries on the right bank. On the 21st the front was partially breached, though the besieged cut the ramparts behind and retrenched them. But when the parallel across the isthmus had been completed, a discovery was made which ought to have caused the fall of the fortress. Driving the parallel had laid bare a subterraneous water-course. Lieutenant Reid, of the Engineers, crawled forward till stopped by a door at the counterscarp of a horn-work. He came back to suggest the formation of a mine, which might fill the ditch and make a way up the counterscarp.

On the 22nd the batteries beyond the Urumea had opened a very practicable breach on the eastern flank. It was advised that it should be stormed next morning, when light and tide would serve, but unfortunately subsequent orders were given to make a second breach to the left. Still more unfortunately, a Spanish civil engineer had directed attention to the walls to the right of the main breach, which were weaker than elsewhere. His information was correct, and they quickly gave to the guns, but the triple breaches subsequently led to dire confusion. Moreover, by the delay in widening this second breach, invaluable time was lost. The morning of the 25th was finally appointed for the assault, and three fatal mistakes were made.

In the first place, it was made in the dark, though in adopting Major Smith's plans, Wellington had insisted that the assault must be delivered in daylight; in the second, in place of being made at low water, the tide was already mounting fast; in the third, the defences dominating or raking the breaches had been left almost uninjured. The attack was advanced to an hour before daybreak, on account of the rising of the tide. The distance of the uncovered approach from the trenches on the isthmus to the breaches was 300 yards. The column stumbled in the dark along a strip of shelving beach, slimy with seaweed; every gun on the heights had been depressed to bear upon them; stones and burning beams were hurled down, and they were enfiladed by incessant discharges of grape or musketry. At that moment Reid's mine was sprung, with even more than the expected effect. The counterscarp and glacis came down in a landslip; the defenders of that part of the works were panic-stricken. A rush would have carried the gap and the Portuguese were ready; but no ladders were forthcoming. The garrison quickly recovered from their alarm, and the opportunity was gone.

Meanwhile two gallant officers, with a handful of men, had gained the top of the main breach. But all below was in wild confusion. Those who should have supported them were running back, nor could they be rallied by any efforts of their officers, and that handful of heroes perished. The discomfiture of the first column involved the failure of the second, destined to pass in rear of it to assail the further breach.

With the dawning the whole was over. There was a loss of 45 officers and 800 rank and file in killed, wounded, or missing.

That day Lord Wellington arrived from Lesaca. He would have widened the second breach and renewed the attack, but scarcity of ammunition compelled him to defer it; and the intelligence of the enemy's dispositions, which reached him immediately afterwards, induced him to withdraw the heavy guns, change the siege to a blockade, and turn his attention elsewhere.

CHAPTER 20

Battles of the Pyrenees
July 1813

Marshal Soult had been sent back from Germany as Commander-in-Chief of the armies in Spain. On the 1st of July he received his appointment. On the 13th so much expedition had he made that he was at his headquarters at Bayonne. So little store had Napoleon set by Joseph's denunciations that Soult had actually secret orders to supersede the King, even by force should force be necessary. It was needless, for the intrusive monarch, sickened of his crown of thorns, was content to lay it down. It would have been well for Napoleon had he overcome his family pride and consented before to the appeals of Joseph. Had he removed his brother when he had recalled Soult, affairs in the Peninsula might have gone very differently. But now that the last stake was to be played, the most formidable of Wellington's opponents was to be again pitted against him, and Soult came south with every inducement that could stimulate his ambition and justify his master's flattering choice.

As he had travelled with extraordinary rapidity, he acted with amazing promptitude and success. He found the demoralised wrecks of three broken armies. In a few days he was facing the menacing enemy with a fairly-disciplined force, numbering nearly 80,000 with the colours. It was no fault of his that a considerable part consisted of raw and unwilling conscripts. But, on the other hand, he was supported by levies of national guards drawn from the mountaineers, well used to hard- ships and thoroughly familiar with their mountains. Such auxiliaries were eminently desirable. For the theatre of war was a hilly quadrilateral, the corners being the fortresses, all held by the French, of Bayonne and St Jean Pied de Port, Pamplona and San Sebastian.

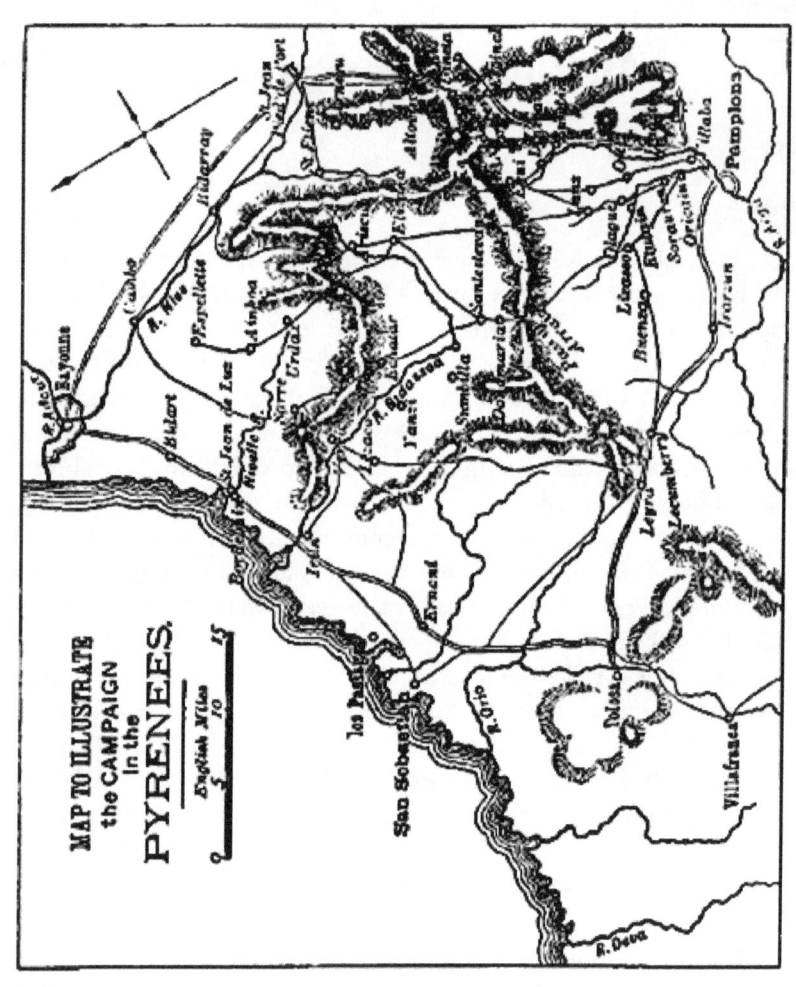

South of the Nive it was traversed by the parallel rivers of the Nivelle and the Bidassoa, which was the Spanish boundary; across it, and diagonally, but trending southward to the west, ran the main ridge of the Pyrenees.

On either side of that ridge were lateral spurs, locking the narrow entrances to rugged valleys, and all the ranges could only be crossed by *cols*, as the French call them—*puertos* in the Spanish speech—always difficult of approach, and not unfrequently virtually impassable. The French Marshal had one great advantage. Behind his screen of mountain and river he could move with facility on excellent roads. Whereas, on the Spanish side, direct communication could only be maintained by the mountain tracks that were often shrouded in mists. The only alternative was by making some circuitous detour when each hour might be of the last importance.

On the 14th—the day after his arrival—Soult was already making his dispositions. In a mere sketch of those infinitely intricate operations it is almost impossible to be both succinct and satisfactory. It will be seen that the frontier takes a turn almost at right angles at St Jean Pied de Port, running thence nearly north to Bayonne. Briefly, Soult's extreme left was at St Jean under Clausel. D'Erlon guarded the centre. To his right was Reille, overlooking Vera. The reserve, under Villatte, watched the Bidassoa from Irun down to the mouth of the river, and two supporting divisions of cavalry were distributed on the Nive and Adour. All along that line of nearly sixty miles the French were confronted by the allied forces, generally comparatively weak in numbers, but holding positions of exceeding strength.

San Sebastian was considered tolerably safe, as, notwithstanding a nominal blockade, it had never lost its sea communications. But Pamplona might soon be reduced to extremity, and Soult decided on a supreme effort for its relief. With that object he began throwing bridges over the Bidassoa, that Wellington might turn his attention in that direction. Meantime he had been accumulating stores at St Jean. And then, being masked by a continuous line of scouts and skirmishers, he quietly shifted his strength to the east. His design was, by surprise and overwhelming numerical superiority, to force the strong mountain positions and march on Pamplona, rallying Paris with the garrison of Zaragoza, who were still halted at Jaca.

Time and surprise were of supreme importance, but the weather was against him. The rains had flooded the streams and broken the roads. His troops were delayed or had to make long detours, and it was only on the 24th, instead of four days previously, that he had assembled all his forces at St Jean. Then no further time was lost, and he commenced operations on the following day. Probably he had counted the chances beforehand, and decided that the ordinary rules of war might be overridden by special circumstances. Certainly his whole scheme was based on a defiance of Napoleon's grand principle, that in mountain warfare, *il faut se faire attaquer et ne jamais attaquer*. But the inevitable accidents of war were against him, for as he had been first delayed by the rains he was afterwards baffled by the fogs.

The famous battles of the Pyrenees began with the attack on General Byng's post at the historical pass of Roncesvalles. For on the 24th 60,000 men were gathered to force the pass of Roncesvalles and that of Maya to the west. At Roncesvalles the fighting was at 5000 feet above the sea-level. Byng had been warned and was ready, but the numbers opposed to him were overwhelming. Cole, who commanded the supports, rode up at noon, but his men had been left far behind. Meanwhile Reille was advancing along a parallel ridge against the Spaniards of Morillo. When he attained the main heights his orders were to turn to the right and operate against the rear of Hill, who was on guard at Maya. He lost his bearings in the mists, or was misled by his guides, and descending instead into one of the southern valleys, fell into the rear of Clausel and for the time was altogether out of the fighting. At nightfall Cole still held the mountains, but his right had been turned, and with 10,000 men he was threatened by thrice that number in Soult's six divisions. Consequently he withdrew in the darkness to positions equally strong, and Soult, as the result of that sanguinary day had gained only ten miles out of thirty.

Reille's column had gone astray, nor were there satisfactory reports from D'Erlon. Soult deferred following up the attack for another day, a mistake as it proved, and a great misfortune for him. For a time Cole, was unsupported, and his men were worn out. The delay till the 27th gave them time to rest, and the scattered forces of the allies had then effected their junction. The French attack on the right had been no more decisive, for though D'Erlon, surprising the general rather than the troops, had forced all the passes in front of him, and established himself in dominating positions, yet, overestimating the forces showing front to him, he failed to press his advantage. General Stewart had been charged with the defence of the passes of Maya, Lessessa and Aretesque. D'Erlon's real object was the main pass of Maya, but his columns moving forward from Urdax could be seen by the British outposts.

On the other hand, the French advance on Aretesque was concealed by an intervening hill, and their men had crowned the crest before the British pickets were aware of them. Thus, while the pickets holding the Maya and the supporting companies were attacked in front, they were assailed simultaneously by the heads of the columns who had gained a footing on the ridge of Atchiola, which runs at right angles to the road traversing the Maya. Fearfully overmatched, they made good the ground; supports were hurried up, and the Maya was still maintained, although the defenders were falling fast, and one battalion of the 92nd was almost annihilated. Repulsed at one point or another, the French always rallied again in gathering masses. When General Stewart came up, the Lessessa and Aretesque had been lost, and soon after the troops were forced back from Maya, leaving a Portuguese battery to the enemy.

Towards evening it seemed that abandoning the Atchiola ridge would be inevitable, for the ammunition had given out, and the soldiers, when they had emptied their pouches, were hurling stones down upon their assailants. Then the situation was saved by the almost simultaneous arrival of night and succours. Stewart bivouacked on the hotly-contested ridge, and D'Erlon concentrated on the Col de Maya. Yet, both at Roncesvalles and Maya, the passes had been seized, and on the whole the day had gone decidedly against the allies. But Reille had blundered; D'Erlon was inert; Soult, as was his habit, was overcautious, and everything still remained in suspense.

Soult had so ably masked his movements towards his left that Wellington had been misled as to his purpose. The French Marshal, as we have seen, had confirmed the misapprehension by throwing pontoon bridges over the Lower Bidassoa. Knowing what Soult did not—that San Sebastian was now in greater straits than Pamplona—he fancied Soult was operating for the relief of the former fortress. Consequently, when the news of these battles in the Pyrenees surprised him, he was at Hill's headquarters in the Bastan valley. Losing not a moment he hurried eastward, arriving at the centre of action, as often before, at the critical moment. All his plans seemed on the point of being baffled. The garrison of Pamplona and the besiegers had been alike informed that Soult was advancing victoriously to its relief Abispal was preparing to raise the blockade, and was already spiking his guns. The garrison, in successful sallies, had stormed some of the batteries.

Already the siege would have been at an end, had it not been for

Carlos D'España. Picton, who had formed a junction with Cole, had commenced a retreat, despairing of Pamplona and abandoning the intention of covering it. In fact Abispal's alarm was by no means unwarranted, for the enemy was closing in around him. Cole had passed Pamplona, and Picton was following him, when Wellington came galloping into the village of Sauroren, situated somewhat to the eastward of Pamplona. From thence he saw Clausel's column advancing along the ridge of Zabaldica. He saw at the same time that Picton's troops in the Lanz valley must be cut off. Springing from his saddle he scribbled an order, and despatched it by Lord Fitzroy Somerset, the only staff officer who had kept pace with his chiefs hunter. As Somerset rode out at one end of the village street, the French light cavalry dashed in at the other: Wellington had barely time to save himself and reach his troops.

Never was anything more 'touch and go.' But Picton, turned sharply aside from Huarte, took up a position on the ridge crossing the Lanz and Zubiri valleys, and so effectually screened Pamplona. The opposing forces were confronted on opposite heights, flanked on either side by a river. The generals were so near to each other that Wellington from his standpoint could distinguish the figure and even the features of Soult. Then ensued a most dramatic incident. When the presence of the allied commander was recognised, loud cheers, taken up by battalion after battalion, rang along the whole length of the line. Wellington looked across to his opponent and ejaculated in audible soliloquy, 'Yonder is a great commander but a cautious one, and he will delay his attack to ascertain the cause of those cheers; that will give time for the 6th Division to come up, and I shall beat him.' So it proved.

The French attack was only begun at noon, when Clausel, covered by swarms of sharpshooters rushing down the valley, had turned Cole's left. At that moment the 6th Division, appearing from behind a ridge, formed in order of battle across the French front. It was a repetition of the stroke made by Soult at Salamanca, and he never retrieved the false move. The French who had sought to encircle the allies were encircled in turn, for, assailed simultaneously on either flank, they were pushed back by the front onset of the 6th Division, though fiercely disputing each foot of the ground. Meantime the remaining divisions of Clausel and Reille had to yield in the centre, though for long the tide of battle fluctuated, with varying fortunes and frightful bloodshed.

Marshal Soult

On the right the Portuguese showed distinguished gallantry, and the Spaniards, to whom the position in front had been entrusted, fought well and stood firmly. Yet it was the heroism of the 40th Regiment which saved the situation there, when the French column, flushed with success, threatened to carry all before it. Soult had been foiled, and he was prompt to recognise it, by sending back his guns, the wounded and great part of his baggage to St Jean Pied de Port. But much was yet to happen before he could extricate himself, and it was a bare chance that saved him from absolute disaster.

On the 39th the armies kept their positions in quiet, but Wellington's anxieties were ended. No longer severed by the *Sierras*, the allied army had become a united force. Soult had likewise been gathering up his scattered divisions, but his difficulties were great. Again he had to acknowledge the qualities of the allies and their commander, for he had been out-manoeuvred, and his best troops had been fairly beaten by a force of half their number. And not the least depressing consideration was, that the Portuguese and even the despised Spaniards had scarcely been surpassed in steadfastness and courage by the British. But he was not the man to throw up the game because the fate of war had gone so far against him. Foiled in his attempt to relieve Pamplona, he now turned his attention to the succour of San Sebastian by operating against the allied left, and at the same time effecting one of his masterly changes of front in face of the united enemy.

His artillery and cavalry had already marched for the Lower Bidassoa. His object now was to draw off the bulk of his army in the same direction. He strengthened D'Erlon, who had come down the valley of the Lanz to Ostiz with 18,000 men, and who was ordered to march on the 30th by Etulain upon Lizasso. Clausel was to follow, and was to be followed in turn by Reille, who in the meantime with his weakened force, but supported from behind by Foy, was to protect the movement and maintain the positions in front of the allies. Then, with superior forces, Soult hoped to crush Hill, whose advance was threatening his right. The consequence was the sharp affair of Buenza, and there Soult was so far successful. He turned Hill, forced him back with considerable loss, thus opening a new and shorter line of retreat to the Lower Bidassoa, by the pass of Doña Maria, leading to San Estevan. Or at San Estevan he might seize the road from the east to Tolosa, and, effecting his junction with Villatte, raise the siege of San Sebastian.

In that scheme he counted without the British light division, of whose movements he was in ignorance, and also without the prompt action of Wellington, who had penetrated his designs. Soult had counted on Reille's positions being practically impregnable. The English general determined to storm them. The operations were admirably conceived, and carried out with the most determined courage. Picton turned the right from behind heights which the French had just abandoned, while Lord Dalhousie was acting against their left. The central attack was as brilliant as it was successful, and the French, notwithstanding superior numbers, were driven from post to post. The village of Sauroren was stormed, the face of the mountain was scaled.

The decisive victory was due to the sudden shock delivered by General Inglis with 500 men of the 7th Division. Breaking the regiments covering Clausel's right, and seizing on the ridges beyond the Lanz, he severed the French line at the centre, throwing the division on the flank and rear of the main body. Repulsed from the crest, Reille's soldiers broke and dispersed. The bulk of them fled up the Lanz valley, the others sought the protection of Foy, who had no time to come to the rescue. Keeping to the heights, he retired into the mountains, and Wellington pressed the pursuit till dark, when it was arrested at Olague, beyond Ostiz.

By that unexpected defeat Soult was gravely imperilled. The choice of plans was no longer open to him; his sole consideration was to save his army by leading it across the Doña Maria pass to San Estevan and calling in Clausel. He marched all the night, but early on the 31st the rear-guard under D'Erlon was brought to action on the summit of the pass. The formidable ground was held with resolution, but the 2nd and 7th Divisions would not be denied, and again the fugitives were dislodged. Meantime Wellington, moving through the pass of Vellate upon Irutita, was thus turning their new position at San Estevan. Byng had already reached Elisondo, capturing a great convoy of stores and ammunition. Soult was surrounded in a narrow valley; Graham was on the march to seize upon the exits on the side of Vera and Echallar; Byng had repossessed himself of the pass of Maya, and Hill was advancing by Almandoz.

A crowning catastrophe seemed inevitable, the rather that Soult was ignorant of the imminence of the peril. Wellington gave strict orders for silence, and forbade any lighting of fires; he placed himself in a commanding position, whence he could scan each movement of the enemy, who seemed to be still unsuspicious. Then occurred one of those trivial incidents which influence the fortunes of war. Some of our marauding soldiers, straggling in defiance of orders, were taken by the French scouts. Unhappily the alarm was thus given, and half an hour afterwards, from his post of observation, Wellington saw the enemy's columns moving out of San Estevan.

They had been saved for the time, but the situation was eminently critical. Instead of taking the road to Echallar, which led to the Col de Maya, Soult pressed forward to Yanzi, where a narrow bridge spanned a deep torrent bed. Had Wellington's instructions been carried out, the bridge, with the gorges beyond, would have been held by Longa with his Spaniards, and the light division under Alten would have come up in time to support them. But Longa had delayed, Alten had gone astray, and Soult's scouts informed him that the way was open. Alten was late, but yet his division arrived on the heights as Reille's column was defiling along the passage beneath the precipices. He had done all that man could do to retrieve a mistake. He had marched through the mountains for forty miles and for nineteen hours, in overpowering heat, without halting the division. The sufferings of the soldiers had been great, and many had dropped and been left behind, succumbing to sunstroke and exhaustion. It was a strange position. The French were within musket-shot from the rocks above, but the precipices prevented the antagonists from coming to close quarters. To the right the British had descended on the low ground near the bridge, where their riflemen found cover in the brushwood.

The bridge was taken, cutting off all retreat, though the French made desperate efforts to recover it. Meantime the plunging fire from the heights turned the road and the river-bed into a horrible shambles. It is said that the assailants held their hands, or fired with averted eyes, in sheer disgust at the butchery of men who could not retaliate. Beyond the bridge two ways branch off. That leading to Vera and the Lower Bidassoa was followed by the troops who had extricated themselves from the gorge, while the greater part of those who had been caught in the defile escaped by way of Echallar. The rout was complete, yet had Wellington's combinations succeeded, the enemy would have had no choice but general surrender. Soult had rallied the wreck of the army, which had sought safety on the side of Echallar, in a strong position between the town and the pass of the same name. Forced from his first line of defence, he retired to a second, only to be driven thence. After that second unavailing stand, his army was in full retreat for France. Suchet was still on the seaboard of Catalonia, but beyond that all that remained to the late masters of Spain were the beleaguered fortresses of Pamplona and San Sebastian.

CHAPTER 21

Fall of San Sebastian
August, September 1813

Those battles of the Pyrenees had lasted for nine days, and besides skirmishing, there had been ten regular engagements. The losses on both sides had been severe. Those of the French were concealed, and have never been reliably stated, but whole divisions had shrunk to skeletons. D'Erlon, for example, had come to Ostiz with 18,000 men; when he re-passed the Bidassoa, there was barely a third of that number with the colours. It may be remembered that the turning point of the brief but bloody campaign was the daring and intelligent action of General Inglis in the fighting around Sauroren. By seizing on the ridges between Reille and Soult's right, and separating the forces of Foy from the main body, he relieved the overwhelming stress on Hill, and upset Soult's second plan of operations.

Now the allies were re-established in all those frontier positions from Roncesvalles westwards from which they had been forced nine days previously. They occupied them in greater strength than before; and the French had been so thoroughly beaten and demoralised, that there was no immediate fear of their resuming the offensive. It might have been supposed that Wellington would have followed up his successes while the enemy were in dismay and confusion. But he adhered to his persistent plan of risking nothing rashly when such vast issues were at stake. Various weighty considerations, military and political, deterred him from an immediate invasion of France. Once committed to a campaign in France, he was bound, for prestige's sake, to persevere, and any serious reverse must have been ruinous. Soult for the moment was almost at his mercy, but he knew not what was passing in Germany.

Our allies there were not to be trusted; they might patch up a separate peace, and then Napoleon might send his liberated veterans to the south. The allied troops, after tremendous exertions, had need of repose, and if they had suffered less than the French, yet all his battalions were depleted. Their shoes had been worn out on the rocks of the Pyrenees, and their ammunition exhausted by constant fighting and skirmishing. Besides that, he had to assure himself on the new sea base he had adopted after the victory of Vittoria. The great roads in the Basque Provinces and Navarre, as well as those in Catalonia, were still blocked by fortresses in occupation of the enemy. The repulse of Soult involved, sooner or later, the surrender of San Sebastian and Pamplona; but to assure his ground, and secure his communications, these fortresses must be reduced.

The more pressing object was the capture of San Sebastian, for it was within reach of possible succour, and indeed Soult did make one final effort for its relief. While the war had been running its course in the mountains, the blockade had been maintained, though the heavy guns had been taken from the batteries and embarked. On the 3rd of August, the garrison and besiegers heard alike of Soult's defeat, and preparations were pushed forward on both sides for a renewed attack. Nothing was neglected by the commandant that energy or engineering skill could effect. As for Graham, he was impatiently expecting the return of his guns and the arrival of fresh artillery and ammunition from England, They came soon, and there was a busy scene in the little cliff-locked harbour of Passages; but when the allies set themselves to recommence the siege, the place was stronger than before.

Operations began on the 24th, and the besieged immediately met them with a sortie. The batteries opened fire on the 26th. The plan now adopted was to level the towers flanking the great breach, and to connect it with the second breach; to open another to the left, and, warned by the former experiences, to demolish a *demi*-bastion flanking the whole. On the 30th Lord Wellington pronounced the breaches practicable, and named eleven on the next morning for the assault, when the tide would be ebbing towards its lowest. Appearances are deceptive, and the breaches might have been pronounced virtually impracticable. To a certain point the ascent was easy, but above and behind was a sheer drop of 20 feet, and among the burned houses was a high wall, loopholed for musketry, and with *travises* at either end. The tower immediately commanding the great breach had been mined and charged with twelve hundredweight of powder, and at the salient angle by which the stormers must pass in single file, there were counter mines ready charged for an explosion.

Guns were in position to rake the breaches, and the Mirador battery belched its fire on the open ground over which the assailants crossed to the attack. The slope of the breach gave fair protection from musketry, but soon the approaches were so choked by the dead and dying that it became necessary to clear away the bodies. The forlorn hope had fallen to a man, with its gallant leader. Sir James Leith, who commanded the stormers, repeatedly and severely wounded, had nevertheless refused to withdraw, though ultimately he was borne back on a stretcher, still encouraging the advancing soldiers. Graham took his stand by the side of Leith in a position fully exposed to the fire. A man of the firmest resolution, he declared he was determined to succeed this time, even if he sent his last companies to the breaches. He was in anxious consultation with Sir Richard Fletcher, and with Colonel Dickson of the Artillery. They decided to open a heavy cannonade on the curtain, although the shot passed close over the stormers.

When the fire began, some of our stormers were killed, but the veterans soon recognised its purpose. For immediately the discharges from the hostile batteries slackened and the curtain that crowned the breaches was swept clear of its defenders. Again the assailants crowded forward, only to be brought up again by the insurmountable obstacles. According to all rules of the game of war the attack had failed, and ought to have ceased. But then chance came in, and fortune turned in favour of the stormers. Already the chambers at the salients had been prematurely exploded; the mine at the great breach had failed altogether, for an accidental shot had severed the sausage; and now there was a grand explosion behind the curtain. A *depôt* of ammunition and combustibles had blown up, spreading death and destruction all around. Panic-stricken for the moment, the French fled back. The fortifications were enveloped in blinding smoke.

Seizing the occasion, the stormers rushed forward, passed the perilous defile, and formed among the crumbling houses. Scaling ladders were fortunately at hand, and they descended into the streets, where desperate hand-to-hand fighting ensued among the barricades. Meantime the Portuguese had forded the Urumea, waist deep, below our Chofre batteries, and forced their way through the lesser breach on the right. The town was taken, and the garrison withdrew to the citadel on Monte Orgullo, retaining only besides their outwork at the Convent of Santa Theresa. Had our success been steadfastly followed up, probably the capitulation would have been immediate. But the soldiers had broken loose from restraint; already they were drunk with blood as well as liquor, and the worst atrocities of the invaders are said to have been equalled if not surpassed at the sack of this Spanish town by the allies. The only extenuation is that it had become more French than Spanish.

Two or three days of mad excess had elapsed before Graham could get the troops in hand again. Then the outlying convent was stormed, and a concentrated fire of vertical shell was rained upon the citadel from three sides. The garrison was short of food, water and ammunition. There was scarcely shelter in the casemates for the soldiers off duty; the helpless non-combatants and prisoners were absolutely unprotected from the rain of death. At last General Rey hung out the white flag, and with a garrison reduced to a third of the original strength marched out with the honours of war. The allies had lost 2500 men, and more than two-thirds of their officers had been killed or crippled. The most serious loss was that of Sir Richard Fletcher, but the gifted engineer had lived long enough to do his country invaluable service.

Immediately before the fall of the fortress, Soult had made a half-hearted effort for its relief He could hardly have hoped that the attempt would succeed against his watchful antagonist, but the allies were still scattered along an extended line, and he longed to do something to retrieve his reputation. Doubtless he felt that fortune had dealt hardly with him, for the skill of his previous strategy has seldom been impeached. His invincible greatness under defeat and discouragement is unquestionable. Already he was reorganising his broken battalions, as the stragglers began to rejoin the colours. The Spaniards, who spared no Frenchmen they came across, did him good service to the south of the Bidassoa as recruiting officers. And from France he was being reinforced by 30,000 conscripts, who would, at least, be serviceable in strengthening the reserves.

But in devising fresh schemes of offence he had to consider his reduced means, which made it impossible to attempt again the relief of Pamplona, hardly as that fortress was known to be pressed. He decided, therefore, to act on the side of San Sebastian, and advance on the allied left by the road of Irun. Wellington held both banks of the Bidassoa down to Vera, and from thence to the sea the river divided the hostile pickets. But below the broken bridge of Behobia on the Irun road the Bidassoa is a tidal estuary: the only points of attack were then believed to be certain fords above the bridge, and at Vera, where the *tête-de-pont* was occupied by the allies. Could Soult make his way to Oyarzum, which is seven miles to the south of the Bidassoa on the great southern highway, the siege must be raised. That main road runs through a broad valley; there are precipitous spurs on the west, jutting out into the Bay of Biscay, while to the east and parallel to the river is the long ridge of San Marcial. That ridge was the key of the position, for over its eastern shoulder came roads that joined the royal highway at Oyarzum.

Soult had meant to attack on the 30th, but, as it happened, the attack was deferred to the 31st, the very day of the assault on San Sebastian. He had taken every precaution to keep his intentions secret, but, nevertheless, Wellington, from observations and otherwise, had become suspicious of them. Three divisions of Spaniards under Freyre, supported by British infantry, held San Marcial. His left was on the mountain overhanging the harbour of Passages, and knowing that the French had been assembling in force before Vera, he strengthened his guards upon the heights in that direction. Reille was charged with the storming of San Marcial; thence he was to press on to Oyarzum, leaving a reserve to form a junction with Clausel's columns coming up from Vera. While Reille was engaged in carrying the ridge, Foy was to throw bridges across the river lower down, and move straight upon Oyarzum with the artillery and cavalry.

Reille began the combat at day dawn in full assurance, for he knew he was opposed only by Spaniards. However, the Spaniards fought with unexpected courage, and charging downhill with the bayonet, repeatedly broke and forced back the assailing columns. But they could not prevent the French *pontonniers* from constructing the bridges, and in the afternoon they were again attacked simultaneously in front and on the flank. At that moment Wellington rode up, to be greeted with deafening cheers. The Spaniards charged again, and literally hurled the French down into the river. So fierce was their onslaught that many of the fugitives were drowned, and several of the boats which came to the rescue were overloaded and sunk.

Clausel had been simultaneously foiled at the fords below Vera by the Portuguese, supported by Generals Inglis and Kempt, and Inglis had established himself in a position so strong that the French recognised they could not dislodge him. D'Erlon, on the extreme left, had been menaced by columns from Echallar and Maya, and sent messages to Soult, suggesting that it seemed to be Wellington's purpose to turn their left and descend the Nive valley to Bayonne. So when preparing on the following day to renew the attack on San Marcial, D'Erlon's intelligence, which seemed probable enough, reached Soult, with the news of Clausel's failure. He heard at the same time of the fall of San Sebastian. In any case, having been repulsed all along the line, his troops on the left of the Bidassoa were seriously endangered. Fortunately Foy had not yet passed the river, and orders were sent to Clausel to re-cross immediately. But there had been one of those torrential storms which so often preceded or accompanied the Peninsular battles.

The Bidassoa was swelling fast, and Clausel could only cross by the bridge of Vera. His division passed that narrow bridge, under fire with heavy loss, and had there been sufficient strength to head them back they must have laid down their arms. Soult's strenuous efforts had been all in vain, and he resumed his former positions and the defensive. Reflections on his last attempt must have been disheartening; choosing his points of attack, so far as was possible, 45,000 French soldiers had been driven back by barely more than a fifth of their number. What gave cause for even graver consideration was that the brunt of the victorious fighting had fallen upon Portuguese and Spaniards. The Portuguese, under Beresford's training, had for long fought shoulder to shoulder with the British in staunch solidarity; now the Spaniards were acquiring confidence with discipline, and seemed likely to prove equally trustworthy. Napoleon and Wellington between them had turned the guerrillas into soldiers.

Events of importance had been passing in Eastern Spain, although there Wellington's grand efforts were but indifferently seconded. There the commanders had been changed seven times in the course of fifteen months. The thoughts of Lord William Bentinck, perhaps the most capable of those generals, were rather turned towards Sicily and Italy, whereas Wellington regarded it as of supreme importance that the efforts of England should be concentrated on the Peninsula. The effect of Vittoria, as has been pointed out, had compelled Suchet to fall back on Catalonia. He had evacuated Aragon, which he had ably administered, and the heroic city of Zaragoza was again in Spanish hands. After the failure before Tarragona, the Anglo-Sicilian army had returned to Alicante, but the French almost simultaneously had retired from Valencia.

The French were in retreat, but Lord William was desirous that they should be prevented from dismantling the strong works of Tarragona. Having entered Valencia on the 9th of July, he despatched a corps to Tarragona by sea under Sir William Clinton. Clinton disembarked at the Col de Balaguer, to the south of the city, and having been joined there by Lord William with the advance guard of the main body, they proceeded to invest the fortress. It was believed that the destruction of the fortress was contemplated, and that Suchet might come up to cover the operation. Yet information was conflicting, and it was doubtful whether he did not intend to continue his retreat. Lord William, fearing to be attacked at a disadvantage, deferred landing his battering-train, lest he might risk such a failure as that of Sir John Murray. He was daily expecting the arrival of the Duque del Parque and of Sarsfield with his Catalans.

The delay may have been prudent, but it gave Suchet time to collect a greatly superior force. He advanced rapidly, and Lord William hesitated to hazard a battle. On the night of the 15th August he abandoned his lines, and at daybreak the garrison saw nothing of the besiegers. Suchet had saved the garrison, and had leisure to blow up the fortifications, though the work was done with so much precipitancy that many of the guns, with great quantities of stores, fell into the hands of the allies.

Suchet fell back on the Llobregat, and in the beginning of September had established his headquarters at Villafranca. Then Soult, in grave anxiety after the fall of San Sebastian and the losses sustained in attempting its relief, with the dubious prospect of replenishing his ranks with a levy of raw conscripts, proposed that Suchet should join him with his veterans, marching through southern France. Then the united armies might advance to the succour of Pamplona. That proposal was soon recognised by both to be impracticable. Suchet urged that he would be followed up by the Anglo-Sicilians, and the departments of France which were left defenceless would be ravaged. He suggested, by way of compromise, that he should march up the northern bank of the Ebro to meet Soult, debouching from Jaca. Suchet would bring his guns; Soult would come with infantry and cavalry. But before even risking so much, Suchet must have reinforcements for his garrisons, and, above all, he must dispose of the Anglo-Sicilians.

The Anglo-Sicilians were posted at Villafranca and in the surrounding villages, their advance guard holding the pass of Ordal, half-way between the main body and the French positions on the Llobregat. Lord William was over-confident in the strength of the pass; but there Suchet surprised the defenders at midnight on the 12th. Though there was a surprise, the pass was obstinately defended, but before Lord William could hurry up in support, all the positions had been carried. He decided therefore on a retreat, and accomplished it in safety, though with considerable loss. Had Suchet pressed his advantage, the result might have been more serious, for the allies could have made no stand in ruined Tarragona, and would have been assailed to great disadvantage in threading the defile of Balaguer.

Immediately afterwards Lord William, on learning the defection of Murat, embarked for Sicily, and then the command devolved upon Clinton. Clinton had much to undertake, with inadequate means. He had to guard against Suchet withdrawing his garrisons, and to occupy him so that he should do nothing to assist Soult. As the preliminary, he resolved to restore the defences of Tarragona and to re-establish it as a place of arms and his basis of operations. Had Suchet shown his earlier ardour and sagacity, or had he realised the relative weakness of his adversary, he might have regained even more than he had lost. He had 25,000 hardened soldiers under his hand. The Anglo-Sicilians numbered only half as many, and though there were 11,000 Spaniards besides, half starved and in rags, they had broken loose from all restraint. But the startling successes of the allies in the north-west, and the determined fighting at Ordal, seem to have paralysed him. He was content again to withdraw to the Llobregat, and again the allied headquarters were at Villafranca, while the armies were observing each other and waiting on events.

CHAPTER 22

Passages of the Bidassoa and Nivelle
OCTOBER, NOVEMBER 1813

Wellington had been anxiously watching those operations in Catalonia. He was inclined to take the command there in person, to reduce the fortress, drive Suchet into France, and so accomplish the deliverance of the Peninsula, could he have previously secured the frontier of the north-western Pyrenees. But Pamplona—and Santona as well—held out. So long as Pamplona was still in French occupation, a regular invasion of France was impossible or at least undesirable. The weeks that elapsed after the surrender of San Sebastian were passed in apparent inactivity. The allies had resumed their former positions looking down from the commanding heights on the French valleys, and across to the positions that were held by the enemy. But from any point of view the delay was inevitable. The troops were being rested and reorganised, and every week came transports from England, bringing recruits to fill the gaps in regiments that had been literally cut to pieces, with ammunition and other supplies to replenish the exhausted stores.

On their side the French were equally active. Reservists and conscripts had been sent to the front. Everywhere from St. Jean Pied de Port to Hendaye they were busy with pick and spade, entrenching themselves behind breastworks, and strengthening a second mountain line of extraordinary natural strength. At first the activity plainly visible among them induced Wellington to apprehend a renewed attack. But he speedily understood that the cautious French Marshal had decided to remain strictly on the defensive. For himself, he would have willingly done the same, and waited at least for the capitulation of Pamplona. But political considerations, connected with events in Germany, came into play, and pressure from ministers at home urged him to some serious aggressive demonstration. He was not to be tempted to risk a catastrophe by pushing forward into the triangle which, with its apex at Bayonne, the left extremity at the entrenchments of St Jean, enclosing the debouches of the eastern passes, and the right resting on the tidal estuary of the Bidassoa, formed a receding angle with easy inner lines of intercommunication, which might well become a fatal trap. But, yielding to that political pressure, he resolved upon a feat which Soult, with all his experience of his antagonist, expected even less than the passage of the Douro.

Soult had been somewhat uneasy as to his left and centre, strongly entrenched and formidably posted as they were. But having taken all ordinary precautions, he scarcely gave further thought to the safety of his right. Moreover, like Wellington, he had the custom of gauging the temperament and character of an adversary, and he dismissed the idea of the patient strategist, who had often baffled him, risking anything so obviously hazardous. As a skilful soldier he had reason for over-confidence, and to that Wellington trusted much. The mountain called the Grand Rhune runs in a south-westerly direction, in a succession of heights, each with a name of its own, gradually sinking towards the Irun road. These heights were to be attacked simultaneously with the passage of the river, below the broken bridge of Behobia. Having once gained a footing on the northern bank, the enemy's own works and positions would be turned against them. On the right the attack would be made from Vera, where roads from the Spanish side lead to the *puerto* of that name.

Between Vera and Behobia, where the river skirts the ridge, there were certain well-known fords. But below Behobia it seems to have been believed, even by the natives, that there were no means of passing. Naturally the passage had never been attempted before. There was a broad tidal estuary; with the rapid flow of the tide the water rose fifteen feet; at low water a wide space of soft sand was left bare on either bank. But while the army was inactive certain Spanish boatmen, while apparently fishing, had been sounding the bottom. Three fording places had been discovered which were pronounced practicable. It is greatly to the credit of these patriots that none turned traitor, when he had invaluable information to sell and might have asked his own price.

On the night of the 6th the final dispositions were made. Again the elements were on the side of the allies. A tremendous thunderstorm broke from the Guipuzcoan hills, driving a drenching rain down on the French bivouacs. The peals of the thunder drowned all other sounds when the crest of San Marcial was being armed with heavy guns. The heads of seven columns told off to as many passages had been kept carefully under cover. At seven o'clock the opening of the cannon fire gave signal for the simultaneous advance. The storm had not cooled the air, and the morning was unusually sultry. The tide was at the lowest, and the three columns attacking below Behobia had to toil across the broad expanse of sand. Reille was in command of the forces opposed to them, holding double lines crossing the sandhills.

The advanced line had been entrusted to Maucune, an experienced veteran and one of the heroes of Salamanca, with 5000 good soldiers. Yet he was so little prepared for an attack that his guns did not open till the assailants had waded to the middle of the stream. Reille hastily sent forward supports, but he was taken equally by surprise and had no time to rally his detached working parties. The landing was effected, the forward line was forced, and its defenders were followed up to the Croix des Bouquets, a sandy eminence, and the key of the positions. Fortunately, trusting to the estuary in front, supposed to be impassable, there and there only the fortifying had been neglected. Nevertheless, with the advantage of ground, Maucune with the supports offered determined resistance.

But the impetuosity of the allies would not be denied, and the French were soon in full retreat from their last defensible position. Soult had been with D'Erlon's corps at Espalette—half-way between the Nive and the Bidassoa—when he was roused from his slumbers by the roar of the cannon from San Marcial. Throwing himself into the saddle, after some delay, owing to a false attack on D'Erlon, he galloped towards Hendaye, to find his lines already in possession of the enemy. The passage had literally been effected against time and tide, for a check or prolonged delay must have ended in a grand disaster.

Yet the safety of the isolated left depended on the result of well-devised combinations elsewhere. It will suffice to give a brief summary of these. The entrenchments on the heights opposite the fords of Biriatu and Bildox, while assailed from the front, were turned on their left and abandoned. The defenders were falling back in extreme confusion when Soult, coming up with reserves, restored some sort of order. The fighting on the side of Vera had been more stubborn, as it well might be. The Grand Rhune was an almost impregnable fortress, where splintered crags and beetling precipices were so many natural

The Duke of Wellington and his staff crossing the Bidassoa

bastions and scarps; there the French had been working industriously for a month, and engineering science had done its utmost to assist Nature. Thither some of the defenders of the heights to the left had withdrawn, and there Clausel had concentrated eight regiments in a position that seemed assured.

The rugged flanks had been retrenched, and each angle was protected by abatis, and commanded by musketry fire. Redoubts and retrenchments were carried by the light division, while Giron's Spaniards, pressing forward on the right front, were only stopped at the foot of inaccessible crags, crowned by a rude edifice called the Hermitage. The evening closed in with dense fog, and when night fell, though the Spaniards kept up a harmless fire, Clausel was still in his rock citadel. When the fog lifted on the following morning, Wellington had come up to reconnoitre the mountain. He pronounced it unassailable from the front or the west, but deemed it practicable to attack it from his right, simultaneously with the works at the camp of Sarre. There was fierce fighting, the French hurling down rocks on the heads of the assailants; but before night Giron had established a battalion on the eastern flanks of La Rhune. The position was insecure—perhaps untenable—but during the night Clausel thought it wise to withdraw, evacuating at the same time the works before Sarre.

On the evening of the 9th the allied armies were established in cantonments in France. With losses comparatively slight they had stormed a series of positions, which, as a distinguished officer said, men ought to have defended forever. For in an almost unbroken succession of defeats the French had become utterly disheartened and demoralised.

The army took up its new positions with headquarters at Vera. Hill commanded the right, with the Spaniards of Morillo and Mina. Beresford had the centre, occupying Maya and the mountain ranges from the Rhune to the Mandale. The left from the Mandale to the Bidassoa mouth was entrusted to Sir John Hope. That distinguished officer, who had succeeded to Moore after the battle of Corunna, now took the place of Sir Thomas Graham, who had gone home invalided. His was the most responsible post, for if there were immediate danger it threatened the left wing. In the event of an attack and a repulse, the fords over the estuary might be unavailable. Yet all precautions were taken; the troops were kept busy entrenching themselves; and beside the fords above Behobia, two pontoon bridges and a bridge of boats were thrown across the river.

But Soult had no idea of immediately resuming the offensive. It seems clear that Suchet, who apparently bore him an old grudge, had knowingly deceived him as to the relative strength of the opposing forces in Catalonia and Valencia. In any case all projects for effecting a junction were finally disposed of by the passage of the Bidassoa, and the approach of winter. It is certain that Suchet had good reason for saying that the pass of Jaca, by which Soult was to have debouched on Aragon, could not have been made practicable for the transport of cannon. With the storms that might be expected in November it would be blocked.

Consequently Soult, though he had rightly urged that the genius of the French lay rather in attack than in passive resistance, was constrained to acquiesce in the inevitable. He made immense preparations for the defence, and indeed he had been occupied with them since his defeats in the Pyrenees, three months before. It was a broad and comprehensive scheme, indicated by the physical features of the country; and its only defects were beyond his control, for his troops were scarcely adequate to maintain, with a prudent regard to contingencies, that far-reaching system of works, from the entrenched camp at St Jean Pied de Port to that other formed before Bayonne. Reille still commanded on his right, and again upon double lines covering St Jean de Luz.

Clausel faced the allied centre, resting on the Little Rhune as an advanced post, and holding the formidable ridges to the north of it. D'Erlon was in the old positions he had occupied when the cannonade of San Marcial roused Soult at Espalette. Behind these lines was a base of entrenched camps stretching from Bayonne towards St Jean Pied de Port, and Foy had been ordered down to Bidarray on the Nive, where he could act, in case of need, in either direction. Soult did all that man could do in the circumstances, and he appears to have won the affections of his generals and to have been seconded with unusual loyalty. Nevertheless his difficulties were great. The Emperor's attention was concentrated on Germany, and he had scarcely a thought to spare for Spain. There was no hope of veteran reinforcements, and the conscripts came slowly forward. The finance department turned a deaf ear to appeals for money; the merchants of Bayonne, fearing for their town, provided for some immediate expenses, but Bordeaux, further removed from the seat of operations, could not be persuaded to follow the example. In fact, Southern France, weary of the war, was almost ready to welcome invasion. The problem was how Soult was to feed his men, and he could not possibly feed his horses. When forage gave out, they were sent back towards the interior, so that he was deprived for the time of his cavalry and his artillery teams.

Soult's position was difficult enough, but that of the allies was infinitely worse. For the most part they occupied bleak mountain ranges, exposed to all the violence of the winter storms. There was an exhausted country behind them, and the difficulties of transport were tremendous. Forage at first was absolutely wanting, and the horses, with the scanty grazing, were reduced to skeletons. The cattle, driven up from great distances, dropped and died by hundreds on the roads. An unusually stormy season had kept the transports off the coasts, and the disembarkation of stores was rare and precarious. As for money, Wellington was even more embarrassed than Soult, and he had to appeal, and not in vain, to the soldierly spirit of his men, not only to endure privations, but to submit to stoppages of pay. The commissary service was forever a trouble to him; and all through this time of terrible suffering it was notorious in the army that commissaries in league with contractors were making fortunes out of the general misery. The Government pack mules were often laden with luxuries, to be sold for private advantage at famine prices.

While the soldiers of both the armies were half starved, the garrison and townsfolk of Pamplona had been reduced to more dire extremities. Moreover, scurvy was raging within the walls. The governor had held out as obstinately as General Rey at San Sebastian, and with as little regard for humanity, so far as the citizens were concerned. Towards the end of the month he had endeavoured to make terms, but Carlos D'España, by Wellington's instructions, would hear of nothing save unconditional surrender. It came to that on the last day of October, when the capital of Navarre was finally given over. It had been rumoured in the besieging lines that the governor meant to imitate Brennier at Almeida— to blow up the fortifications and force his way out. The breaking out being impossible made the cases totally different, and the Spaniard summarily intimated to the Frenchman that if he destroyed anything it should be at his peril, and he and the garrison would be put to the sword. Assuredly the threat could not have been carried out, but it sufficed to salve the governor's honour.

The fall of the fortress left Wellington free to act. Political motives again urged him forward, for each post brought fresh news of French disasters in Germany. Moreover, it was no slight consideration that he might bring his men down from among the summits of the Pyrenees to regions less exposed and a more clement climate. Already pickets

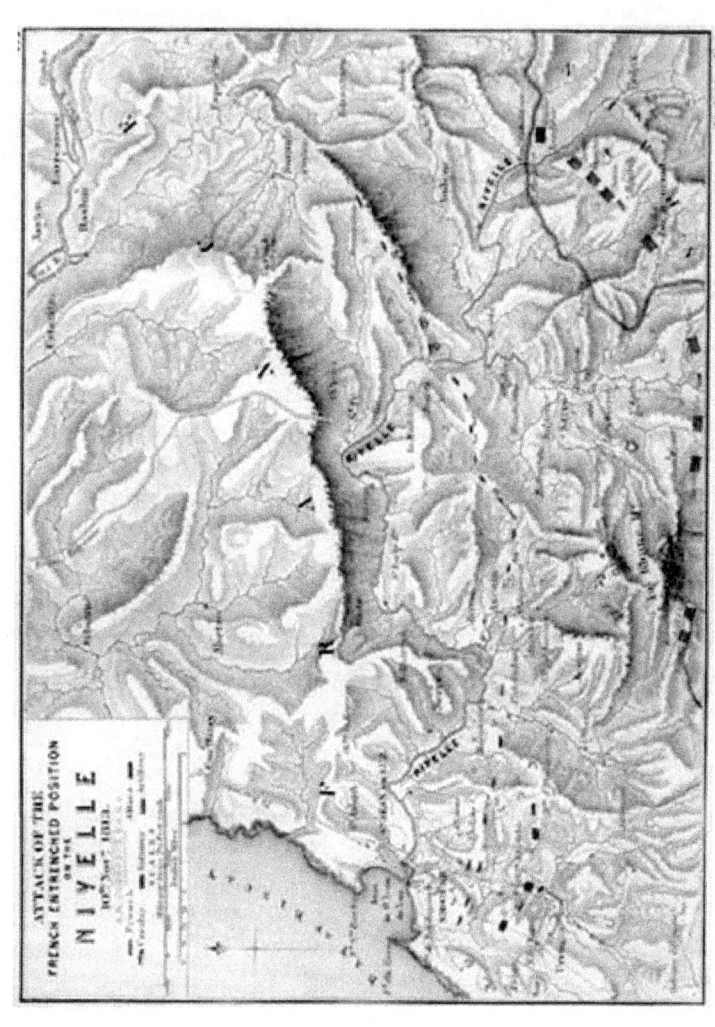

had been snowed up between Roncesvalles and Maya in gorges which it seemed scarcely necessary to guard, and the relieving parties had driven bullocks before them, to test the snow cornices overhanging the abysses. Wellington had only waited to move till Pamplona was in his possession. The surrender had been delayed some days beyond his expectations, and had been followed by torrential rains.

But by the 7th November the weather had cleared. His first idea had been to turn the French left by way of Roncesvalles through St Jean, but on second thoughts he had abandoned it from strategical considerations. As Soult could operate more rapidly on inner lines, unnecessary odds would have been given in his favour. Now it was decided boldly to attack the centre, for strong as the positions were, they were always open to flank assaults, and the fighting when the Bidassoa was passed had shown the deterioration of the French *moral*. On the 7th the commander-in-chief met the chiefs of the divisions of the right and centre at Urdax, whence the opposite heights of Ainhoa could be closely reconnoitred. Then all the arrangements were made. These heights were to be carried; the army was to be advanced to the rear of the French right, and the attack was to be made by columns of division, each led by the general commanding, and forming its own reserve.

Again the rains came down, and the battle was postponed to the 10th, but on that day 90,000 men were ranged in order of battle, and, what was remarkable, considering the state of the mountain tracks, ninety-five guns were ready for the action. Hill led the right; Beresford came next to him, on the right of the centre; Giron with the Andalusians was on Beresford's left. Baron Alten and Longa were to attack the little La Rhune. Cotton's cavalry were to support the centre, and further to the left Freyre with his Gallicians was to descend from the ridge of Mandale towards Ascain, to be in readiness to act according to circumstances. On these corps was to fall the brunt of the fighting. Hope was to play a subordinate, though an important, part.

At six o'clock Wellington was, with Sir Lowry Cole, at the head of Cole's column, on a sloping ridge above the village of Sarre. In a valley to the west was Giron, in another to the right was Le Cor. Facing the column was a formidable redoubt on the culminating point of the ridge. As soon as the light served, the signal was given. Five-and-twenty field-pieces opened their fire; the enemy's pickets were driven in with a rush, and the column charged up towards the redoubt covered, by a heavy fire from the horse artillery, which had been brought up within 300 yards. For an hour the French showed no signs of wavering, but when they saw the Spaniards in their rear, and the red-coated infantry coming forward with scaling ladders, they turned and fled precipitately, and their flight involved the abandonment of a redoubt on the right. Wellington rode up to the captured works, to be greeted as usual with vociferous cheering. Thence he could see and direct the further operations. The strongly-fortified village with the low heights beyond were carried, and Cole halted to breathe his men and await further orders.

Alten in the meantime, with the light division, had literally rushed the little La Rhune, emerging from a ravine at the foot of the greater mountain, within 300 yards of the French entrenchments. There the enemy made no stand, and the labours of months were given away with scarcely a shot or blow. The redoubts clustered in the rear were abandoned with as little fighting, and those positions were won almost simultaneously with these which were stormed by Cole. Wellington had waited till Clinton, following D'Armagnac on the right of the Nivelle, was well forward. Then he crossed the river with the 3rd and 7th Divisions, and so the battle in the centre was decided. These divisions, with the 6th, had assured their positions in rear of Soult's right.

Reille, on the allied left, had been holding two advanced positions in front of Urogne. Both had been taken early in the day, and there the battle continued to rage all along' the line, with slight advantage to either side. Yet Hope had accomplished all that was asked of him, for he had given full occupation to Reille and his reserves. Twenty-five thousand French had been detained there, none had been sent from the camp of Serres to the aid of Clausel, when making his stand with only 16,000 men against converging attacks by superior numbers. Villatte, in occupation of the camp at Serres, covered the retreat of Reille to St Jean de Luz. There the French general made no long halt, but, having broken down the bridges on the Lower Nivelle, withdrew during the night to Bidart on the Bayonne road.

The results of the day were another heavy blow to Soult, and the beaten generals indulged in angry recrimination. Soult declared that he had relied so confidently on the strength of the central works, that he might have counted on the allies losing 25,000 men in forcing them, if they did not fail after all. He said that had Clausel concentrated on the main position, he must have maintained it. As for Clausel, he complained that he had fought hard for five hours, and that no help had been sent him, either from the camp at Serres or St Jean de Luz. There seems to have been justice in the complaint, for Soult was evidently deluded into believing that Hope's advance was seriously meant, instead of being merely a feint and distraction. And on the other wing, Foy was as much out of the battle as Grouchy was to be at Waterloo. Foy had been ordered to attack Mina by the Gorospil Mountain, and was away beyond reach of recall when urgent messages were sent from D'Erlon.

It had rained heavily through the night, and the morning of the nth was misty. When the haze had cleared, and Wellington had trustworthy information, the orders were given for a general advance. Hope forded the Nivelle with his infantry, while the bridges were being hastily restored to permit the passage of the horses and guns. Beresford moved forward in the centre on parallel lines, and Hill on the right made painful progress along flooded roads to attempt the fords at Ustaritz and Cambo. But Foy had come down to defend the passages, and with the rains in the mountains the river was in heavy flood. On the 11th, Soult had rallied his forces in a line of camps, extending from Ustaritz to the coast at Bidart. But warned, perhaps, by the former day's experiences of the danger of fighting such adversaries on too extended a front, he fell back next morning on the ridge before Bayonne, with his right at Anglet on the Biarritz road, and his left in the entrenched camp which had been in course of construction since the disaster of Vittoria had driven Joseph out of Spain.

CHAPTER 23

Battles of the Nivelle and Surrender of Eastern Fortresses
December 1813—April 1814

Had the weather and other circumstance been favourable, Wellington would have immediately followed up his success and struck again while the enemy was demoralised. His troops were in the highest spirits, overflowing with confidence and eager to press onward. When they had rushed down from bleak bivouacs and scanty rations in the Pyrenees, they had looked forward to comfortable quarters in the rich provinces of Southern France. But for a week from the nth it rained incessantly, and the country, deep in clay and water, was virtually impracticable. The royal roads—those leading from Bidart and St Jean Pied de Port to Bayonne—were in possession of the French. So long as the river was flooded the fords were impassable. There was nothing for it but to go into cantonments. They commenced on the sea, behind Biarritz, and were carried to the river at Arcangues; from thence they were thrown back, almost at a right angle, along the left bank to the villages opposite Cambo. The troops were chafing at the delay and the prolongation of their privations, and were threatening to give trouble.

Already on the morrow of the battles on the Nivelle, even the British had begun to break out in such excesses as had followed the storm of the Spanish fortresses. These had been summarily checked by the sharp discipline of the provost-marshal. But the Spaniards, used to guerrilla warfare, and with a long series of atrocities to avenge, had broken loose from all restraint. Mina's battalions were in open mutiny. Determined that the French should have no cause of complaint, Wellington sent those turbulent auxiliaries back to their own country, although that strong measure was bitterly resented and his army was unseasonably weakened.

In cantonments he was in some anxiety for his right flank. Soult had ordered the construction of a *tête-de-pont* at Cambo, and Foy, with command of the passage, might venture on an offensive movement. Hill was ordered to make demonstrations, but on his advance the French officer in charge anticipated his purpose by breaking down the entrenchments and blowing up the bridge. Thus, in the meantime, Wellington was reassured as to any danger of attack by Foy. It was Soult who now entertained apprehensions, for the mountain rivers subside suddenly as they rise, and the Nive, when the water is low, is fordable in many places. And he knew that Wellington had every inducement to effect the passage, in order that he might regain his liberty of action and replenish his magazines. As it was, he could only wait behind works, with his cavalry and trains of artillery paralysed.

However, in the beginning of December, the weather began to mend, and on the 8th the allies moved out of their cantonments. They were excited at the prospect of action, and, moreover, there was news from the north to exhilarate them. The French had evacuated Hanover; the Dutch had declared independence. Soult had, of course, made his dispositions for defending the Nive, but the inaction of the allies had lulled him into temporary security, and in some measure he was taken by surprise. Reille held the Lower Adour, covered by inundations, and aided by gunboats. He was *à cheval* on the road leading to Biarritz from Hope's headquarters at St Jean de Luz. His left, under Clausel, extended to the Nive, also partially protected by swamps and overflow. Beyond the Nive was another entrenched camp, and the passages at Ustaritz, and higher up at Cambo, were held respectively by D'Armagnac and Foy, D'Erlon being in command of the whole. Hill was instructed to cross at Cambo, and Beresford, with Clinton's division, at Ustaritz. Meantime Hope and Alten were to drive in the outposts before Bayonne, and prevent the detachment of supports to the real points of attack.

The operations succeeded perfectly. Neither at Cambo nor Ustaritz was there more than desultory resistance; the enemy were driven back from the right bank, and the allies were soon in possession of the road from St Jean Pied de Port. But the heavy marching had delayed the rears of the columns, and D'Erlon had time to establish himself firmly on a range of heights parallel to the Adour. There he was joined by Soult, and they were prepared to offer battle; but already the short day was drawing to a close, and the allies bivouacked on the ground they had secured. On the left, Hope, with three divisions and a handful of cavalry, had given full occupation to double his numbers. He had fought his way up to the front of the entrenched camp, but towards nightfall he drew back, according to his instructions.

When his troops returned to their quarters, they had been twenty-four hours under arms. Wellington appears not to have apprehended an immediate counter-stroke. His forces were in two divisions, arrayed in separate orders of battle, and separated by the river, yet he was already throwing a bridge of communication across the river below Ustaritz. But Soult had decided to concentrate for the counter-attack, and was only hesitating on which side to strike. Partly owing to false information as to the allied dispositions, he resolved to break out upon Hope, but on that side he had really fair prospects of victory. Hope's wearied troops had withdrawn to St Jean de Luz, and the ridges, centring in the plateau of Barouillet in front of the camp, were only weakly held. On the key of the position at Barouillet there was but a single brigade, and the supports were far in the rear. The light division was at Arcangues, two miles to the right, but the connection was only maintained by slight and scattered posts.

Between Arcangues and Barouillet was a broad valley, almost undefended, as it was believed the enemy could never attempt it, being menaced from the positions on either flank. Soult's first intention was to have launched his united force on that ill-defended opening. For some unexplained reason, and unfortunately for himself, he changed his mind, and the attack was delivered in two columns. Reille advanced along the main road to Barouillet; Clausel attacked on the side of Arcangues and Bussussary. Soult was aware of his numerical superiority, but had he realised the diffusion and exhaustion of the allied forces, and the extreme difficulty of bringing up their guns, he must have pressed home his attacks and almost certainly succeeded. As it was, the ground was desperately disputed by the allies, while feeble succours only arrived at critical moments when each station of vantage was on the point of being lost.

Hope, with his staff, had galloped to the front, and his gigantic figure was to be seen everywhere in the foremost of the battle, encouraging his men and rallying the battalions in supreme indifference to his own safety. Yet fresh field batteries were for ever being brought up from Bayonne, and the French had forced their way through the woods of Barouillet, where they were checked by a timely charge on their left flank, and hurled back with the loss of some hundreds of prisoners. That sharp repulse saved the situation; the brigade of guards arrived from St Jean de Luz, and Wellington, who had hurried over from his right wing, rode on to the field. When night fell, little had been lost or gained. But the 1st Division, which had come up from its cantonments, relieved the troops that had borne the brunt of the battle.

At Arcangues, Clausel's attack had been comparatively weak, though there was sharp, desultory fighting, but he had succeeded in occupying the plateau of Bussussary, though he had failed to dislodge the light division from its other positions. Soult was deeply mortified by the result, for he had once more been foiled by far inferior numbers when fighting with everything in his favour. And during the night there came another shock to the *moral* of his forces, for two German regiments went over to the allies. It was a question between military honour and patriotism, but recent events in Germany had absolved them from allegiance to Napoleon.

On the 11th the conditions had changed. Wellington, when he left Hill's quarters, realising the state of affairs, had ordered three divisions to follow. So Clausel had been kept in check, and there had been no renewal of the onslaughts on Barouillet. On the contrary, his troops had been withdrawn and concentrated in expectation of a counter attack. When that did not come off, Soult in the afternoon resumed the offensive. It was unexpected, and the allies were taken by surprise, but it led to nothing, though the losses were severe. It rained hard through the night, and neither side was eager for action. The day passed with some promiscuous skirmishing, and in the evening, as the upshot of the bloody sortie, Soult had withdrawn again to his entrenchments.

But the indefatigable Marshal had no idea of resting there. Resolved to try his fortunes against our right wing, where Wellington on the 9th had been with Hill in expectation, he passed a great body of his forces through Bayonne in the night. Hill was not unprepared, but nevertheless his position was critical. He defended a crescent line, four miles in length, between the Nive and the Adour, his centre resting at the village of St Pierre on the high road from St Jean Pied de Port. He had 14,000 men and fourteen guns, but for the time he was cut off from the rest of the army, for the Nive had risen with the rains and swept away the new bridge of communication.

Against his 14,000 men Soult was bringing three times the number, while another division under Paris, with Pierre Soult's cavalry, was threatening his rear. The odds were heavy; nevertheless, they were rather apparent than real. For the ground before him was swept by his guns; it was impracticable for horsemen; and even the infantry could only approach in single columns. The attack was as vigorous as the defence was resolute; the slight allied line swayed backwards and forwards under the stress of the onset: as our shot and shell tore through the assailing columns, fresh combatants pressed forward to replenish the ranks; once D'Armagnac's leading brigade had actually pushed forward to the rear of our defences; and twice the defence was gravely imperilled by two English colonels withdrawing their regiments. But there was no faltering in the courage of the rank and file, and these errors of judgment were promptly retrieved.

The Portuguese fought in the front with signal gallantry, and Hill, who exposed himself as freely as Hope had done on the 8th, directed the operations with consummate skill, strengthening each threatened point to the utmost of his feeble means. Nevertheless, it was a welcome relief when, the bridge being restored, Wellington appeared on his left, leading back the three divisions. But by that time the day was virtually won, and Hill had all the honour. That battle was one of the most sanguinary of the war; Wellington, as he rode over the scene of the contest, declared he had never seen a field more thickly strewn with dead, and it was said that the causeway before St Pierre was literally running with blood, as it was covered with corpses.

Those five days of fighting on the Nive were the logical consequence of the passage of the Nivelle. Wellington could not suffer himself to be confined between those rivers, and the next step in his progress must be the passage of the Adour. Soult took prompt measures to obstruct the further advance. It was a question now of the defence of France, and both generals were bound to contest the rich districts from which they could draw supplies. Soult, for the moment, might be comparatively easy. Leaving a sufficient force in the camp at Bayonne, which besides was overlooked by the citadel, he established his headquarters at Peyrehorade on the Gave de Pau; Clausel was on the Bidouze, a tributary of the Gave, communicating on his left with General Paris and St Jean Pied de Port. Sundry posts were thrown forward to villages far in advance, and Soult was now on a new line facing the allied right, and compelling Wellington to make corresponding dispositions.

Soult might be easy for the moment, for he was defending navigable rivers, but circumstances would change with a change of the seasons, when those rivers would shrink and the shallows be passable. Nor was it possible for Wellington to take immediate action. The country was impracticable as ever: Bayonne must be invested or reduced: and when men were wanting for indispensable work he had weakened his army by sending back the Spaniards. As he wrote Lord Bathurst, in the invasion he meant to conciliate the people and act with justice and moderation. He had pledged himself not to levy requisitions, and so the difficulties of supply were as great as ever.

There were differences with the admiral on the coast, for the wise measures as to navigation and the opening of St Jean de Luz to the ships of powers still in alliance with France interfered with naval prize money. A change of admirals settled these differences amicably, but the financial pressure was severe as before. Even the pay of the muleteers was long in arrear, and the commander-in-chief could not walk out of his lodgings without being beset by clamorous creditors. Moreover, when he had weakened himself by sending back the guerrilla bands, the veteran soldiers in his provisional battalions were being withdrawn for service elsewhere, notwithstanding his urgent protests.

Condemned thus to temporary inaction by circumstances he could not control, he had grave anxieties elsewhere. Soult had brought General Harispe, a member of an old Biscayan family, from Catalonia to the Basque Provinces, to call the peasants to arms for a partisan war. Morillo and Mina had aided his recruiting, by breaking back into the French valleys and committing savage atrocities. Harispe repulsed them, but Wellington in the meantime had arrested his farther progress by more peremptory orders to the Spanish chiefs, and by stern warnings to the Basques. He warned the peasants that they must either be regular soldiers or non-combatants; if they chose to wage irregular war out of uniform, they would be shot or hung and their villages burned. In fact, he acted as the French marshals had acted in Spain, or as the Germans when, on the invasion of France, they were harassed by swarms of *franctireurs* in civilian dress.

A more serious affair was an adroit move of Napoleon, by which he sought to obtain the friendship or neutrality of Spain, and so secure the withdrawal of his armies in the south for service on his northeastern frontier. He had extracted a treaty from the obsequious prisoner of Valançay, by which Ferdinand, on certain conditions, was to be sent back to his kingdom. The integrity of the Spanish Kingdom was recognised, and in consideration of the French evacuating Spain,

Ferdinand was to procure the embarkation of the British allies. The scheme, which had been incubating some considerable time, seemed plausible. For the friction between the Regents and the Cortes had risen to such a pitch that Wellington had not only suggested to the home Government the contingency of withdrawing our troops, but even the possible propriety of declaring war upon Spain.

However, when Ferdinand's confidential agent, the Duke of San Carlos, came to Madrid, he broached the proposals in an unfortunate hour for Napoleon. There was no counting on the instability of Spanish faction. After much secret discussion and intrigue, all parties came to a gratifying semblance of unanimity, and the decision of the Regency was patriotic and rational, though dictated, undoubtedly, by selfish considerations. The Cortes would recognise no deed of Ferdinand done under constraint, nor would they enter on any negotiations for peace while the invaders still garrisoned their fortresses. So Napoleon's scheme for recruiting his northern army failed; and when he made heavy drafts subsequently on Suchet and Soult, he seriously weakened them without materially strengthening himself During November nothing of importance had passed in Catalonia, although the intrigues connected with the abortive treaty of Valançay had done something to embarrass Clinton.

The chiefs of the Spanish auxiliaries were looking towards Madrid, and more inclined to wait upon events than to give him efficient assistance. One well-devised stroke had failed, because Copons at the critical moment had interfered with the arrangements between his lieutenant and the English general. It might have been treachery or simply caprice, but Clinton, making head against Suchet, with forces largely composed of irregulars, was constrained to be content to block the passes and remain generally on the defensive. The dominating fact was, that all the time the British on the west or east of the Peninsula were finding occupation for nearly 20,000 veterans who, had they been liberated, might have repelled the invasion in the north.

And when Wellington was preparing for a farther advance, the final evacuation of the Peninsula was imminent. Suchet had held to Catalonia with admirable tenacity, but he had been already weakened by the withdrawal of 10,000 men and many pieces of artillery. Still determined to make the best of things, he had proposed the dismantling of Barcelona, merely holding on to the citadel and Monjuich. That wise suggestion was rejected till too late. When it was accepted, the allies were blockading Barcelona. In the meantime, having appointed

Habert to command in Lower Catalonia, and entrusted the Lower Ebro to General Robert, the Governor of Tortosa, he had retired with the rest of his attenuated army to Gerona. While these measures were in progress, Clinton had planned an attack on Molino del Rey, which must have been delivered with damaging effect if Copons again had not failed to co-operate. But treachery accomplished what arms had failed to effect.

The victories in Germany and of Wellington in the west had made it clear that the French ascendancy was to be ended. Those Spaniards who had cast in their lot with the invaders began to tremble for the consequences. Among the most trusted members of Suchet's staff was a certain Van Halen, a Spaniard, but of Flemish descent. This man, whose courage and subtlety were equal to his treachery, conceived the idea of abusing the French Marshal's confidence, and betraying the garrisons to the south of the Llobregat. He placed himself in communication with Eroles and Copons. He forged despatches—he was even acquainted with the secret sign which intimated to Suchet's subordinates that the despatches were genuine—and passing southwards under a flag of truce, interviewed successively the governors of the garrisons. He professed to be the bearer of messages, averring that the Treaty of Valançay had been signed; that the fortresses were to be given over, and the garrisons to march into France.

Each detail that might infer plausibility or carry conviction was carefully worked out. He only failed with Robert at Tortosa, through an accident and the arrival of a genuine despatch. Unfortunately for the French, Robert was slow of action, and did not promptly arrest the traitor. For the garrisons of Lerida, Mequinenza and Monzon successively fell into the snare, though the two more important places were victualled and stored for two months' defence. Those strongholds were surrendered, the garrisons marched out, followed up by Eroles; they were surrounded in the rocky gorges through which the road runs from Lerida to Barcelona, and consented to lay down their arms on conditions which were shamefully violated. Clinton's forces had assisted in the seizure as an act of legitimate war against armed enemies in the field, but he had held aloof from all the previous intrigues, and had been no party to the agreement or its infraction.

After that the result was a foregone conclusion, and events followed an inevitable course. Suchet dismantled Gerona, with the minor Catalonian fortresses, and withdrew to Figueras. On the 19th March the liberated Ferdinand returned to his dominions, promising everything, with the intention of keeping no embarrassing pledges. He arrived in General Clinton's camp on the 30th March, and thence proceeded to Valencia. Suchet re-passed the Pyrenees at last, leaving a single division in Figueras. Clinton had orders to break up his army; but owing to various causes his departure was delayed till, in the middle of April, he embarked at Tarragona. The last combat in the bloody and protracted struggle was a sally of Habert from Barcelona while the troops were embarking.

Like a more important battle in southern France, it was a needless sacrifice when the war was over. But Habert was blameless, for the news of the general peace only arrived some days afterwards. By that peace, Barcelona, Tortosa, Figueras and four smaller places were handed back to the Spaniards. Had it not been for Van Halen's treachery, Suchet would have held to the last all that was best worth keeping in the north-eastern provinces, and it must be admitted that that skilful and resourceful Marshal, though discomfited, withdrew with the honours of war. The only fortress that still displayed the tricolour was the negligible Santona, on the coast of Biscay.

CHAPTER 24

Battle of Orthes and Submission of Bordeaux

FEBRUARY, MARCH 1814

Soult had been more seriously weakened than Suchet, though left to stem the tide of invasion. The Emperor had reluctantly withdrawn two infantry divisions and one of cavalry. With 14,000 men locked up in Bayonne, and deducting the defenders of St Jean Pied de Port, the Marshal could only muster some 40,000 veteran combatants. So much had circumstances altered that he suggested abandoning a regular system of defence, and waging such a *partida* war on the frontiers as the Spaniards had carried on against the French. Clausel and Harispe, natives of those parts, were the men best fitted to direct it. For himself, he desired to be relieved and transferred where his services would be more useful. His suggestions were not accepted, and he loyally set himself to repel, or at least obstruct, the allied advance on the Garonne.

During January, Wellington had been active in preparation, and his position had sensibly improved. Reinforcements had reached him, the military chest had been replenished, and he had been forming *depôts* in the towns on the coast. Again he could venture to employ and terrorise the insubordinate Spaniards, as he could assure them pay and rations. French Royalists from the southern provinces had been coming into his camp, and finally the Duc d'Angoulême had arrived there. Though he could not altogether credit their sanguine assurances, nor would he commit himself to a rash descent on Bordeaux, yet he might entertain good hopes of substantial aid from Bourbon partisans. It was clear that the commercial classes were wearied of the war, and eager to welcome deliverance in any shape. The traders of Bayonne entered into underhand dealings with him, even undertaking to cash his bills; and when Soult commenced covering works at Bordeaux, he met with passive resistance from the wealthy citizens. It had been Wellington's policy to encourage commerce on the coast, and he would have been even more successful had he not been crossed by his Government. As it was, supplies were flowing in, and the small French traders were facilitating his operations.

In numbers, and notably in veterans, he was far superior to Soult. He had 70,000 good Anglo-Portuguese, and there were 30,000 Spaniards. But the blockade of Bayonne involved a deduction of nearly three times the strength of the garrison; for, situated as it was, astride on the rivers, he must be prepared to repel a sortie in force from any one of three sides. He decided not to pass the Upper Adour, where the French Marshal had his headquarters at Peyrehorade, but to cross the river with his left wing below Bayonne, and simultaneously to press Soult back by steadily turning his left, operating on the slopes of the Pyrenees and among the upper waters of the Gaves. The second operation was sure, if slow. As to the former, it must seem to the enemy so difficult, if not altogether impracticable, that he felt good assurance of effecting it successfully, remembering the passages of the Douro and Bidassoa.

By the middle of February the snows had almost gone from the lower ranges of the mountains. On the 14th Hill set his divisions in motion, passed the Joyeuse, surprised Harispe and drove him back. Then Harispe established himself on the heights of La Montagne, where he was strengthened from the centre, and by General Paris recalled from his march towards the north. The same day Mina began the blockade of St Jean Pied de Port, and Sir William Stewart, with the 2nd Division, supported by Morillo after some sharp fighting arrived on the Bidouze. There was a corresponding movement from the right of the centre. Next day the bridges that had been broken were repaired. Hill crossed the Bidouze and forced Harispe beyond the Gave de Mauleon. There no time was given him to destroy the bridges; the stream was forded besides, and in the night he withdrew again behind the Gave d'Oleron.

Harispe was again reinforced, and took up an exceedingly strong position on the heights of Sauveterre. But when Soult heard of the succession of repulses over ranges and rivers that were eminently defensible, he sent orders that Sauveterre was also to be abandoned.

Destroying all the bridges on the Adour, he left Bayonne to its own resources, and retiring behind the Gave de Pau, removed his headquarters to Orthes.

These operations had effectually diverted the Marshal's personal attention from Bayonne, and the guard of the lower river was left to the garrison. A *corvette* was moored below the town, and the river was regularly patrolled by gunboats. The natural difficulties of crossing were so great that the generals in Bayonne might well be careless. At the spot selected for Wellington's bridge, the Adour was 270 yards in width; the rush of the ebbing tide was at the rate of seven miles an hour. The use of ordinary pontoons was impossible, and it was not easy for ships fit for the purpose to be brought up from the sea. The river mouth, six miles below the town, is blocked by a labyrinth of shifting sand-bars, over which the tides and surf break with extreme violence On the other hand, here, as at the Douro, the allies were favoured by the winding of the river. For the scene of operations was masked from the town, partly by a bend of the Adour, and partly by the famous wood of pines, which comes down to the water on the southern bank.

At midnight on the 22nd Hope set the troops in motion. Diverging from the road at Anglet, they stole silently past the front of the hostile entrenchments, and although delayed by a gun falling into a ditch, at daylight they were among the sandhills at the mouth of the river. Then the guns were mounted in a battery on the bank, the pickets on the right of the entrenched camp were driven in, and meanwhile, as concerted, demonstrations from Anglet and at Urdains diverted the attention of the garrison. Never dreaming of the danger which threatened him, General Thouvenot had neglected to guard in any force the right bank of the river.

It had been arranged that the British gunboats at the river mouth, with the *chasse-marées* which were to form the bridge, were to pass the bar simultaneously with the appearance of the troops. The wind being adverse they were unable to approach it. Yet Hope determined to persevere with the crossing. His guns opened on the French gunboats with destructive effect, and the rocket-batteries, then a novel invention, not only did deadly execution, but spread panic among the French seamen. Meanwhile a party of the Guards had crossed in a pontoon, carrying a hawser with them. The remaining pontoons were coupled, formed into rafts and hauled across; but the process was slow, and when barely 600 of the Guards, with one of the rocket batteries, had been landed, the rush of the tide stopped operations. News of the landing had reached the citadel, and two regiments were sent to attack. But there was a heavy flanking fire from the left bank; the rockets were as demoralising to the soldiers as to the sailors, and they beat a precipitate retreat.

The passage went forward slowly but steadily. On the morning of the 24th the sails of the flotilla were seen. The wind had changed, and become more than favourable, for it was blowing half a gale from the bay, and the surf was breaking wildly upon the bars. The first attempt was made towards the ebb, and failed, with some lamentable casualties. When the water was deepening again the weather had become worse—nevertheless the squadron dashed gallantly at the breakers, led by the boats of the British men-of-war. Pilotage there was next to none at first, for the experts were all abroad as to the surroundings. There were many accidents, and not a few valuable lives were lost, but when the navigable channel was struck at last, one by one the *chasse-marées* were brought into calm water at the point where they were to be formed into a bridge. Moored stem to stern with anchors and old guns, they were further secured by three cables stretched across as a foundation for the elastic planking which would yield to the rush of the stream and yet be strong enough to bear up the cannon. This marvellous work of rough-and-ready engineering was secured from fire-craft by a boom above, and the boom again was guarded by the gunboats.

Having assembled 6000 men on the right bank on the 25th, Hope moved on to complete the investment. After some lively skirmishing, with considerable loss on both sides, he established himself *à cheval* on the ridge of St Etienne, running at right angles to the northern works of the fortress. Thus the investment was completed, though there were no slight difficulties in signalling and maintaining communications between three distinct investing corps divided by navigable rivers.

At Orthes Soult was to make his last stand in stemming the invasion setting directly northward. There he held the last of the strong natural positions on the parallel ridges of the mountain streams. Above, his fortified posts on the Gaves had been successively turned nearer to the sources. Below, the Adour had been bridged and Bayonne was invested. Now the course of Wellington's operations was bringing his severed wings again into communication. Hope was to establish a permanent bridge at the Port of Landes. But the great length of the allied front had compelled the commander-in-chief to bring up Freyre and his Gallicians. This he had done with no little reluctance, for his apprehension was that the vindictive licence of the Spanish levies would excite a peasant rising or *Jacquerie* in his rear, and he had written to Freyre, 'Maintain the strictest discipline; without that we are lost.'

Hitherto, and afterwards, thanks to his stern discipline and liberal payments for all supplies, the sympathies of the population had been for the most part with the invaders. The allies paid in ready money for everything. Soult, as he lost his magazines one after the other, was compelled to enforce requisitions, and his military chest was empty. Moreover, demoralisation had been making rapid progress in his ranks, and many of the fugitives who had straggled after his various defeats were sheltered by the peasants and failed to rejoin their colours. Yet he had still 35,000 veterans, besides the conscripts, with him at Orthes, and though their *moral* had suffered, and with the mortifications of constant retreat they had lost much of their old dash and self- confidence, they had seldom fought more stubbornly than in the battle which takes its name from the town. Soult faced the Gave from heights commanding the bridge of Orthes and fronting the road from Peyrehorade towards the west.

That bridge, solid as the grand structures on the Tagus, had been blocked with mason work, but its strength had resisted the efforts of the engineers to blow it up. All the other bridges were in ruins, and the fords above the town, doubtful and indifferent at best, were strictly guarded. The Marshal had drawn in his detachments. Beresford crossed at Peyrehorade, which Foy had abandoned; the 6th and Light Divisions passed at Berenx, where a pontoon bridge had been thrown over in the night of the 26th, and Picton with the 3rd Division yet higher up. Hill was to menace the bridge of Orthes, and, if practicable, force the fords on the Upper Gave, cutting the enemy off from the road to Pau. Soult had arranged his main battle on the ridge facing Beresford and Picton. The position seemed protected from a front attack by the nature of the flanking ridges of the swamps and marshes in the bottoms of the gorges. From a conical hill in the centre, crowned with heavy batteries, Soult could observe all the hostile operations, save where they were masked by a corresponding eminence within the allied lines, which was the look-out station of Wellington.

The front being unassailable, Beresford was to turn the French right, where his success would cut the French off from Bordeaux, as Hill was to intercept their retreat to Pau, where the combination would throw them back on the barren Landes. But Beresford met

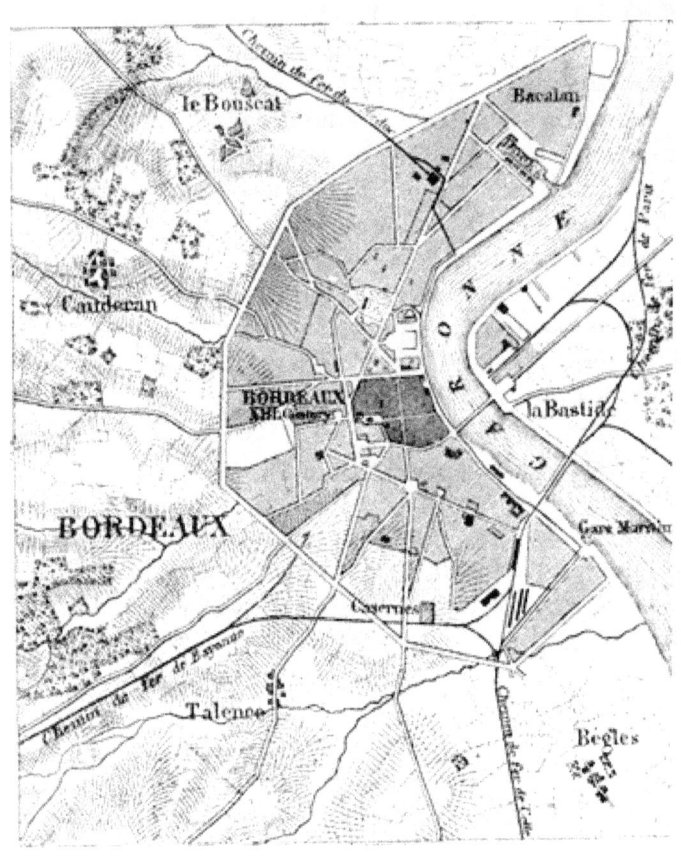

with unexpected difficulties. He took the village of St Bois on the extreme right of the enemy, and so far made his ground good. But the only issue was through a narrow pass, and whenever he attempted to emerge or deploy, the head of the column was crushed by a converging cannonade, and hurled back in confusion by furious bayonet charges. For three hours the fighting went on; Picton on the other flank had done no better, and it was clear that the attack had failed, as it seemed likely the battle would be lost.

Then Wellington, with one of his flashes of inspiration, changed his tactics. Abandoning the attempt to turn the enemy's right, he ordered up three divisions to assail the hill between their right and centre, on Foy's left flank. The 52nd Regiment, which had been held in reserve behind the look-out hill, was ordered to cross the marsh below, ascend the ridge beyond, and take in rear the French who were holding the mouth of the gorge at St Bois. The stroke proved decisive. The 52nd, knee-deep or waist-deep in mud, struggled through the swamp which had been deemed impassable under a galling fire, and charging the assailants of St Bois, threw them into confusion, while batteries brought forward on the advancing spurs sent shot and shell through the disordered masses. Wellington seized the opportunity to pass Beresford's battalions through the disputed gap and form them beyond in fresh order of battle. Picton pushed forward with the 3rd and 7th Divisions, and the wings of the army were united. Meanwhile Hill had forded the river and was confronting Clausel.

But Soult, seeing that his centre was forced and his wings were turned, gave orders for a retreat. He directed it, as usual, in masterly fashion, for one of the Marshal's chief merits was that he never lost coolness or firmness in misfortune. But the country behind him was broken, it was traversed by several unbridged torrents, and necessarily the disorder soon became great On the left Hill kept the fugitives literally on the run, and the result, in place of being merely discomfiture, might have been annihilation, had not Wellington received a contusion which prevented his pressing the pursuit. As it was, the French losses in killed and wounded were very considerable; many prisoners were taken, and the conscripts, for the most part throwing away their arms, scattered beyond recovery. One result was that Soult lost his remaining magazines. The seizure of Mont Marsan followed the occupation of Orthes, and Aire was taken by Hill after another sanguinary combat.

Heavy rain continued to fall after these battles. The rivers were still flooded; the bridges were to be repaired, and everything conspired to delay operations. Soult, forced against his will in the direction of Bordeaux by Hill's corps, had time to deliberate. He was naturally inclined to turn towards the east, where he might hope for succours from Suchet, although, whether from jealousy or otherwise, he was but indifferently seconded by his brother Marshal. Consequently he decided to cling to the spurs of the Pyrenees, although he left Bordeaux with its disaffected citizens open to the allies, and ascending the valley of the Adour he took the road to Tarbes and Toulouse.

Meanwhile the allies took possession of Pau, establishing their hospitals in the picturesque old capital of Beam. A more important acquisition was that of Bordeaux. After the battle of Orthes, the city sent a deputation and invitation to Wellington at St Jean de Luz. The partisans of the Bourbons were in the ascendant; the Duc d'Angoulême was escorted thither by Marshal Beresford; the mayor divested himself of the tricolour scarf, mounted the white cockade, and handed over the keys; the Imperial Governor, General L'Huillier, withdrew with his insufficient garrison, and when the fortress of Blaye in the Gironde surrendered, the great southern port was reopened to British commerce. The royalists of Bordeaux had taken a bold resolution, to which Wellington had at last consented with reluctance, for Napoleon was still negotiating with the allied sovereigns, and it was far from certain that he would be compelled to abdicate.

CHAPTER 25

The Battle of Toulouse, and Close of the War

MARCH, APRIL 1814

Soult had a double motive for moving eastwards along the Pyrenees. He hoped to join hands with Suchet, and, ignorant of Beresford's advance on Bordeaux, he desired to draw the allies after him and to prevent the apprehended revolt in favour of the Bourbons from spreading towards the north. But though undaunted by his defeats he resumed the offensive, he believed Wellington to be stronger than he really was, imagining that Beresford was still with him. The English general, on his side, was also in doubt, suspecting that Soult might have been reinforced from Catalonia. In reality the armies were then nearly numerically equal, though Wellington had reluctantly called up more Spaniards, besides sending for his heavy cavalry, who had hitherto been quartered in Spain. Soult, having sent back most of his baggage to Toulouse, made demonstrations against the right flank of the allies. Wellington ordered two divisions to the support of Hill, and made Aire for the moment the pivot of his operations. Soult, having felt the forces in front of him, and misdoubting the capabilities of his own positions, withdrew on the night of the 14th March to Lambege, and after a temporary halt on the following day, retired upon Vic Bigorre.

On the 17th Wellington had drawn in his detachments and been joined by the heavy horse and the artillery from Spain. Next day his army moved on in three columns, the right by Conchez, the centre by Castelnau, the left by Plaisance. The French retreated again, leaving a rearguard among the hills and vines in front of Vic. Thence they were driven by Picton with his 3rd Division, and before morning the enemy's rear had closed up on the main body at Tarbes. There, on the heights behind the town, they were found in order of battle on the morning of the 20th. Soult was determined to dispute the allied advance, although he had already decided to rest upon Toulouse, and was covering the southern road leading thither by St Gaudens. The allies lost no time in attacking, nor did they meet with very serious resistance, although they fought at a certain disadvantage, as their corps were separated by the Adour.

Clinton, with Wellington, turned the French flank on the left. Alten, with the light division, mastered the rising ground in the centre, while Hill, on the other bank of the river, attacked the town by the high road, forced his way down the main street, and charged victoriously up the hill beyond. But when his soldiers topped the crest, they saw the troops that had fled before them quietly ascending a parallel range, which was held by formidable reserves in heavy masses. Picton halted, for there was no attempting that position till the column coming from Rabastens had made a corresponding advance. But the night came down while operations were in suspense, and long ere morning Soult had resumed the retreat.

He reached Toulouse on the 24th, and, thanks to a renewal of the rains which impeded the pursuit, he had gained three days upon his pursuer. He turned the advantage to the best account in strengthening works which were already strong. Toulouse had been selected as the chief southern arsenal, partly from its strategical position on the Upper Garonne, at the centre of several radiating roads, and partly from its great natural advantages. The city was encircled by massive walls on which the heaviest guns could be mounted; it was girdled on the west by the rapid Garonne, while on the north and east a broad moat was formed by the canal of Languedoc. The remaining side was scarcely more vulnerable, for beyond the suburbs defended by outworks were fortified hills flanking the approaches to the canal, and marshes which were often overflowed by the Ers River.

On March 27th the allies were on the left of the Garonne, opposite the city. Next day an unsuccessful attempt was made to throw a pontoon bridge across above the town and below the junction of the Arriége. The object was either to induce Soult to evacuate the place, or at least to cut him off from communication with Suchet. An attempt made elsewhere some days afterwards was unsuccessful. Hill had actually crossed when it was found that the roads were in such wretched condition that attack from that side was impracticable. Consequently the corps was brought back, and Wellington turned his attention to bridging the river below the town. The pontoons were laid down on the 31st, and no serious effort was made to obstruct the passage. The great danger was from the swiftness of the swollen current, and after Beresford had passed with three divisions, the pontoons were temporarily removed. Soult might have been tempted to attack when the army was divided; but he had resolved to remain on the defensive in the city, and he set soldiers and citizens to work on entrenchments between the canal and the Ers, in preparation for the assault he expected on his front.

The news he received on the 7th of the entry of the allied sovereigns into Paris made no change in his purpose. Sending his cavalry out to observe the enemy, he continued busily engaged on his defences. It was not till the 8th that the waters subsided sufficiently to admit of the pontoons being replaced, when Freyre's Gallicians and the Portuguese artillery passed over. They were accompanied by Wellington in person, who carefully examined the situation from a height five miles from Toulouse. His columns were still separated by the Ers; there were no pontoons to bridge it, and it became an object to seize on the bridge near the city. That was dashingly accomplished by Colonel Vivian with his hussars; at the same time orders were given for moving the pontoons over the Garonne to a point higher up, in order to facilitate communications, and the great attack was to come off on the morrow, Easter Sunday, 10th April. For seventeen days Soult had been preparing.

His positions encircled three sides of the city, while on the south his left was entrenched in the suburb of St Cyprien, whence supports could be sent when needed—as they subsequently were—across the great bridge connecting the suburb with the town. The south, otherwise the weakest point, was found to be effectually defended by the marshes as it was covered by the Ers. The attack was therefore delivered on the north and east, although there the fortified positions were strongest. As for the north, it was virtually impregnable, for the canal, with its embattled and retrenched bridges, was within musket-shot of the ramparts. The east front was a ridge, two miles in length, covered by the unfordable and bridgeless Ers, with *plateaux* to right and left, named respectively the Calvinet and St Sypiére. The French right rested on the latter, and between them two roads led into the suburbs, both crossing the canal.

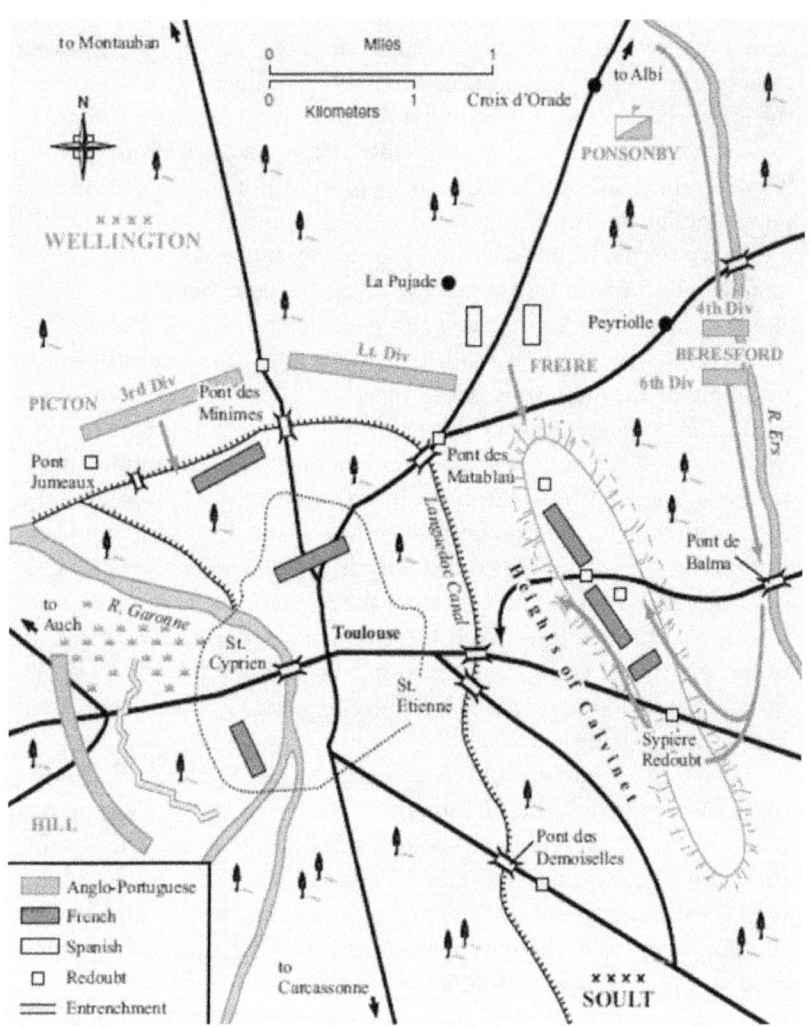

BATTLE OF TOULOUSE, APRIL 10TH, 1814

The battle began unfortunately. The Spaniards, assailing the Calvinet, were repulsed with loss; a second attempt ended in a regular rout, and disaster was only averted by Wellington hurrying up with Ponsonby's dragoons and some reserve artillery. Further to the right, Picton had been directed to make a feigned attack on the bridge of Jumeaux, at the junction of two canals. He forced the bridge, and with reckless disregard of orders, assailed under a withering fire works that could only be carried by escalade. The division lost 400 men, and thus the attacks from Calvinet to the river had only resulted in sanguinary failure. It seemed that the battle was lost, and Soult had a great opportunity had he promptly assumed the offensive. His successes, and the strength of his entrenchments at St Cyprien, enabled him to withdraw the whole of Taupin's division, besides another brigade, to reinforce his battle on the Mont Rave, where Beresford was attacking to the east.

That general had been executing a flank movement over swampy ground and under heavy fire. He was compelled, for the time, to leave his guns behind, yet the French refused the opportunities he inevitably offered. He advanced between the Ers and the fortified heights bristling with batteries till without a single gun he gained his objective, and was forming his men beneath the positions he was to storm. When scarcely yet in formation, he was charged downhill by the French, but they were checked and appalled by an unexpected discharge from a rocket battery. Two British brigades took advantage of the panic, gained the crowning *plateau*, carried the redoubts with the bayonet, and General Taupin fell at the front while attempting to rally his men.

Then came a brief pause. Soult was calling up his reserves, and Beresford bringing up his artillery. At two in the afternoon, Pack and Douglas, with the Portuguese and Highland brigades, rushed from the hollows in which they had been concealed, and carried the French defences all along the line from the Colombette redoubt to the Calvinet. Strengthened by reserves, and backed up by tremendous artillery fire, the French returned to the assault, and one redoubt was regained, but the remains of the Highlanders made good the hill till relieved by the advance of the 6th Division, when the French finally withdrew. Beresford had at last got up his guns and was marching along the ridge that had been mastered. Picton was again threatening the bridge of Jumeaux; the Spaniards, having re-formed, were making a fair show of offence, with the light division ready to support them.

Then Soult, declining further contest, fell back, abandoning the heights of Mont Rave with the works beyond the canal. He still retained two fortified advanced posts, but in the dead of night he evacuated the city, defiling within range of the allied guns, but suffering scarcely any further loss. Next day Lord Wellington entered Toulouse, amid general rejoicings and acclamations. Not a few of the citizens were partisans of the Bourbons. Most were weary of the war, and all, without exception, congratulated themselves on having escaped the horrors of siege or storm. That same evening came the envoys from Paris announcing the abdication of the Emperor. Their journey had been delayed by treachery or blundering, and the battle that had cost so many gallant lives had been fought when there was peace between the nations.

Unfortunately the battle of Toulouse was not the last of the bloodshed. Notwithstanding assertions to the contrary, it has been demonstrated conclusively that Soult fought in ignorance of the abdication. No such excuse can be made for Thouvenot's idle sally from Bayonne. Technically, and in strict formalism, it might be justified; in reality he knew more than enough to have made him hold his hand. The emissaries from Paris, passing through Bordeaux on their way to Toulouse, had sent intelligence of the peace to Hope before Bayonne. It was unfortunate that Hope, standing too rigidly on military etiquette, did not send formal notice to the French governor, without awaiting instructions from the commander-in-chief. But he caused the news to be transmitted to the enemy's advanced pickets, in the expectation that further operations would be suspended.

Thouvenot either discredited, or professed to discredit it; it may be suspected that he hoped to find the besiegers off their guard—as he actually did—though it is more charitable to assume that he set it down for a *ruse* of war. In any case, very early on the morning of the 14th April, two deserters came from the town to the British lines on the north. They announced that the garrison were getting under arms, and preparing for a sortie in great force. Some time was lost in finding an interpreter, and then General Hay, who was in command of the outposts, would seem to have disbelieved the men, for he took no additional precautions. Happily General Hinuber, commanding the Germans and the reserves of the Guards, took the matter more seriously, and got all his troops under arms.

At three o'clock the French, with feints and alarms, disturbed the lines on the left of the Adour and the south of the city; and almost simultaneously there came an eruption from the citadel, sweeping away the chains of posts on the hillsides, and surging into the village of St Etienne, on the Bordeaux road. For a time the surprise carried all before it; but two circumstances restored the battle. The first was the determination of Forster of the 38th, who held doggedly to a fortified house in the village; the second, the readiness of General Hinuber, who promptly advanced, rallied the broken parties of the 5th Division, and recovered the village.

The line of the allies had been pierced at the centre, but to the right the action had gone even worse for them. There they were posted to exceptional disadvantage, for the pickets and advanced guards were separated from their main body by a road running parallel to the line of supports. In places it was time-worn into a deep hollow way, in others it was shut in by high garden walls. Beyond and on the city side was an enclosed labyrinth of gardens, paddocks and vineyards. These were fiercely disputed hand-to-hand, though the besiegers were being steadily forced back by overwhelming superiority in numbers. The darkness was intense; as the supports came up, they were guided to the several scenes of action by the flashes from the muskets, and meantime the citadel from seventy cannon was directing undiscriminating fire on those fitful flashes.

The shells and fire-bombs set houses and the fascine stores on fire, and the French gunboats, dropping down the stream, opened on the exposed flanks of the allies. And the misfortunes of the night were not at an end, for a crowning mishap was in store for the unfortunate general. It was a striking illustration of the chances, and what may be called the 'flukes,' of war. Hope had hurried forward to the front. Knowing the ground, but groping in the darkness, he had plunged into the hollow way, in ignorance that it was held by the French. A man of gigantic stature, he was heavily mounted. A discharge swept the road; horse and man went down; the horse was killed, and Hope, shot through the arm, was pinned by his leg under the fallen animal. His *aide-de-camp*, a nephew of Sir John Moore, and Captain Herries were in close attendance, and made gallant efforts to extricate their chief. A second volley laid both prostrate, and all three were carried prisoners into Bayonne. But with the breaking of day the allies could see each other and rally, to roll back their assailants with irresistible vigour. These left behind them nearly 1000 men, and the loss of the besiegers was little less. A few days afterwards hostilities had ceased with the arrival of a regular intimation of the convention.

Colonels Cooke and St Simon had reached Toulouse the very day of Wellington's entry. The envoys hurried on to Soult's camp and informed the Marshal of the abdication of his master and the end of the war. It is certain that Soult must have believed their report, but in natural mortification he was in no mood to acquiesce, and he was loath to accept the inevitable by precipitately laying down his arms. Besides, he was still snatching at a last chance, for he had no recent intelligence from Suchet. Accordingly he dallied by making overtures for an armistice, which Wellington rejected on incontrovertible grounds; though, understanding and sympathising with the feelings of the Marshal, he left him time for further reflection. So far as Suchet was concerned, Soult's hopes and doubts were soon set at rest. Colonel St Simon found Suchet at Narbonne and in a reasonable frame of mind. To the last he had fought manfully against untoward circumstances, but his military strength was broken.

The wrecks of the armies of Aragon and Catalonia—all the men he had been able to bring out of Spain—barely numbered 12,000. The rest were locked up in half-a-dozen fortresses, doomed to speedy capitulation. He was disappointed, besides, by the news from Toulouse, for Soult had confidently assured him that he could maintain himself in that city. Suchet called a council of his superior officers, and it was decided without a dissentient voice, to send in their adhesion to the new *régime*. The decision necessarily reacted on Soult. The dies were cast and the war was over. Already the allies were closing in upon him with gentle but irresistible pressure. Reluctantly he laid down his arms, recognising the Provisional Government, and on the 19th April the convention for the suspension of hostilities brought the Peninsular campaigns to a close. He had the consolation of knowing that it was a surrender with honour, and that he had been vanquished gloriously. He had protracted a determined struggle through nine most anxious months, disputing each inch of ground, inspiriting his soldiers under a succession of defeats and retreats exceptionally trying to the fiery French temperament.

They fought as fiercely under the walls of Toulouse as in the passes of Navarre or on the banks of the Bidassoa, and that is the best tribute to the qualities of their general. And they had good reason for their faith. Through all the reverses his constancy never failed, his able combinations changed quickly with the unexpected, and his sagacious brain was never at fault. Driven back upon the defensive, and standing resolutely at bay, his foresight had taken all possible precautions, nor as the tide of invasion flowed forward did he for a moment relax his efforts. He had forced labour to assist science in strengthening the natural defences; he had anticipated that use of spade and pickaxe which was carried beyond perfection in the American Civil War, and with his entrenched camps and skilful combinations had almost equalised the odds which were greatly against him.

All that is incontrovertibly true, and all is the glorification of the genius of Wellington. Soult was great in defeat, but, after all, his is a record of failures. The last long act of the sanguinary drama, in which Wellington pushed him back from Pamplona to Toulouse, was only the triumphant finale of an unbroken series of successes. From the day when he landed in Portugal with his 9000 men, leading almost a forlorn hope against the 24,000 of Junot, he was often forced to fall back, but he never faltered. *Tant bien que mal* we have sketched the story of his difficulties and his triumphs, and to recapitulate would be only vain repetition. But, as Napier sums it up, he inspired or personally directed the operations which won nineteen pitched battles, besides innumerable combats, made or sustained ten sieges, took four great fortresses, twice expelled the French from Portugal, and preserved al the Spanish strong places in the south.

When the war began, Napoleon had well-nigh succeeded in reducing Europe to the condition of the Roman Empire under the Caesars, as De Quincey has described it—a prison-house guarded by the legions, where no one could escape the autocrat's resentment or elude his tyrannical caprices. Vaulting ambition overleaped itself. He failed in attaining the summit of his aspirations, thanks to the snows of Russia, the sierras of Spain—above all, to the persistent resistance of Britain, as free-handed with her subsidies as she was lavish of her blood. But it was Wellington, with his unbroken career of victory, who animated the martial spirit of the nation, whose patient tenacity, never risking a catastrophe which must have discredited him, held timid Cabinets to a consistent purpose, and who, as much a man of destiny as Napoleon, is the immortal hero of the emancipation of the Peninsula.

ALSO FROM LEONAUR
AVAILABLE IN SOFTCOVER OR HARDCOVER WITH DUST JACKET

THE FALL OF THE MOGHUL EMPIRE OF HINDUSTAN by H. G. Keene—By the beginning of the nineteenth century, as British and Indian armies under Lake and Wellesley dominated the scene, a little over half a century of conflict brought the Moghul Empire to its knees.

LADY SALE'S AFGHANISTAN by Florentia Sale—An Indomitable Victorian Lady's Account of the Retreat from Kabul During the First Afghan War.

THE CAMPAIGN OF MAGENTA AND SOLFERINO 1859 by Harold Carmichael Wylly—The Decisive Conflict for the Unification of Italy.

FRENCH'S CAVALRY CAMPAIGN by J. G. Maydon—A Special Correspondent's View of British Army Mounted Troops During the Boer War.

CAVALRY AT WATERLOO by Sir Evelyn Wood—British Mounted Troops During the Campaign of 1815.

THE SUBALTERN by George Robert Gleig—The Experiences of an Officer of the 85th Light Infantry During the Peninsular War.

NAPOLEON AT BAY, 1814 by F. Loraine Petre—The Campaigns to the Fall of the First Empire.

NAPOLEON AND THE CAMPAIGN OF 1806 by Colonel Vachée—The Napoleonic Method of Organisation and Command to the Battles of Jena & Auerstädt.

THE COMPLETE ADVENTURES IN THE CONNAUGHT RANGERS by William Grattan—The 88th Regiment during the Napoleonic Wars by a Serving Officer.

BUGLER AND OFFICER OF THE RIFLES by William Green & Harry Smith—With the 95th (Rifles) during the Peninsular & Waterloo Campaigns of the Napoleonic Wars.

NAPOLEONIC WAR STORIES by Sir Arthur Quiller-Couch—Tales of soldiers, spies, battles & sieges from the Peninsular & Waterloo campaigns.

CAPTAIN OF THE 95TH (RIFLES) by Jonathan Leach—An officer of Wellington's sharpshooters during the Peninsular, South of France and Waterloo campaigns of the Napoleonic wars.

RIFLEMAN COSTELLO by Edward Costello—The adventures of a soldier of the 95th (Rifles) in the Peninsular & Waterloo Campaigns of the Napoleonic wars.

AVAILABLE ONLINE AT **www.leonaur.com**
AND FROM ALL GOOD BOOK STORES

ALSO FROM LEONAUR
AVAILABLE IN SOFTCOVER OR HARDCOVER WITH DUST JACKET

ZULU:1879 *by D.C.F. Moodie & the Leonaur Editors*—The Anglo-Zulu War of 1879 from contemporary sources: First Hand Accounts, Interviews, Dispatches, Official Documents & Newspaper Reports.

THE RED DRAGOON *by W.J. Adams*—With the 7th Dragoon Guards in the Cape of Good Hope against the Boers & the Kaffir tribes during the 'war of the axe' 1843-48'.

THE RECOLLECTIONS OF SKINNER OF SKINNER'S HORSE *by James Skinner*—James Skinner and his 'Yellow Boys' Irregular cavalry in the wars of India between the British, Mahratta, Rajput, Mogul, Sikh & Pindarree Forces.

A CAVALRY OFFICER DURING THE SEPOY REVOLT *by A. R. D. Mackenzie*—Experiences with the 3rd Bengal Light Cavalry, the Guides and Sikh Irregular Cavalry from the outbreak to Delhi and Lucknow.

A NORFOLK SOLDIER IN THE FIRST SIKH WAR *by J W Baldwin*—Experiences of a private of H.M. 9th Regiment of Foot in the battles for the Punjab, India 1845-6.

TOMMY ATKINS' WAR STORIES: 14 FIRST HAND ACCOUNTS—Fourteen first hand accounts from the ranks of the British Army during Queen Victoria's Empire.

THE WATERLOO LETTERS *by H. T. Siborne*—Accounts of the Battle by British Officers for its Foremost Historian.

NEY: GENERAL OF CAVALRY VOLUME 1—1769-1799 *by Antoine Bulos*—The Early Career of a Marshal of the First Empire.

NEY: MARSHAL OF FRANCE VOLUME 2—1799-1805 *by Antoine Bulos*—The Early Career of a Marshal of the First Empire.

AIDE-DE-CAMP TO NAPOLEON *by Philippe-Paul de Ségur*—For anyone interested in the Napoleonic Wars this book, written by one who was intimate with the strategies and machinations of the Emperor, will be essential reading.

TWILIGHT OF EMPIRE *by Sir Thomas Ussher & Sir George Cockburn*—Two accounts of Napoleon's Journeys in Exile to Elba and St. Helena: Narrative of Events by Sir Thomas Ussher & Napoleon's Last Voyage: Extract of a diary by Sir George Cockburn.

PRIVATE WHEELER *by William Wheeler*—The letters of a soldier of the 51st Light Infantry during the Peninsular War & at Waterloo.

AVAILABLE ONLINE AT **www.leonaur.com**
AND FROM ALL GOOD BOOK STORES

ALSO FROM LEONAUR
AVAILABLE IN SOFTCOVER OR HARDCOVER WITH DUST JACKET

OFFICERS & GENTLEMEN *by Peter Hawker & William Graham*—Two Accounts of British Officers During the Peninsula War: Officer of Light Dragoons by Peter Hawker & Campaign in Portugal and Spain by William Graham.

THE WALCHEREN EXPEDITION *by Anonymous*—The Experiences of a British Officer of the 81st Regt. During the Campaign in the Low Countries of 1809.

LADIES OF WATERLOO *by Charlotte A. Eaton, Magdalene de Lancey & Juana Smith*—The Experiences of Three Women During the Campaign of 1815: Waterloo Days by Charlotte A. Eaton, A Week at Waterloo by Magdalene de Lancey & Juana's Story by Juana Smith.

JOURNAL OF AN OFFICER IN THE KING'S GERMAN LEGION *by John Frederick Hering*—Recollections of Campaigning During the Napoleonic Wars.

JOURNAL OF AN ARMY SURGEON IN THE PENINSULAR WAR *by Charles Boutflower*—The Recollections of a British Army Medical Man on Campaign During the Napoleonic Wars.

ON CAMPAIGN WITH MOORE AND WELLINGTON *by Anthony Hamilton*—The Experiences of a Soldier of the 43rd Regiment During the Peninsular War.

THE ROAD TO AUSTERLITZ *by R. G. Burton*—Napoleon's Campaign of 1805.

SOLDIERS OF NAPOLEON *by A. J. Doisy De Villargennes & Arthur Chuquet*—The Experiences of the Men of the French First Empire: Under the Eagles by A. J. Doisy De Villargennes & Voices of 1812 by Arthur Chuquet.

INVASION OF FRANCE, 1814 *by F. W. O. Maycock*—The Final Battles of the Napoleonic First Empire.

LEIPZIG—A CONFLICT OF TITANS *by Frederic Shoberl*—A Personal Experience of the 'Battle of the Nations' During the Napoleonic Wars, October 14th-19th, 1813.

SLASHERS *by Charles Cadell*—The Campaigns of the 28th Regiment of Foot During the Napoleonic Wars by a Serving Officer.

BATTLE IMPERIAL *by Charles William Vane*—The Campaigns in Germany & France for the Defeat of Napoleon 1813-1814.

SWIFT & BOLD *by Gibbes Rigaud*—The 60th Rifles During the Peninsula War.

AVAILABLE ONLINE AT **www.leonaur.com**
AND FROM ALL GOOD BOOK STORES

ALSO FROM LEONAUR
AVAILABLE IN SOFTCOVER OR HARDCOVER WITH DUST JACKET

ADVENTURES OF A YOUNG RIFLEMAN *by Johann Christian Maempel*—The Experiences of a Saxon in the French & British Armies During the Napoleonic Wars.

THE HUSSAR *by Norbert Landsheit & G. R. Gleig*—A German Cavalryman in British Service Throughout the Napoleonic Wars.

RECOLLECTIONS OF THE PENINSULA *by Moyle Sherer*—An Officer of the 34th Regiment of Foot—'The Cumberland Gentlemen'—on Campaign Against Napoleon's French Army in Spain.

MARINE OF REVOLUTION & CONSULATE *by Moreau de Jonnès*—The Recollections of a French Soldier of the Revolutionary Wars 1791-1804.

GENTLEMEN IN RED *by John Dobbs & Robert Knowles*—Two Accounts of British Infantry Officers During the Peninsular War Recollections of an Old 52nd Man by John Dobbs An Officer of Fusiliers by Robert Knowles.

CORPORAL BROWN'S CAMPAIGNS IN THE LOW COUNTRIES *by Robert Brown*—Recollections of a Coldstream Guard in the Early Campaigns Against Revolutionary France 1793-1795.

THE 7TH (QUEENS OWN) HUSSARS: Volume 2—1793-1815 *by C. R. B. Barrett*—During the Campaigns in the Low Countries & the Peninsula and Waterloo Campaigns of the Napoleonic Wars. Volume 2: 1793-1815.

THE MARENGO CAMPAIGN 1800 *by Herbert H. Sargent*—The Victory that Completed the Austrian Defeat in Italy.

DONALDSON OF THE 94TH—SCOTS BRIGADE *by Joseph Donaldson*—The Recollections of a Soldier During the Peninsula & South of France Campaigns of the Napoleonic Wars.

A CONSCRIPT FOR EMPIRE *by Philippe as told to Johann Christian Maempel*—The Experiences of a Young German Conscript During the Napoleonic Wars.

JOURNAL OF THE CAMPAIGN OF 1815 *by Alexander Cavalié Mercer*—The Experiences of an Officer of the Royal Horse Artillery During the Waterloo Campaign.

NAPOLEON'S CAMPAIGNS IN POLAND 1806-7 *by Robert Wilson*—The campaign in Poland from the Russian side of the conflict.

AVAILABLE ONLINE AT **www.leonaur.com**
AND FROM ALL GOOD BOOK STORES

ALSO FROM LEONAUR
AVAILABLE IN SOFTCOVER OR HARDCOVER WITH DUST JACKET

OMPTEDA OF THE KING'S GERMAN LEGION by *Christian von Ompteda*—A Hanoverian Officer on Campaign Against Napoleon.

LIEUTENANT SIMMONS OF THE 95TH (RIFLES) by *George Simmons*—Recollections of the Peninsula, South of France & Waterloo Campaigns of the Napoleonic Wars.

A HORSEMAN FOR THE EMPEROR by *Jean Baptiste Gazzola*—A Cavalryman of Napoleon's Army on Campaign Throughout the Napoleonic Wars.

SERGEANT LAWRENCE by *William Lawrence*—With the 40th Regt. of Foot in South America, the Peninsular War & at Waterloo.

CAMPAIGNS WITH THE FIELD TRAIN by *Richard D. Henegan*—Experiences of a British Officer During the Peninsula and Waterloo Campaigns of the Napoleonic Wars.

CAVALRY SURGEON by *S. D. Broughton*—On Campaign Against Napoleon in the Peninsula & South of France During the Napoleonic Wars 1812-1814.

MEN OF THE RIFLES by *Thomas Knight, Henry Curling & Jonathan Leach*—The Reminiscences of Thomas Knight of the 95th (Rifles) by Thomas Knight, Henry Curling's Anecdotes by Henry Curling & The Field Services of the Rifle Brigade from its Formation to Waterloo by Jonathan Leach.

THE ULM CAMPAIGN 1805 by *F. N. Maude*—Napoleon and the Defeat of the Austrian Army During the 'War of the Third Coalition'.

SOLDIERING WITH THE 'DIVISION' by *Thomas Garrety*—The Military Experiences of an Infantryman of the 43rd Regiment During the Napoleonic Wars.

SERGEANT MORRIS OF THE 73RD FOOT by *Thomas Morris*—The Experiences of a British Infantryman During the Napoleonic Wars-Including Campaigns in Germany and at Waterloo.

A VOICE FROM WATERLOO by *Edward Cotton*—The Personal Experiences of a British Cavalryman Who Became a Battlefield Guide and Authority on the Campaign of 1815.

NAPOLEON AND HIS MARSHALS by *J. T. Headley*—The Men of the First Empire.

AVAILABLE ONLINE AT **www.leonaur.com**
AND FROM ALL GOOD BOOK STORES

ALSO FROM LEONAUR
AVAILABLE IN SOFTCOVER OR HARDCOVER WITH DUST JACKET

COLBORNE: A SINGULAR TALENT FOR WAR by *John Colborne*—The Napoleonic Wars Career of One of Wellington's Most Highly Valued Officers in Egypt, Holland, Italy, the Peninsula and at Waterloo.

NAPOLEON'S RUSSIAN CAMPAIGN by *Philippe Henri de Segur*—The Invasion, Battles and Retreat by an Aide-de-Camp on the Emperor's Staff.

WITH THE LIGHT DIVISION by *John H. Cooke*—The Experiences of an Officer of the 43rd Light Infantry in the Peninsula and South of France During the Napoleonic Wars.

WELLINGTON AND THE PYRENEES CAMPAIGN VOLUME I: FROM VITORIA TO THE BIDASSOA by *F. C. Beatson*—The final phase of the campaign in the Iberian Peninsula.

WELLINGTON AND THE INVASION OF FRANCE VOLUME II: THE BIDASSOA TO THE BATTLE OF THE NIVELLE by *F. C. Beatson*—The final phase of the campaign in the Iberian Peninsula.

WELLINGTON AND THE FALL OF FRANCE VOLUME III: THE GAVES AND THE BATTLE OF ORTHEZ by *F. C. Beatson*—The final phase of the campaign in the Iberian Peninsula.

NAPOLEON'S IMPERIAL GUARD: FROM MARENGO TO WATERLOO by *J. T. Headley*—The story of Napoleon's Imperial Guard and the men who commanded them.

BATTLES & SIEGES OF THE PENINSULAR WAR by *W. H. Fitchett*—Corunna, Busaco, Albuera, Ciudad Rodrigo, Badajos, Salamanca, San Sebastian & Others.

SERGEANT GUILLEMARD: THE MAN WHO SHOT NELSON? by *Robert Guillemard*—A Soldier of the Infantry of the French Army of Napoleon on Campaign Throughout Europe.

WITH THE GUARDS ACROSS THE PYRENEES by *Robert Batty*—The Experiences of a British Officer of Wellington's Army During the Battles for the Fall of Napoleonic France, 1813.

A STAFF OFFICER IN THE PENINSULA by *E. W. Buckham*—An Officer of the British Staff Corps Cavalry During the Peninsula Campaign of the Napoleonic Wars.

THE LEIPZIG CAMPAIGN: 1813—NAPOLEON AND THE "BATTLE OF THE NATIONS" by *F. N. Maude*—Colonel Maude's analysis of Napoleon's campaign of 1813 around Leipzig.

AVAILABLE ONLINE AT www.leonaur.com
AND FROM ALL GOOD BOOK STORES

ALSO FROM LEONAUR
AVAILABLE IN SOFTCOVER OR HARDCOVER WITH DUST JACKET

BUGEAUD: A PACK WITH A BATON by *Thomas Robert Bugeaud*—The Early Campaigns of a Soldier of Napoleon's Army Who Would Become a Marshal of France.

WATERLOO RECOLLECTIONS by *Frederick Llewellyn*—Rare First Hand Accounts, Letters, Reports and Retellings from the Campaign of 1815.

SERGEANT NICOL by *Daniel Nicol*—The Experiences of a Gordon Highlander During the Napoleonic Wars in Egypt, the Peninsula and France.

THE JENA CAMPAIGN: 1806 by *F. N. Maude*—The Twin Battles of Jena & Auerstadt Between Napoleon's French and the Prussian Army.

PRIVATE O'NEIL by *Charles O'Neil*—The recollections of an Irish Rogue of H. M. 28th Regt.—The Slashers—during the Peninsula & Waterloo campaigns of the Napoleonic war.

ROYAL HIGHLANDER by *James Anton*—A soldier of H.M 42nd (Royal) Highlanders during the Peninsular, South of France & Waterloo Campaigns of the Napoleonic Wars.

CAPTAIN BLAZE by *Elzéar Blaze*—Life in Napoleons Army.

LEJEUNE VOLUME 1 by *Louis-François Lejeune*—The Napoleonic Wars through the Experiences of an Officer on Berthier's Staff.

LEJEUNE VOLUME 2 by *Louis-François Lejeune*—The Napoleonic Wars through the Experiences of an Officer on Berthier's Staff.

CAPTAIN COIGNET by *Jean-Roch Coignet*—A Soldier of Napoleon's Imperial Guard from the Italian Campaign to Russia and Waterloo.

FUSILIER COOPER by *John S. Cooper*—Experiences in the 7th (Royal) Fusiliers During the Peninsular Campaign of the Napoleonic Wars and the American Campaign to New Orleans.

FIGHTING NAPOLEON'S EMPIRE by *Joseph Anderson*—The Campaigns of a British Infantryman in Italy, Egypt, the Peninsular & the West Indies During the Napoleonic Wars.

CHASSEUR BARRES by *Jean-Baptiste Barres*—The experiences of a French Infantryman of the Imperial Guard at Austerlitz, Jena, Eylau, Friedland, in the Peninsular, Lutzen, Bautzen, Zinnwald and Hanau during the Napoleonic Wars.

AVAILABLE ONLINE AT **www.leonaur.com**
AND FROM ALL GOOD BOOK STORES

ALSO FROM LEONAUR
AVAILABLE IN SOFTCOVER OR HARDCOVER WITH DUST JACKET

CAPTAIN COIGNET *by Jean-Roch Coignet*—A Soldier of Napoleon's Imperial Guard from the Italian Campaign to Russia and Waterloo.

HUSSAR ROCCA *by Albert Jean Michel de Rocca*—A French cavalry officer's experiences of the Napoleonic Wars and his views on the Peninsular Campaigns against the Spanish, British And Guerilla Armies.

MARINES TO 95TH (RIFLES) *by Thomas Fernyhough*—The military experiences of Robert Fernyhough during the Napoleonic Wars.

LIGHT BOB *by Robert Blakeney*—The experiences of a young officer in H.M 28th & 36th regiments of the British Infantry during the Peninsular Campaign of the Napoleonic Wars 1804 - 1814.

WITH WELLINGTON'S LIGHT CAVALRY *by William Tomkinson*—The Experiences of an officer of the 16th Light Dragoons in the Peninsular and Waterloo campaigns of the Napoleonic Wars.

SERGEANT BOURGOGNE *by Adrien Bourgogne*—With Napoleon's Imperial Guard in the Russian Campaign and on the Retreat from Moscow 1812 - 13.

SURTEES OF THE 95TH (RIFLES) *by William Surtees*—A Soldier of the 95th (Rifles) in the Peninsular campaign of the Napoleonic Wars.

SWORDS OF HONOUR *by Henry Newbolt & Stanley L. Wood*—The Careers of Six Outstanding Officers from the Napoleonic Wars, the Wars for India and the American Civil War.

ENSIGN BELL IN THE PENINSULAR WAR *by George Bell*—The Experiences of a young British Soldier of the 34th Regiment 'The Cumberland Gentlemen' in the Napoleonic wars.

HUSSAR IN WINTER *by Alexander Gordon*—A British Cavalry Officer during the retreat to Corunna in the Peninsular campaign of the Napoleonic Wars.

THE COMPLEAT RIFLEMAN HARRIS *by Benjamin Harris as told to and transcribed by Captain Henry Curling, 52nd Regt. of Foot*—The adventures of a soldier of the 95th (Rifles) during the Peninsular Campaign of the Napoleonic Wars.

THE ADVENTURES OF A LIGHT DRAGOON *by George Farmer & G.R. Gleig*—A cavalryman during the Peninsular & Waterloo Campaigns, in captivity & at the siege of Bhurtpore, India.

AVAILABLE ONLINE AT www.leonaur.com
AND FROM ALL GOOD BOOK STORES

ALSO FROM LEONAUR
AVAILABLE IN SOFTCOVER OR HARDCOVER WITH DUST JACKET

AFGHANISTAN: THE BELEAGUERED BRIGADE *by G. R. Gleig*—An Account of Sale's Brigade During the First Afghan War.

IN THE RANKS OF THE C. I. V *by Erskine Childers*—With the City Imperial Volunteer Battery (Honourable Artillery Company) in the Second Boer War.

THE BENGAL NATIVE ARMY *by F. G. Cardew*—An Invaluable Reference Resource.

THE 7TH (QUEEN'S OWN) HUSSARS: Volume 4—1688-1914 *by C. R. B. Barrett*—Uniforms, Equipment, Weapons, Traditions, the Services of Notable Officers and Men & the Appendices to All Volumes—Volume 4: 1688-1914.

THE SWORD OF THE CROWN *by Eric W. Sheppard*—A History of the British Army to 1914.

THE 7TH (QUEEN'S OWN) HUSSARS: Volume 3—1818-1914 *by C. R. B. Barrett*—On Campaign During the Canadian Rebellion, the Indian Mutiny, the Sudan, Matabeleland, Mashonaland and the Boer War Volume 3: 1818-1914.

THE KHARTOUM CAMPAIGN *by Bennet Burleigh*—A Special Correspondent's View of the Reconquest of the Sudan by British and Egyptian Forces under Kitchener—1898.

EL PUCHERO *by Richard McSherry*—The Letters of a Surgeon of Volunteers During Scott's Campaign of the American-Mexican War 1847-1848.

RIFLEMAN SAHIB *by E. Maude*—The Recollections of an Officer of the Bombay Rifles During the Southern Mahratta Campaign, Second Sikh War, Persian Campaign and Indian Mutiny.

THE KING'S HUSSAR *by Edwin Mole*—The Recollections of a 14th (King's) Hussar During the Victorian Era.

JOHN COMPANY'S CAVALRYMAN *by William Johnson*—The Experiences of a British Soldier in the Crimea, the Persian Campaign and the Indian Mutiny.

COLENSO & DURNFORD'S ZULU WAR *by Frances E. Colenso & Edward Durnford*—The first and possibly the most important history of the Zulu War.

U. S. DRAGOON *by Samuel E. Chamberlain*—Experiences in the Mexican War 1846-48 and on the South Western Frontier.

AVAILABLE ONLINE AT **www.leonaur.com**
AND FROM ALL GOOD BOOK STORES

www.ingramcontent.com/pod-product-compliance
Lightning Source LLC
Chambersburg PA
CBHW031625160426
43196CB00006B/276